Praise for *Mudlarking*

THE *SUNDAY TIMES* BESTSELLER

A BBC RADIO 4 BOOK OF THE WEEK

AN *OBSERVER* AND *DAILY EXPRESS* BOOK OF
THE YEAR

'The very best books that deal with the past are love letters to
their subject, and the very best of those are about subjects that
love their authors in return, embracing them, and showing
their readers just why the author is so deeply committed. Such
books are very rare, but this is one' Ian Mortimer, author of
The Time Traveller's Guide to Medieval England

'There is nothing that Maiklem does not know about the
history of the river or the thingyness of things ... *Mudlarking*
is a treasure trove of such curiosities ... There is a great deal
to learn from these pages, not least the insight that finding
lost things is the best way of losing yourself. It is, above all,
her wisdom that makes Lara Maiklem such restful company'
Guardian

'This book is as great a treasure as any of the fascinating
and eclectic finds that the author has unearthed along the
Thames over the years. The narrative ebbs and flows like the
river itself, revealing London's rich history, its modern day
landscape and a wealth of poignant personal reflections. One
of the best books I've read in years' Tracy Borman, author
and historian

'Maiklem persists in seeking out a curious beauty ... [Her]
description of the fog is worthy of Dickens or Joseph Conrad'
Sunday Telegraph

'A flowing river of human stories; beautiful, wondrous and
eternal' Hallie Rubenhold, Baillie Gifford Prize-winning
author of *The Fi*

'Mudlarking, once the preserve of society's most impoverished, now delivers fragments of history to excited scavengers ... It made even a capsized cynic like me feel more sentimental about the Thames. In fact, I am quite tempted to join Maiklem on the riverbed looking for treasure' *Sunday Times*

'A lovely, lyrical, gently meandering book, filled with fascinating diversions and detail' *Literary Review*

'Lara Maiklem has amassed a battered and stained collection of everyday things turned talismanic by time and immersion ... [She] augments the Thamesian tally, summoning old Londoners out of silty suspension from a discarded Victoria Cross or a pot-lid' *Spectator*

'Maiklem's imagined histories for her special finds read like waterborne fairy stories, a hard kernel of truth clothed in mythical finery ... The most arresting portions are those that deal with the practicalities of mudlarking. Reading it, I felt like I was down on the foreshore myself, sifting through the pages for titbits' *Daily Telegraph*

'As deep and as rich as the Thames and its treasures. Fascinating' Stanley Tucci

'Maiklem's enthusiasm is infectious, and her reimagining of the lives of those who parted with these items is an illuminated joy' *i*

'Maiklem has found the most extraordinary treasures – not always valuable so much as hauntingly evocative of past lives and lost loves' *Daily Mail*

'This is the Thames and London's history as you've never heard it, revealed slowly bit by bit, tide by tide, rinsed out and glittering and fresh ... This accretive, joyful and leisurely book welcomes us to stamp and slither along with Maiklem from the source to the estuary, from this side to the other, down dank, treacherous historic stone steps to secret entry points' *Country Life*

NOTE ON THE AUTHOR

LARA MAIKLEM moved from her family's farm to London in the 1990s and has been mudlarking along the River Thames for nearly twenty years. She now lives with her family on the Kent coast within easy reach of the river, which she visits as regularly as the tides permit. This is her first book.

There is a companion Instagram page for this book where pictures are featured in chapter order: @Laramaiklem_Mudlarking. Lara also regularly posts about new finds as @LondonMudlark on Facebook and Twitter, and as @London.Mudlark on Instagram.

MUDLARKING

Lost and Found on the River Thames

LARA MAIKLEM

BLOOMSBURY PUBLISHING
LONDON · OXFORD · NEW YORK · NEW DELHI · SYDNEY

BLOOMSBURY CIRCUS
Bloomsbury Publishing Plc
50 Bedford Square, London, WC1B 3DP, UK

BLOOMSBURY, BLOOMSBURY PUBLISHING and the Bloomsbury Publishing
logo are trademarks of Bloomsbury Publishing Plc

First published in Great Britain 2019
This edition published 2020

A catalogue record for this book is available from the British Library

ISBN: HB: 978-1-4088-8921-3; eBook: 978-1-4088-8920-6;
PB: 978-1-4088-8923-7

2 4 6 8 10 9 7 5 3 1

Typeset by Newgen KnowledgeWorks Pvt. Ltd., Chennai, India
Printed and bound in Great Britain by CPI Group (UK) Ltd, Croydon CR0 4YY

MIX
Paper from
responsible sources
FSC® C020471

To find out more about our authors and books visit www.bloomsbury.com
and sign up for our newsletters

Searching the bed of the tidal Thames (Mudlarking) requires a permit for
which you can apply to the Port of London Authority. There are areas
where searching is not allowed and other locations that are subject to legal
protection. Objects of historic importance and interest should be reported
to the Museum of London or a Finds Liaison Officer from the Portable
Antiquities Scheme. The foreshore is an unpredictable and a potentially
dangerous place. Anyone venturing onto it should familiarise themselves with
the tides, rules and regulations and take necessary safety precautions. The
author accepts no responsibility for anyone venturing on to the foreshore
independently.

For more information, visit the Port of London
Authorities' website: https://www.pla.co.uk/Environment/
Thames-foreshore-access-including-metal-detecting-searching-and-digging

For Sarah

... an old woman with a nut-cracker nose and chin, which almost dipped into the filthy slush into which she peered, and dirty flesh as well as a scrap or two of dirty linen showing through the slashes of her burst gown, over which, for 'warmth's sake', she wore a tippet of ragged sack-cloth ... She slinks off to her lair, followed by an imp bearing a rusty crumpled colander, piled with its find. Its sex is indistinguishable. It has long mud-hued hair hanging down in a mat over its shoulders. Through the hair one gets a glimpse of a never-washed little face, whose only sign of intelligence is an occasional glance of wicked knowingness.

Richard Rowe, 'A Pair of Mudlarks',
Life in the London Streets (1881)

CONTENTS

Maps   xii

Mudlark   1

Tidal Head   7

Hammersmith   21

Vauxhall   43

Trig Lane   65

Bankside   91

Queenhithe   117

London Bridge   139

Tower Beach   163

Rotherhithe   185

Wapping   205

Greenwich   229

Tilbury   255

Estuary   275

Acknowledgements   297
Select Bibliography   301
Index   309

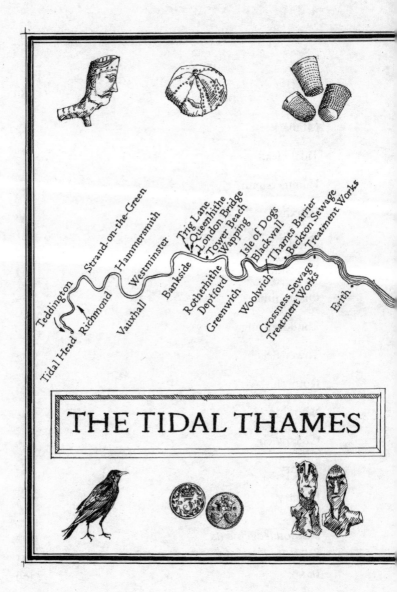

Teddington · Tidal Head · Richmond · Strand-on-the-Green · Hammersmith · Vauxhall · Westminster · Bankside · Trig Lane · Queenhithe · London Bridge · Tower Beach · Wapping · Rotherhithe · Deptford · Greenwich · Isle of Dogs · Blackwall · Woolwich · Thames Barrier · Beckton Sewage Treatment Works · Crossness Sewage Treatment Works · Erith

THE TIDAL THAMES

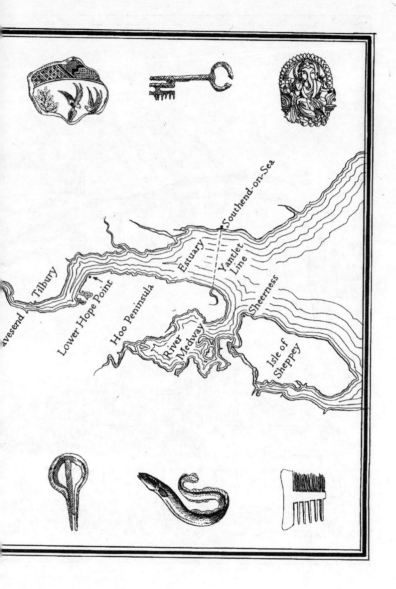

Tilbury

avesend

Lower Hope Point

Hoo Peninsula

River Medway

Estuary

Yantlet Line

Southend-on-Sea

Sheerness

Isle of Sheppey

CENTRAL LONDON

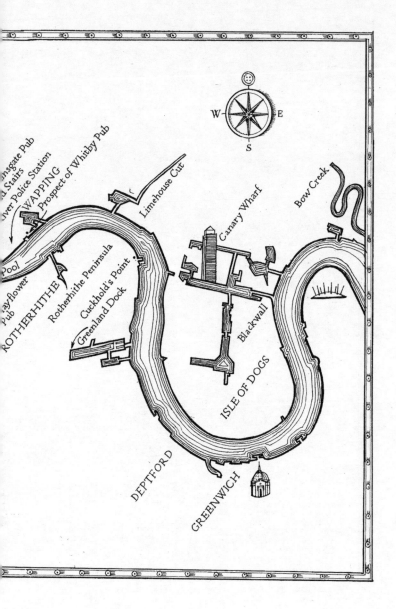

MUDLARK

Mudlark /'mAdla;k / n. & V. L18. [F. MUD n.1 + LARK n.1] A n.
+ 1 A hog. slang. L18 – E20. 2 A person who scavenges for usable
debris in the mud of a river or harbour. Also, a street urchin; joc.
a messy person, esp. a child. colloq. L18. 3 A magpie-lark. Austral.
L19. 4 = MUDDER. slang. E20. B. v.i. Carry on the occupation of
a mudlark. Also, play in mud. M19.

Mudlarker n. + MUDLARK n. 2 E19.

New Shorter Oxford English Dictionary
on Historical Principles (1993)

It is hot and airless on the 7.42 from Greenwich to Cannon
Street. I am squeezed between strangers, straining to avoid
the feel of unknown bodies. No one makes eye contact and
no one speaks. There is an unwritten rule of silence on the
early-morning London commute and barely a murmur can
be heard, just the rustle of newspapers and the high-pitched
squeal of the rails as we lurch and sway towards the city.

I know every inch of this route. For nearly twenty years
it has been taking me to the centre of London, for work, to
meetings, to see friends and to visit the river in search of
treasure. I know when to hold on tight, where the tracks jolt
the train to one side, how long the gaps are between stops
and when the driver will start to slow down for the next

station. For years I have watched old graffiti fade and new graffiti appear. For six months now I have been watching a sports sock, discarded and stuck to the tracks, turn from white to tattered dirty brown.

This journey will take me seventeen minutes and I am impatient. I check my watch again and work back three hours from today's predicted low tide. The river will be at its lowest at 10.23 a.m. My timing is perfect. I twitch and shift from foot to foot as the train pulls out of London Bridge station, willing it to speed up: I am almost there. We trundle over a railway viaduct, past Southwark Cathedral with its dappled flint dressing and Gothic spires, and through the centre of Borough Market. I look out over its glazed roof and try to spot the cast-iron pineapples balanced above one of the entrances. Then the sky opens up and I am above the river on Cannon Street Bridge, water flowing towards me from the west and away from me to the east. I scan the river on both sides, peering through the bodies, over newspapers and around rucksacks to check the tide. A patch of slime-covered rubble is just beginning to show through. It is close to the river wall, but the tide is falling. By the time I get down there the river will have dropped even further and enough of the foreshore will be exposed for me to begin my search.

It amazes me how many people don't realise the river in central London is tidal. I hear them comment on it as they pause at the river wall above me while I am mudlarking below. Even friends who have lived in the city for years are oblivious to the high and low tides that chase each other around the clock, inching forwards every twenty-four hours, one tide gradually creeping through the day while the other takes the night shift. They have no idea that the height between low and high water at London Bridge varies from fifteen to twenty-two feet or that it takes six hours for the water to come upriver and six and a half for it to flow back out to sea.

I am obsessed with the incessant rise and fall of the water. For years my spare time has been controlled by the river's ebb and flow, and the consequent covering and uncovering of the foreshore. I know where the river allows me access early and where I can stay for the longest time before I am gently, but firmly, shooed away. I have learned to read the water and catch it as it turns, to recognise the almost imperceptible moment when it stops flowing seawards and the currents churn together briefly as the balance tips and the river is once more pulled inland, the anticipation of the receding water replaced by a sense of loss, like saying goodbye to an old friend after a long-awaited visit.

Tide tables commit the river's movements to paper, predict its future and record its past. I use these complex lines of numbers, dates, times and water heights to fill my diary, temptations to weave my life around, but it is the river that decides when I can search it, and tides have no respect for sleep or commitments. I have carefully arranged meetings and appointments according to the tides, and conspired to meet friends near the river so that I can steal down to the foreshore before the water comes in and after it's flowed out. I've kept people waiting, bringing a trail of mud and apologies in my wake; missed the start of many films and even left some early to catch the last few inches of foreshore. I have lied, cajoled and manipulated to get time by the river. It comes knocking at all hours and I obey, forcing myself out of a warm bed, pulling on layers of clothes and padding quietly down the stairs, trying not to wake the sleeping house.

When I first started looking at tide tables, they confused me. I'm not a natural mathematician and numbers just bewilder me, so a page filled with lines and columns of them sent me into a flat spin. But I've been studying them for so long now that they've become second nature. A quick glance and I can see which tides are good and when it's worth visiting the river. The most important thing is to choose the correct tide table for the stretch you are planning to visit. There can be a difference of around five hours between low tide at Richmond and low tide at Southend, since the tide falls earlier in the Estuary than it does at the tidal head. Even the length of the low tide varies depending on where you are. While the rise and fall of tides in the open sea are of almost equal duration, twenty-five bends in the tidal Thames and the dragging effect of the riverbed and its banks shorten the river's flood tide and lengthen its ebb tide. This means that the river stays at low tide for longer at Hammersmith than it does in the Estuary, which in theory equates to more mudlarking time the higher up the river you go, but even then, depending on the weather and the slope of the fore-shore, the river can still catch you out.

I never look at the high-water levels, but I know that a good low tide of 0.5 metres and below will expose a decent amount of foraging space, so I scan the tide tables for these and circle them with a red pen. Spring tides mark the highest and lowest tides of the month. The name comes from the idea of the tide 'springing forth' and not, as some mistakenly think, the time of year when they occur. There are two spring tides every month, during full and new moons, when the earth, sun and moon are in alignment and the gravitational pull on the oceans is greater, but the very best spring tides are after the equinoxes in March and September when they can fall into negative figures. They are known as negative tides because they fall below the zero mark, which is set by the average level of low tide at a specific place. A few years ago there was a run of freak low tides that were lower than most mudlarks could remember. Those were the best tides I've ever seen. They revealed stretches of the foreshore that hadn't been mudlarked for over a decade and uncovered countless treasures.

It is the tides that make mudlarking in London so unique. For just a few hours each day, the river gives us access to its contents, which shift and change as the water ebbs and flows, to reveal the story of a city, its people and their relationship with a natural force. If the Seine in Paris were tidal it would no doubt provide a similar bounty and satisfy an army of Parisian mudlarks; when the non-tidal Amstel River in Amsterdam was recently drained to make way for a new train line, archaeologists recorded almost 700,000 objects, of just the sort we find in the Thames: buttons that burst off waistcoats long ago, rings that slipped from fingers, buckles that are all that's left of a shoe – the personal possessions of ordinary people, each small piece a key to another world and a direct link to long-forgotten lives. As I have discovered, it is often the tiniest of objects that tell the greatest stories.

TIDAL HEAD

The Thames about Richmond and Twickenham seems to be rapidly approaching the condition of those tropical streams which disappear altogether in the summer months. Anyone who has found it his duty to steer a boat between Richmond Bridge and Teddington Lock must have often been sorely perplexed by the deviousness and scantiness of the navigable channel.

St. James's Gazette, June 1884

There isn't much to draw the average mudlark west, and I had been mudlarking for more than a decade before I decided to make a pilgrimage to Teddington. But it makes sense to begin our journey where the tidal Thames starts (or ends, depending which way you imagine the water flowing). The stretch of river between Richmond and Teddington is unusual in that the water levels are controlled. The lock at Teddington artificially ends the tidal Thames, which would otherwise continue further upstream – something it still does, in effect, when there's a very high tide and the water overflows the lock. But the tide hasn't always turned this far west. In the first century AD, it turned where the Romans built their bridge, near to where London Bridge is today.

The demolition of Old London Bridge in 1831 also had an effect on the tidal head. For centuries its narrow arches and wide pier bases had blocked the flow of water and held back enough of the tide to maintain a navigable stretch along the entire tidal Thames, but when it was removed, water levels at Teddington dropped by thirty inches and the river was reduced to a mere stream running between mudbanks. Cricket matches were held on the riverbed. On Wednesday 25 June 1884, the *Globe* reported on a picnic that was held just downstream from Teddington Lock: 'It has been reserved for this generation to dine where the Thames ought to be ... spreading their cloth on the bed of the river and drinking "Prosperity to the new lock, which is, or is not to be. That is the question."' Richmond Weir and Lock was opened in 1894 to counteract this effect and to maintain the water levels between Richmond and Teddington at half tide or above to ensure the river remained navigable.

It is still in use, and every autumn it is left open for about three weeks while the locks and weir at Teddington stay closed, in what is known as the annual Thames Draw Off. This allows the stretch of water between them to rise and fall naturally with the tides, and when the tide is out the water falls so low that vast amounts of riverbed are exposed. For that brief period, it becomes the only part of the tidal Thames where, in places, you can walk from the north (Middlesex) shore to the south (Surrey) shore without getting your feet wet. While the lock is lifted, essential maintenance takes place, environmental surveys can be conducted on the riverbed, local action groups can clear the river of rubbish, and mudlarks can mooch around a unique part of the foreshore.

The best and most fruitful spots to mudlark on the Thames are those where there has been intense human activity over a long period of time and where busy river traffic churns up the foreshore and erodes the compacted mud that contains the river's treasures. I have never found that much west of Vauxhall, but when I read about the annual draw off, I decided I had to see it for myself. Just once, in any case. It was the photographs that had really captured my attention: pictures of the naked riverbed with stranded boats leaning precariously to one side and people wandering around at will on the dry riverbed. Perhaps the river this far west had something to offer after all.

Draw-off days are always at the end of October and early November when damp mists hang over the water mingling with the smell of burning leaves. During the first week locals descend on the newly exposed riverbed to collect the casual losses and lucky pennies tossed in the previous year. Families pick their way through the shingle and mud, heads down, plastic bags in hand, exploring the newly unfamiliar, wondering at the river's-eye view. It was this that I had in mind as I began my walk from Richmond Bridge one chilly afternoon in November a few years ago.

I chose to follow the riverside path along the Middlesex side of the river and continue over the bridge, turning hard left down a road that leads to a slipway. From here I joined a tarmac path that was edged with sludgy leaves and gritty mud and set my pace for the long walk to Teddington. I'd worked out my route the night before and knew I had quite a distance to cover, so I'd decided to wear walking boots instead of wellingtons, which are uncomfortable over long distances. I just hoped I wouldn't need them. The pictures

I'd seen didn't show much mud, but I didn't want to be walking back with it squelching through the lace holes in my boots as I've done after other visits to the foreshore.

Everything was leisurely upstream. I passed a few people, but not many: women pushing buggies with babies bundled up against the cold ambled in contented pairs; joggers apologised as they bounced past. This is the part of the river where people relax and play on the water. There are motorboats, narrowboats and barges turned into houseboats along the banks. In the summer you can hire traditional Thames skiffs here, with old-fashioned names like *Linda* and *Violet* painted on the back seat. Even the river is calmer and slower than it is in central London and the Estuary. It lacks the pace and ferocity it acquires as it flows through the city and away to the sea. And to me that is what is missing.

But there was no denying it was beautiful. Willow trees clung to the bank and ancient plane trees lined the other side of the path. There was a scent of earth, rotting leaves and river mud, and birds were everywhere. A group of ducks were sitting fluffed up and huddled on some steps that led to the river and two Canada geese eyed me warily from the bank nearby. Gulls and cormorants flew past, a reminder that I was just over sixty miles from the pier at Southend-on-Sea. Blackbirds rustled in the bushes beside the path and for a time a robin kept pace with me, reappearing now and then and fixing me with his bead-like eye. My great-aunt once told me that robins are the souls of the departed: this is why they come so close and their company feels so intimate. They are the people you once knew visiting from beyond, coming to say hello, and I always say hello back because you never know who they might be. Perhaps my great-aunt herself.

Only the regular roar of planes descending into Heathrow Airport reminded me that I was still in London. But if I ignored that, I could very well have been walking along a country lane back near the farm where I grew up in the 1970s and 80s: 300 acres of heavy Weald clay, 120 milking cows, a collection of old barns and a lopsided farmhouse built in the reign of Henry VIII, all nestled in a green valley at the end of a long concrete road.

A small river ran through the farm and skirted the back of the house, a large ash tree shading its water in the summer and a single willow reaching into its shallows. With my two much older brothers away at boarding school and in the absence of neighbours, the farm dog and the river were my playmates. While the dog chased ducks and swam around in circles, I spent hours fishing with nets tied to long bamboo canes for the tiny fish and water snails that sheltered in the weeds near the bank. I lay in the long grass and watched dragonflies dart and hover among the reeds, dipping their tails into the water to lay their eggs. If I stayed still long enough, I saw water voles emerge from their river-bank burrows at dusk and very occasionally a grass snake twisting silently through the water, its tiny head held proud, forked tongue flicking.

The river flowed from east to west through the middle of the farm and I knew every inch of it: the bends that caught rubbish, sometimes a football and once even an escaped battered rowing boat. I knew the deep bits to avoid and where it was shallow enough to wade across from one side to the other without flooding my wellington boots. I knew where the sticklebacks hid in the weeds, where ducks nested, and how to get into the low space under the concrete bridge where I listened to our cows patiently shuffling back to pasture after being milked. I learned to love rivers on the farm and they have proved to be my most enduring passion.

There are no walls or barriers on the river path at Teddington. For much of my route the riverbank was natural, sloping down to the river at an angle created by the water rather than by man, and the river was right next to me. If I had wanted, I could have stepped off the path, crossed a few feet of dead weeds and grass and dropped right into the water. The brittle stems of dead nettles pushed through the yellowing grass and every so often I passed a wide short set of concrete steps set into the bank. Rowing clubs have their clubhouses along this stretch and I assumed this was where they launched their boats.

I passed an eyot, otherwise known as an 'ait' from the Old English *īgeth*, based on *īeg* meaning 'island'. This is Glover's Island, named after a waterman called Joseph Glover who paid £70 (around £4,400 in today's money) for it in 1872 and caused a scandal by putting it up for sale twenty-three years later for £5,000 (around £410,000). It was eventually sold in 1900 for an undisclosed sum to a local resident and gifted to the council. It is one of three eyots between Richmond Bridge and Teddington Lock and one of nine on the upper reaches of the tidal Thames. Eyots characterise this part of the river. These mudbanks and slices of land have been carved away from the mainland, deposited by the river and sculpted into long blunt strips and teardrops by the flow of the water. Most of them are uninhabited, wild and overgrown, covered with dense scrub and willow trees that reach down into the water to dabble in the currents.

The opposite bank seemed even more rural and I wondered if I should have taken that route. The houses had gone and there were green open spaces, parks and woodland. According to the map on my phone I should have been able to see the flat scrubby expanse of flood meadows at Ham Lands quite soon, a 178-acre nature reserve that lies in a bend in the river on the south side between Richmond and Kingston, somewhere safe for the river to go if it swells and breaks its banks.

People living along the river at the tidal head are used to the river flooding on high spring tides. There are no river walls or embankments to protect them from these natural forces and the river overflows quite regularly. The houses along the river path at Strand-on-the-Green in Chiswick are well prepared with garden walls and Perspex or glass barriers in front of the windows. Sandbags are at the ready and the wooden planks that slide in to block the doors are on standby. Over the centuries, the doorways of the oldest houses have physically moved up and away from the creeping water. The number of steps up to them has increased and each step has stolen a foot from the height of the door. Some are now little more than three-foot hobbit doors at the top of a flight of steps – incontrovertible proof that water levels are rising. At London Bridge, the tides rise by about three feet every hundred years; as the ice caps melt, London sinks and various other geographical and environmental conditions come into play. The tides today are higher than they have been at any time in history.

The tide had been falling as I'd walked. The closer I got to Teddington, the more the riverbed was exposed. Some boats were already stranded awkwardly, leaning on their keels, and I started to think about getting down onto the foreshore. I reached Eel Pie Island, the most famous of the inhabited eyots, named for the eel pies once sold there. Eel Pie Island splits the river in two. The channel nearest me was almost dry, apart from a few small pools that had been left behind in shallow dips. Ducks circled them, quacking angrily at the human interlopers who were poking around and marvelling at the novelty of being able to walk where the Thames should be. I decided to join them and cast around for a suitable place to descend. I didn't fancy scrambling through the scrub and weeds into mud of unknown depth and consistency, so the wide slipway that led directly to the foreshore from the road was a godsend.

The riverbed was firm, not muddy at all, just a fine layer of silt the consistency of thin custard. There was an even layer of gravel mixed with small, round pea-mussel shells that popped and crunched beneath my boots. It was clean and natural with none of the rubble and urban waste that litters the foreshore in the city. I looked down at the unfamiliar riverbed, my eyes darting between the freshwater mussel shells, which were everywhere. They were just like the ones I used to search for as a child, convinced that one day I'd find a pearl. I never did, but from latent habit I bent down and picked one up to admire the creamy opalescence inside. Just a few yards away, crows flapped down to turn stones, looking for shrimps and other tiny creatures stranded by this rare occurrence. All around me were the carefully constructed cases of what looked like caddis fly larvae; perhaps the crows were eating those too.

I looked hard along the bank and under the footbridge, but all I found was rubbish – an empty duffel bag, two scooters, an old lighter, a shirt, a wellington boot, headphones, a submerged shopping trolley, a car exhaust, a traffic cone, a mobile phone and 14p in change. Near some steps, a bit further along, it was more promising: a few clay pipe stems, to prove you can indeed find them the entire length of the Tideway, and a fair amount of broken glass. I recognised the thick dark-brown glass of beer bottles from the late nineteenth to early twentieth centuries and the aqua-coloured shards of old soda water and lemonade bottles. Perhaps they'd fallen out of creaking wicker picnic baskets or slipped from tired happy hands at the end of the day when this part of the Thames was a mecca for day trippers and boating parties. People swarmed here from the railway stations, while steamers brought crowds of noisy cockneys upriver from the East End.

Among the shards of glass I found a green marble, which was in fact the stopper from a Codd bottle. The Codd bottle is one of those brilliant Victorian inventions that you wish would be brought back into general use, although they still have the sense to use them in India and Japan. In 1872 the wonderfully named Hiram Codd patented his solution to the problem of sealing fizzy-drink bottles. The marble in his bottle sat on a glass 'shelf' within a specially designed pinched neck. Gas from the fizzy drink created pressure that forced the marble onto a rubber ring in the collar of the bottle, thus forming an effective seal. To pour the drink the marble was pushed back into the bottle using a little plunger or by giving it a swift bash on something, which is said to have given rise to the term 'codswallop'. If the bottles weren't smashed by children for their marbles, they were returned to the manufacturer where they could be washed and refilled. I've been told by those old enough to have bought drinks in Codd bottles that the lure of the imprisoned marble proved too great for many children and a lot of bottles got smashed. I must admit, while I've found scores of marbles, I've only ever found one complete bottle.

Over the years, I have amassed quite a variety of different stoppers, from river-worn cut-glass decanter stoppers and large earthenware plugs for hot-water bottles, to pressed-glass HP Sauce bottle stoppers and delicate perfume dabbers. The oldest stopper I have is Roman, from the second to third century AD. It is a large plug of unglazed red clay, shaped like a fat mushroom, which is thought to have originated in the Bay of Naples where it was pushed into the neck of an amphora, perhaps containing olive oil, before it was sent to London. What I like most about it is the faint line that runs just below the top, from once resting on a sealing bung of clay or plant stuff.

Corked and broken bottlenecks have no real value and are overlooked by most people, but they are precious to me. It amazes me that while the rest of the bottle has broken, the neck remains firmly corked, exactly where it was pushed by the last person to pour or drink from it. I have brought home some very old bottlenecks, seventeenth-century free-blown wine bottles and tiny apothecary bottles. The corks survived while they were wet, but once they dried out, they shrank and slipped out. With the magic gone there was no point in keeping them, so I returned them to the river.

Plenty of mudlarks don't bother collecting the black vul-canite stoppers that roll around at the water's edge and nestle among the pebbles and stones either. They are often smoothed and eroded into mere suggestions of their original form, but I've also found them perfectly preserved, still tightly screwed into beer bottles, faithfully preserving what's left of its contents. Unscrewing them is like opening a smelly time capsule, with a hissing rush of air followed by the smell of hundred-year-old beer dregs turned foul and rotten.

Many stoppers were branded with the manufacturer's trademark and name, and it's these I look out for: long-forgotten breweries and local soft-drink manufacturers with gloriously old-fashioned names like 'Bath Row Bottling Co.' and 'Style and Winch'. Most come from London or Kent or Essex, but at Teddington I found one from much further away. It was thick with mud when I picked it up and what I saw when I wiped it clean with a swipe of my thumb gave me quite a shock. It was a large swastika with the name St Austell Brewery around the edge.

The symbol on the stopper was so powerful and forbidden it intrigued me. I was sure it pre-dated the war, but there had to be a story behind it, so I took to the Internet when I got home. I discovered that the St Austell Brewery in Cornwall, like other companies, including Coca-Cola and Carlsberg, chose the symbol for its original meaning of health and fertility in around 1890, but withdrew their swastika stoppers in the early 1920s when Hitler adopted it as the symbol of the Nazi party. Stuck with a pile of old stock and with materials in short supply the brewery ground off the offending image so that they could use them through the war. At the same time, vulcanite stoppers were produced with a dip in the top to reduce the amount of rubber needed, and the words 'War Grade' stamped around the edge. I used to find a lot of them on the foreshore, but

I haven't found one for a while. Perhaps more people are realising their worth.

Happy with my unusual vulcanite stopper and with another Codd bottle marble for my collection safely stashed in my pocket, I decided it was time to leave. The light was fading and the blackbirds in the bushes were beginning to stutter their evening chink-chink call. I still had a way to walk to Teddington Lock where I wanted to see the obelisk that marks the beginning point of the tidal Thames. So I began to head west again. This time the path took me inland through suburban streets and around the lucky houses that have lawns running right down to the river.

This is where my mother was born. She grew up playing and picnicking along the Thames at Twickenham and her early years were spent here with her grandmother Kate. When my grandfather came out of the army after the war, she moved with her parents to a neat suburban house close to the river at Thames Ditton. My grandparents lived there for years and I grew up playing in their immaculately manicured garden, which they filled with red geraniums and tomatoes year after year. My grandmother was a very fast driver and visits to their house invariably involved a terrifying journey in her maroon Triumph Herald to watch the boats on the river and feed the ducks while we ate the tomatoes and soggy white-bread salmon-paste sandwiches. Heaven.

I looked down into the mud along the edge of the river at the bottom of Radnor Gardens and tried to imagine a four-year-old version of my mother stuck in the mud, crying her eyes out. She and her older brother spent a lot of time wandering around on their own and one day they found themselves in Radnor Gardens, a small public park beside the river. In the deep mud at the water's edge was a beautiful cricket bat, which my uncle sent her to retrieve. Thankfully, two ladies passing by saw what was happening. They pulled her out, cleaned her up with their handkerchiefs and sent them both off home.

I was not far from my great-grandmother's house. If I hurried, I could take a peek at it and still get to Teddington Lock before dark. When I found it in the middle of a long straight road, I recognised it straight away. I'd seen an old faded photograph of it in a box of other family pictures. It must have been taken around the mid-1920s because my grandmother is standing outside with a friend and she's a teenager. She doesn't look like the person I remember, but her eyes are the same. Eyes don't lie, and they don't age either. The house was the same too, a large Victorian villa built of yellow London brick with bay windows. I stared at it, thinking of all the people in my life who'd crossed its threshold, looked out of its windows and lived in its rooms. It was a curious feeling of familiar and unfamiliar. Like looking at the riverbed at draw off. I know that Kate and my great-grandfather Albert worked as 'antique dealers', and I know that what they did was not always above board. Both had been born in the East End and were determined to pull themselves up in the world, by any means necessary. Albert ran a ring that fixed auction prices and Kate fenced the goods he acquired. My grandmother told me how her parents sold antiques in bulk, furnishing entire rooms in their house at Richmond and then selling everything in one go. She'd often come home from school to find her room empty, everything sold except a mattress on the floor for her to sleep on.

I'd have loved to knock on the door, explained who I was, invited myself in, but there was no time, it was getting dark and they'd probably have thought I was mad anyway. So I walked back to the main road, consumed by thoughts of family, people I never met and those who had gone and who I still missed. Eventually I turned off down a quieter street leading to Teddington Lock, and a thin iron footbridge that took me over the river. I could just about see the full channel of the non-tidal river beyond and once on the south side it was a relatively short walk to the obelisk that has marked the upper reach of the tidal Thames since 1909, the year the Port of London Authority (PLA) came into being and took control of the tidal Thames. As well as marking the start of the PLA's jurisdiction, it also marks the upper limit of the old Thames Waterman Licence, the lower limit being marked by another obelisk in the Estuary.

The stone at Teddington is at least less underwhelming than its wind-blown sister in the Estuary, which lists slightly landwards and is surrounded by rubbish blown in off the strandline. Someone has made the effort to protect it with iron railings and it is set straight. I always touch the Estuary stone, so I knelt down on the cold flagstones and reached as far as I could through the railings to try to brush my fingers against the base. I'd finally completed the line between the western and eastern ends of the tidal Thames. The box was ticked and I didn't need to come back this way for a while.

HAMMERSMITH

It is very kind of you, but pray do not trouble … I am a destroyer &
not a collector & am always reducing my possessions as near to zero
as may be.

Letter to a customer from T. J. Cobden-Sanderson,
14 February 1918

Ten and a half winding miles downstream from
Teddington, the river starts to look like the one I am
familiar with. Hammersmith is the tipping point, where
you really get a sense that the river has grown up and is
gaining momentum in preparation for its journey through
the city and out to sea. It is wider and faster, more urgent
and grimy. Trees and bushes line the muddy path along
the south bank, which is much like that at Teddington, but
the houses on the north side are squeezed into a dense line
along the riverfront and protected from the water by a tall
wall. This is a sign of what is to come. Further downriver,
past Hammersmith Bridge, modern apartment blocks have
appeared, crowding the river and changing its character.

Richmond Lock and Weir control the river at Teddington,
but here the tides rise and fall naturally with the sea, lifting
the narrowboats, converted barges and floating homes that
are moored along the north side at Hope Pier and Dove

Pier. Gangplanks lead down to floating jetties from wide gaps in the river wall, which are blocked most of the time with wooden planks. Some of the jetties belong to rowing clubs; almost all of them have notices warning that they are private.

It's fairly easy to get down to the foreshore on the south side, although it can involve a muddy scramble through tall weeds. There is no wall or barrier here to climb over, just a few gently sloping feet of rough ground, cobbled halfway to prevent the river from eating away the soil of the natural bank. Here and there narrow, slippery concrete steps are cut into the cobbles. They can be overgrown and muddy, green with slimy weed and algae at the bottom where the river climbs up at high tide, but they make access to the foreshore relatively simple. Getting to the foreshore on the north side, however, is far more difficult. I have tried climbing over the railings next to the bridge and wading through the mud and tall reeds where I assume there was once a slipway, but I have to admit it is much easier to invade 'private property' – hop over the gaps in the wall, scoot down a gangplank and jump off one of the wooden platforms that are grounded on the foreshore at low tide.

I know the north side of the river at Hammersmith quite well. I was a regular visitor for some time in the late 1990s, when I was working in a soul-destroying job in an anonymous office block wedged beside the flyover. The river was hidden by the city and all I could see from my office window was a tangle of roads and endless concrete and brick, so it took me a while to realise I was as close to the river as I was. I had come to London a few years earlier to get away from peace and quiet. I had had enough of mud in the countryside. I wanted to immerse myself in the city, the seediness and excitement of it all, and I threw myself at it with gusto. The Thames was something I barely saw as I passed over it in the early hours of the morning on my way home from clubs and parties, usually slumped in the dirty back seat of a minicab that reeked of pine air-freshener. But then I began to notice it: a silver ribbon reaching east and west, a line of natural tranquillity through an urban mess, a sudden moment of calm after a crazy night.

Sometimes it pricked my conscience, making me feel sad, remorseful and even guilty. I began to realise how disconnected I was becoming from the world I had grown up in. I was part of two worlds. I was the farm kid who had dreamed of bigger, more exciting places, but deep down I was missing home and pining for what I'd left behind. At lunchtime at work, I escaped from the office and ate my sandwiches in parks and squares, but so did everyone else. I ended up sitting by regimented beds of tulips, squeezed in next to strangers, wondering what they were eating and listening in to their conversations. At weekends, I searched for green space near where I lived, but all I found were random patches of worn grass with broken slides and swings, graffiti and menacing gangs of kids who scared me away. I tried further afield, but Regent's Park made me feel as if I was visiting someone's well-ordered garden and even Hampstead Heath felt too controlled.

Then one day I found myself beside the Thames. I was meeting a friend after work and she had suggested we meet at a pub down by the river. I was early and having spent the day hunched over my desk, I decided to stretch my legs while I waited for her. The tide was high and the water had risen up close to the top of the river wall. I looked out across the thick brown expanse and I felt my muscles relax, my shoulders fall away from my ears. Somehow, for a moment, the moving water had taken the city away. It was just me and the river, nothing else but an overwhelming sense of comfort, of finally coming home. It turned out my playmate had been with me all along.

It was still some years before I discovered the foreshore, but in the middle of my dirty, noisy, thrilling city I had found something familiar – a wild brooding place with a wide-open sky. Here I found the space and solitude I needed to offset the clamour and chaos my city twin pursued, where I could connect with nature and the two parts of my being could come together. The river became my secret place of peace, where I went alone to watch the seasons change and feel real weather on my face. Without buildings to block the wind and catch the rain, I was as exposed as I would have been at home in the middle of a field, and it was liberating. Even birds are different on the river. Unlike the greasy, maimed London pigeons, they fly unhindered and free. Pure white gulls swoop and soar over the water; cormorants fly low along its length.

When I was by the river, I was somewhere else, disconnected from the city and a world away from my problems. It was my escape, from people, work, awkward situations, even sometimes from myself. It was where I went to forget about my failing relationship and my unfulfilling jobs, it healed my broken heart, helped me to make sense of the senseless and threw a watery arm around my shoulders when life became too much. Sometimes, just a stolen half-hour was enough. Other times I walked beside it for miles, casting my problems into the retreating tide, telling it my secrets.

But I'm not unique, there are others who come to the river in search of peace and to keep themselves together. For some, their visits are a way to control their demons, to deal with what's going on in their lives or with what's happened in their past. For them, the foreshore is an anonymous world without judgement or demands, purpose or destination, inhabited only by the ghosts of people who no longer exist. My friend Johnny likens his trips to the foreshore to entering a portal to another world. He calls it Portal 670, because when he first started mudlarking, his route to the river took him past a sign that read 'P670' (parking for 670 cars). It became a marker on his journey, the point where he knew he had almost reached his sanctuary.

Over the years Johnny has honed his preferred part of the foreshore down to a patch not much larger than fifty square feet, which he scrutinises regularly for up to four hours at a time. I know I will always find him in this spot and I can tell if he's had a good day from the way he reaches into his pockets for the little plastic bags that contain his treasures. For the longest time our conversations were limited to the river and the foreshore. We respected each other's privacy and space and had never intruded into each other's lives. Then one day he took me by surprise. From his bag he produced a small bulging notebook, held shut with an elastic band. Inside were exquisite miniature paintings, accompanied by neat writing. It was Johnny's river diary, a record of his visits to the foreshore in which he documented the weather, what he had seen, the people he had met and the things he had found. The work of this man of six foot five was elfin in its proportions. Each of his finds had been beautifully rendered in such detail that they looked as if they could tumble off the page and fall back into the mud again. He's let me use a few pages from his notebooks for the endpapers of this book, and some of his drawings for the cover.

For most of the people I know, mudlarking is a peaceful pastime, a contemplative escape from the world and a momentary distraction from their worries. But there is another side to it. For some, the foreshore is a battlefield, albeit a quiet one, and the site of petty feuding, territorial disputes, jealousies, fierce competition and paranoia.

Modern mudlarks fall into two distinct categories: hunters and gatherers. I am one of the latter. I find objects using just my eyes to spot what is lying on the surface. Eyes-only foragers like me generally enjoy the searching as much as the finding, and derive pleasure from the simplest of objects: an unusually shaped stone, a colourful shard of pottery or a random blob of lead. There is an element of meditation to what we do, and as far as I'm concerned the time I spend looking is as important, if not more so, than the objects I take home with me.

Hunters, by contrast, are more demanding of the river. They are usually driven by the find, its monetary value or its rarity. Most hunters use metal detectors, sieves and trowels to cut into the mud, breaking open the foreshore and peeling back its skin, too impatient to let time and nature take its course. In my experience, the hunters are often men, while gatherers tend to be women. It is rare to see a woman on the foreshore with a metal detector.

There has been a mudlarking permit system in place for years for those who wish to metal detect, scrape and dig, but until recently there was some confusion over whether a permit was necessary for eyes-only searching. Concerns have also grown about safety, people mudlarking in restricted areas and the unreported removal of historic artefacts. So in 2016, the Port of London Authority, which administers 100 per cent of the riverbed and foreshore up to the mean high-water mark, decided to clarify the situation. Anyone searching the foreshore in any way at all now needs to hold a valid permit. There are two kinds of permit: a 'standard' permit, for which anyone can apply, allowing metal detecting and digging down to 7.5 centimetres in permitted areas, and a 'mudlark' permit, which allows the holder to dig to a depth of 1.2 metres and use metal detectors on parts of the foreshore that standard permit holders aren't allowed to detect on.

But it is not as easy as you might think to get your hands on a mudlark permit. Currently, you have to be a member of the Society of Mudlarks, and in order to be eligible to join the Society of Mudlarks, you need to have held a standard permit and have been reporting your finds to the Museum of London for two years. But even that doesn't guarantee a mudlark permit, since membership is at the discretion of the society, which maintains a deliberate air of mystery and exclusivity. Their loose invitation-only, one-in-one-out policy limits its numbers, and it can take years to receive an invitation, if at all.

You would be forgiven for thinking the society's roots lie in some nineteenth-century cult, but in fact they only date back to the 1970s, when hobbyist metal detecting was in its infancy. In an attempt to control and monitor what was being taken and to discourage illegal digging, permits were issued that allowed people to dig the foreshore in return for recording their finds with the Museum of London. Over time, the society has developed into a select group of around fifty members, predominantly men and mostly metal detectorists, who meet regularly at a secret location (actually, it's a not-so-secret London pub). I don't know exactly what happens at these meetings, nobody does except the members – even the Finds Liaison Officer who records their finds for the Portable Antiquities Scheme and the experts who are invited to come and talk on various subjects have to sit outside the room and wait until they are called in – but I suspect it follows a similar pattern to most metal-detecting club meetings and involves nothing more mysterious than comparing and discussing recent finds.

Our knowledge of the city and the lives of its inhabitants over millennia has undoubtedly been increased by the objects society members have dug up over the years, but I think the time has come to ban digging completely. There is no need to keep disturbing an already fragile and fast-eroding foreshore for more and better objects. They are better left where they are for the future, rather than putting them at the mercy of an indiscriminate spade or fork. While only a handful of people still legally dig, the damage they do can be considerable. They hack through centuries in an afternoon, and in their rush to beat the incoming tide, they smash delicate objects and miss the small and non-metallic pieces that don't register on the sweep of their metal detectors. They leave the foreshore pocked with soft mud and poorly filled-in holes that are lethal to unwary ankles, and the objects they overlook are left to the mercy of the tides. I have made some of my best finds where the diggers have been at work and I hate to think how much more the river has claimed.

Some people commit their troubles to the river in a more tangible way by physically throwing them in and letting the water take them away. The more modern flotsam and jetsam that washes up on the foreshore can sometimes feel quite intrusive. I have found prayers and curses, remembrance wreaths, single roses, love letters, torn-up photographs, and wedding and engagement rings. They are all windows onto private moments and uncomfortable evidence of unhappiness. In many ways, I dread these encounters. They make me feel uneasy, as though I am rifling through personal possessions or eavesdropping on a stranger's life. It is a very different feeling from finding an old object that belonged to someone long ago. There is a good chance the owners of these objects are still alive and that they threw them into the river in the belief that the water would swallow their problems up and make them disappear for ever. They thought they were throwing them into a private space; they didn't consider scavengers like me.

I've kept or given away the modern rings I've found, except for one. It was a simple plain nine-karat gold wedding band, worn in places, nothing unusual apart from the inscription 'WJ 1970' engraved on the inside. I put it in my pocket without thinking, but as I continued with my day it began to weigh on my mind. If it hadn't had the initials and date I would have kept it, but something about them made it too personal. It carried an extra sadness that I didn't want to let into my life, so I threw it back into the water where it was intended to be. Even more troubling than the ring was an object that looked quite innocuous at first sight. It was a grey plastic brick that had been washed up next to a crook in the river wall in a drift of empty water bottles and broken polystyrene packaging. I had never seen anything like it before. I expected it to be light, but when I picked it up, it was surprisingly heavy. I shook it, and it sounded like sand and gravel mixed together, then as I turned it over in my hands, a soggy label revealed its contents: 'Remains of the Late ...' I had found someone's ashes.

I stared at the lonely little box for some time, pondering my options carefully. I even walked away from it a couple of times. But I couldn't just leave it there in the mud. Eventually, I wished the grey box and its contents a solemn goodbye, dropped it back into the river and watched as it floated east towards Tower Bridge. I like to think whoever was inside made it past the Estuary and out to sea, but it's more likely they're marooned, further downstream, on a more isolated part of the foreshore, with the old car tyres, plastic bottles and orphaned flip-flops.

But I think T. J. Cobden-Sanderson, the nineteenth-century bookbinder who tipped 500,000 tiny pieces of his beloved metal type into the river at Hammersmith – to be vouchsafed 'for ever and for ever' – really wanted his secret to be discovered. The story of Doves Type is mudlarking legend, although I hadn't heard of it in the days of the anonymous office block by the flyover, which was just as well otherwise the temptation to break free from the office to look for it would have been too great. I found out about Doves when I started mudlarking and began to find pieces of lead type on the foreshore in central London. I was curious about them and asked other mudlarks what they knew.

With so many printers north of Blackfriars Bridge the general consensus was that the type had accidentally washed down the drains, into what was once the Fleet River, which now trickles beneath Fleet Street and emerges from a storm drain under Blackfriars Bridge. But there were other theories. One man told me about a lead recycling plant that was beside the river near Rotherhithe until the 1970s. He said the type was delivered by barge, so perhaps it had fallen into the water in the process. Others suggested it had been deliberately thrown in by typesetters emptying their pockets on their way home over the bridges. When the pages of set type were destroyed after printing, each tiny piece had to be put back into a separate compartment in a type case. This is where the terms 'upper case' and 'lower case' come from: capital letters went in the top part of the case and small letters went beneath them in the lower part. It was a fiddly job and I've been told the typesetters often stuck the smaller pieces in their pockets to save themselves the trouble of re-casing them. Like so many Thames mysteries there seemed to be no definitive answer, but the recurring question from the people I showed the type to was, 'Is it Doves?' and this piqued my interest. What was Doves?

The story begins in 1900, when Thomas James Cobden-Sanderson together with Emery Walker founded the Doves Press beside the River Thames at Hammersmith. Walker was a typographer and printer; Cobden-Sanderson was the leading bookbinder of his generation. Both men were involved with the Arts and Crafts movement, and both had houses overlooking the river. They named their press after the riverside pub, the Dove, which is a few doors down from where Cobden-Sanderson lived at 15 Upper Mall, a three-storey house now painted white with a yellow door, a black porch and black railings.

The two men set about creating a type using fifteenth-century Italian Renaissance books for inspiration. Each letter was carefully developed and the punches, from which the type was produced, were carved by hand. It was made in only one size (16pt), with upper and lower case and no italics. The books they created were as pared down as the type, with plain white vellum covers and gold spine lettering. There were no illustrations inside to interfere with the type – the only variation was larger capital letters that were wood-engraved or hand-drawn. For Cobden-Sanderson, this was a quest to create the perfect book, suitable for only the highest works of literature – the Bible, Milton, Shakespeare, Goethe, Wordsworth. As the biographer Colin Franklin put it in his book about private presses, Cobden-Sanderson believed 'books could reduce God to a page of visible type, as sunlight on a still morning showed the river in His form'. Cobden-Sanderson wrote in his journal on 11 December 1898: 'I must, before I die, create the type for today of The Book Beautiful, and actualise it – paper ink, printing, writing, ornament, and binding. I will learn to write, to print, and to decorate.'

For six years the two men worked together to print, bind and publish Cobden-Sanderson's dream, but in 1906 they fell out. Cobden-Sanderson had become increasingly obsessed with the quality of his work and less able to cooperate with anyone else, and he told Walker he wanted to sever their arrangement, offering to buy him out. Walker refused. He wanted half of everything connected with the press and that included the type – an idea that Cobden-Sanderson couldn't countenance. To him the type was sacrosanct and he couldn't risk it becoming commercialised and in his mind defiled. Although it was finally agreed that Cobden-Sanderson could continue using the type to print books until he died, upon which time it was to pass to Walker, he was prepared to prevent it from falling into his old business partner's hands at any cost.

Having worked beside the Thames since 1893, Cobden-Sanderson was familiar with the movement of the river. He even once described its surface as a 'sheet of molten lead' and perhaps this is what gave him the idea to do what he did next. In his journal, on 9 June 1911, he spelled out his intentions:

> To the Bed of the River Thames, the river on whose banks
> I have printed all my printed books, I bequeath The Doves
> Press Fount of Type – the punches, the matrices, and the
> type in use at the time of my death, and may the river in its
> tides and flow pass over them to and from the great sea for
> ever and for ever, or until its tides and flow for ever cease;
> then may they share the fate of all the world, and pass
> from change to change for ever upon the Tides of Time,
> untouched of other use, and all else.

And so, in March 1913 he began to commit the type to the river, first throwing in all the punches and matrices and recording what he did from then onwards in his journals: 'Yes; yesterday, and the day before, and Tuesday I stood on the bridge at Hammersmith, and looking towards the Press and the sun setting, threw into the Thames below me the matrices from which had been cast the Doves Press Fount of Type, itself to be cast by me, I hope, into the same great river, from the same place, on the final closure of the Press in __?'

But it wasn't until the night of 31 August 1916 that he began to dispose of the type itself. 'I had gone for a stroll on the Mall, when it occurred to me that it was a suitable night and time; so I went indoors, and taking first one page and then two, succeeded in destroying three. I will now go on till I have destroyed the whole of it.' It took him until January 1917 to get rid of it all, throwing over a ton of lead type into the river in the course of around 170 nightly visits. Under the cover of darkness he walked a mile from his house on the Mall, along the river and over the bridge, to a point where the water was deepest and where he was concealed from the road. There he waited until a vehicle passed, to drown out the splash of the type hitting the water, before scuttling back over the bridge and home. Rather than feeling remorseful, Cobden-Sanderson's journals suggest he was in his element. Although he feared being caught by the police, he also revelled in being found out. 'I rather like the idea of the discovery. I shall not attempt to hide it up if I am discovered, but shall own up and explain the object I had in view, "to dedicate the type".'

Each visit was a carefully planned adventure. He tried carrying the type in his pockets, or in linen bags, or by wrapping it in paper. One Friday night he threw two packets that landed on a projecting pier of the bridge. Instead of panicking he found the whole affair quite comical, and after deciding not to hire a boat to retrieve them, waited to let the river decide his and their fate. Eventually he found a wooden box with a sliding lid, which proved to be the best solution. 'I heave up the box to the parapet, release the sliding lid, and let the type fall sheer into the river – the work of a moment.' But this method was not without its risks either and one night he nearly emptied the contents into a passing boat.

By the time Cobden-Sanderson had finished, the only existing pieces of Doves Type left belonged, rather ironically, to Walker. He had used them to set a Christmas message to his wife that read: 'May this Christmas of the Century Prove the best kept unto the last for thee. M.G.W. 3 Hammersmith Terrace W. Christmas 1900.' But it represented just a fraction of the 98–100 glyphs – or characters – in the original metal font and without the rest of the type it was unusable. Cobden-Sanderson had succeeded.

But the story doesn't quite end there. When Cobden-Sanderson died in 1922, his ashes were tucked into a nook in a wall at the end of his garden, overlooking the river. His wife's ashes joined them in 1926. Then in 1928 there was a great flood. The Thames burst its banks at Hammersmith and the ashes of Cobden-Sanderson and his wife were taken away by the current to join his beloved font. He guards it from the river now.

This was the stuff of fiction. I couldn't believe it had happened on the Thames, and the more I read the more fascinated I became. Then, when I posted a picture of some of the type I had found on the foreshore further downstream at Blackfriars on my Facebook page, a man called Robert Green responded. He doubted it was Doves, he said, because he had most if not all that had been found. Who was Robert Green and what else did he know about the type? I asked if he'd meet me and some weeks later I was sitting in a cafe in Shoreditch listening to him describe how he had become a man obsessed.

Robert looked about my age, I thought on first meeting him. Stocky with a shaved head, his eyelids drooped to cover tired eyes and his brow furrowed as he talked over coffee about his work as a designer and how the design world had changed since he had graduated from art college. His mood lifted, however, when we got on to Doves. His obsession with recreating what he sees as the most perfect font began in 2010, when he was looking for a specific font for the project he was working on. He knew, as soon as he saw images of Doves online, that he had found what he wanted, and unable to get hold of a digital version of it he decided to create it himself.

He began by copying the font from what were, in his words, 'rubbish references': over-contrasted images of the printed type reproduced in reference books, which made everything look thick, blobby and amorphous, and impossible to reproduce accurately. He then sought out examples of Doves Press books in the British Library. The Library wouldn't let him scan the precious pages at high resolution, which is what he needed, without prohibitive charges and he worked out he would need so many that it was cheaper and more practical to buy some original pieces of his own. So he began to scour London's book dealers and managed to track down a single page of the famous Doves Bible and enough pieces of Doves ephemera to give him an example of each glyph. For the next three years, he worked on trying to recreate the font from this, but metal type pressed into soft paper distorts and weakens the print and the results just weren't good enough. The only way he could see to recreate an accurate version, was to use the actual type itself – so he determined to find some. Reading everything he could find about Cobden-Sanderson, he inserted himself into the old man's state of mind, until he worked out where the type might have been disposed of and he was ready to go down to the river to look for it.

He went onto the foreshore when the tide was out, looked around the riverbed and found the first piece within twenty minutes. It was the letter 'i'. 'I knew it was there, I knew it was waiting for me,' he said. He felt as if Cobden-Sanderson had handed it to him personally as a reward for his tenacity. He found two more pieces within five yards of the first before the tide came back in. He returned a month later with a crew from the PLA, including three divers who searched with their fingertips in near zero visibility, spiralling into the find spot from around ten yards out, but in total they only recovered another 148 pieces. Of the 98–100 glyphs in the original metal font, Robert has around thirty – no numbers and only a few pieces of punctuation. The divers reported a lot of poured concrete at the dive site, from repair works to the bridge, and Robert believes this has entombed many of the 500,000 individual pieces of type he estimates Cobden-Sanderson threw in the river.

Hammersmith Bridge is a suspension bridge with two pairs of pillars at each end, and it's never been very stable – three IRA bomb attacks haven't helped. The first, on Wednesday 29 March 1939, was foiled by Maurice Childs, a hairdresser from nearby Chiswick, who was walking home across the bridge in the early hours of the morning when he saw smoke and sparks coming from a suitcase lying on the walkway. He opened it, discovered a bomb and quickly hurled the bag into the river. The explosion sent a sixty-foot column of water up into the air, which could also have scattered the type far and wide. 'Even if you went down there you wouldn't find anything,' Robert said. 'Those bits I found are my reward for five years of hard work, the rest is all gone now ... and I'm not telling you where to look anyway.' Spoken like a true mudlark. But I know the river and I know how it produces objects at random when you're least expecting it, so I thought it was worth giving it a try.

I went to Hammersmith on an early-spring day. Pasty-faced people were emerging from winter hibernation and the riverside was busy. Joggers puffed past and office workers sat eating their lunchtime sandwiches on benches, enjoying the year's first rays of sunshine. As I approached the bridge the traffic petered out. It was closed for the week for yet more maintenance work and was blissfully free of its usual lines of cars. Men in hi-vis vests were hard at work; saws buzzed, hammers clattered and a light cloud of dust hung in the air. I had spoken to Robert earlier in the week and he had let slip a couple more clues as to where to begin my search. Using those and trying to think like someone committing a potentially illegal act, I headed to one of the bays by a pillar where, just like Cobden-Sanderson, I was obscured from one direction and had a good view of oncoming traffic from the other. I could see where Doves Press had once been; it felt right and it felt strange to be standing there, knowing I was treading the same route he had all those years ago.

I walked to the end of the bridge and dropped down onto the river path. The lime-green buds on the trees and bushes were bursting open and the soil smelled of new life and spring. I scrambled down the riverbank, through last year's dead weeds and onto a soft layer of silty mud that eventually gave way to gravel. A broken safe lay half submerged and an empty champagne bottle had been abandoned by the retreating tide. Apart from that, the foreshore was relatively clean and I spent some time walking along the shingle, trying to locate patches of small pieces of metal where I thought the type might gather in the same way that it did near Blackfriars, but I couldn't find any and soon gave up.

As I walked to the edge of the water, I disturbed the pigeons pecking around the stones. They flew up among the metal girders beneath the bridge and cooed softly down at me while I searched the tideline, following the water as it retreated. The bright spring sunshine was a surprise accomplice, cutting through the clear water and magnifying the riverbed. Gradually the tide pulled back, away from the pillar, revealing chunks of concrete with nuts and bolts and bits of iron from old repairs embedded in it. My heart sank. Perhaps every bit had gone after all; maybe it was, as Robert had said, encased in concrete. Then, lying in a thin layer of shingle the river had deposited on top of some of the concrete, I saw it. A dull grey slug of type. I couldn't believe it. I'd found what I had come for and I felt just as Robert had: as though Cobden-Sanderson had reached out through the years and handed me a prize for my efforts.

I squinted at the piece of metal between my wet, frozen fingers and could just make out the curve and tail of a comma. Robert didn't have a comma; it was, as far as I knew, the only Doves Type comma in the world. To think it had been touched by the man I had read so much about. I stashed it safely in my finds bag and hunted around for more. Two more pieces followed quickly from the same patch, both blank spacers, and then nothing. I searched for another two hours until the river drove me away. I had plundered Cobden-Sanderson's secret and it was all I was getting that day.

I was beaming from ear to ear as I skipped back over the deserted bridge, desperate to share my discovery with someone who understood. Without really thinking, I retraced Cobden-Sanderson's footsteps west, along the river path, past the Georgian houses and the houseboats moored against the piers, down the cobbled alley past his white three-storey house to the Dove pub for a well-earned drink. Feeling more than a little smug, I texted Robert a photograph of my treasures. He called me immediately, a little incredulous. 'I thought it was all gone,' he said. 'I'll have to take another look.'

I didn't go back to Hammersmith for another year. I wasn't going to go back at all. I thought I'd cured my obsession and I had a little bit of history to show for it, but it was still playing on my mind. I wanted an actual letter and I had a feeling there was more to find. So one very low, late-night tide, I trekked back to west London for another look. The tide was at its lowest close to midnight, and since I hadn't wanted to be there alone, I'd asked my friend Lisa to come with me – ostensibly to hold the torch, but also to bolster my nerves. Our excited chatter hushed to a whisper as we descended the stairs to the dark river path. I felt my eyes stretch wide open as I tried to take in as much of my surroundings as I could in the weak light and every step we took was loud and clumsy in the silence.

While Lisa shone the torch, we both peered into the mud. It took perhaps forty-five minutes, but then I saw it. Another slug of type, caught against a chunk of concrete. I snatched it up and trained the light on it – an 'f'. My wish had been granted. Lisa wanted one too, so we carried on searching for another hour or so. By then it was very late, but we hadn't found anything more so we called it a night. Since Hammersmith is off my regular mudlarking patch I won't be going back there – I have what I wanted – but I did recently read about another set of type called Vale that was flung into the Thames in 1903 by a man named Charles Ricketts. His efforts to become 'a publisher in earnest' bear similarities to Cobden-Sanderson's obsession with the Book Beautiful. Perhaps I'll start looking for that next ...

In the meantime, Robert has created a digital version of Doves based on printed references and the type he found in the Thames. As there were no italics in the original version, he is creating them himself and has designed an @ to bring it up to date. According to Robert, it is not Doves but a version based on his interpretation of it: an 'apparition' of the original. Perhaps this would be enough to pacify Cobden-Sanderson, who wrote in his journal, 'It is my wish that the Doves Press type shall never be subjected to the use of a machine other than the human hand.' If you want to know what it looks like, look carefully at the title on the jacket, the running heads at the top of each page and the epigraphs and first letter of every chapter. They are all set in Doves – and the comma ... the comma is mine.

VAUXHALL

I have seen the Mississippi. That is muddy water. I have seen
the Saint Lawrence. That is crystal water. But the Thames is
liquid history.

John Burns, Liberal MP 1892–1918

I don't visit Vauxhall often, but on unusually low tides, I
will occasionally travel west to descend to the foreshore near Vauxhall Bridge. This is my favourite bridge, a
mudlark's bridge, best seen from the foreshore. From the
road it looks quite ordinary and as if it could do with a
lick of paint, but from the foreshore and the river it is a
work of art that relatively few ever properly see. Mounted
above the granite piers and facing the river on both sides
are eight allegorical figures representing industry. They are
all women, which is quite something since they were cast
at the turn of the twentieth century when men dominated
almost every sphere of the working environment. Twice
life-size, they are also some of the largest bronze figures
in London. Each one is classically swathed and holding an
object to represent her discipline. Facing upstream, Pottery
is solid and strong with a pot cradled in the crook of one
arm and the other resting on her hip, Engineering is similarly Amazonian and holds a miniature steam engine, while

Architecture, with her scale model of St Paul's Cathedral, is more delicate and youthful. The hooded figure of Agriculture carries a scythe in one hand and a sheaf of corn in the other. On the opposite side, facing downstream, Education holds a naked infant in her arms and shelters a boy with a book under her cloak, Fine Art looks dreamily down into the water with a palette and brushes held to her breast, and Science and Local Government have a solemn, serious look about them.

The high grey granite wall of the Albert Embankment extends from Vauxhall Bridge to Westminster Bridge along the south bank. It is imposing from the foreshore, carpeted in bright green weed and swagged with three lines of thick chain, and it lends an air of urban sophistication to the river that it lacks further upstream. Before the Embankment was built, this stretch at Vauxhall had a reputation for filth, overcrowding and unsanitary conditions. Fetid alleyways, decrepit houses, wharves, boatyards and stinking factories tumbled towards the river and the foreshore was thick with sewage and industrial waste. But with the construction of the Embankment between 1866 and 1870 all of this was swept away and the riverbank was transformed. It allowed the Metropolitan Board of Works to construct a main drainage system for the capital and its high walls prevented the low-lying areas of Vauxhall from flooding, which they previously did regularly on particularly high tides. Large carved stone lion faces frown at the river from the wall. Some still hold metal rings in their mouths, while the mouths of others are empty, leaving them with a sad and incomplete look. According to the saying, if the lions are seen drinking on a high tide, London will flood. I've seen the lions drinking a few times, but I've yet to see London flood.

At very low tides at Vauxhall, the remains of an ancient structure can be seen emerging at the water's edge. The two rows of wooden posts were first noticed by a mudlark in 1993 and have been dated to the Middle Bronze Age, approximately 1500 BC. Since they were discovered the foreshore has continued to erode and they now stand quite clearly proud of the mud. There are also the remains of a possible Iron Age fish trap nearby and what could be, although it's yet to be proved, an even older prehistoric structure just to the east of the bridge.

Two thousand years ago, the Thames was a slower moving river, twice as wide as it is now and far more shallow. It flowed over and between a collection of islands and through marshes, scrubland and mudflats. Only a handful of hills and gravel terraces stood proud of the water in what is now central London, and this is where the Romans founded the city. The native Britons called their river 'Tamesa' or 'Tamesis', from the Celtic *tam*, meaning smooth or wide-spreading. As well as the land, the Romans also took the river's name, translating it into 'Thamesis'.

The river is why the Romans came. Its tidal waters allowed their ships to come inland, bringing troops and imported goods and taking away local produce and slaves. They built jetties, quays and wharves, and eventually, a river wall. As the city grew, the spaces between the shore and natural river islands were filled in, tributaries were covered over and more land was reclaimed behind a series of wooden and stone river walls. Over the centuries, the riverside crept further and further towards the river's deepest part and the river channel narrowed to become the familiar thin brown ribbon that loops and wiggles its way through the city today.

In its natural state the riverbed has a gentle incline towards the centre of the river, but to facilitate the loading and unloading of ships that by the start of the eighteenth century were coming to London from every corner of the globe in ever increasing numbers, it needed to be flat. Strips of foreshore were stabilised and level platforms known as 'barge beds', or 'hards', were constructed next to wharves and jetties. The barge beds that are left on the foreshore today are contained within strong wooden plank and pile structures – called revetments or campsheds – built several yards from the river wall. The revetments were filled with the city's rubbish, anything that was available – soil, old building rubble and general waste – then capped with a hard surface, often chalk, which was rammed down until it was solid and flat.

Constant use and the persistent efforts of the river to wash it away meant that the barge beds had to be regularly maintained, but by the 1960s and 70s, the working wharves and warehouses had closed and boats and barges no longer unloaded at the river wall. Without anyone to look after the barge beds the river has been slowly picking away at its scabs, breaking through the revetments and scooping out the contents, returning the foreshore to its natural state. In many places, all that it is left of the barge beds are ghostly streaks of white chalk and broken planks that flap and strain at the metal trusses that tether them on every tide, until they finally break free and float away, washing up further downstream. At Vauxhall, the river is eating away at a layer of old concrete and scooping out the soft chalk below it, creating a craggy lunar landscape of volcanic dips and hollows.

Some mourn the loss of these riverside structures, but their demise is my gain, their contents my treasure. Within the revetments are demolished houses, road sweepings, domestic refuse, kiln waste and spoil from foundations and cellars dug deep into the medieval and Roman layers of the city. It is one of the reasons the foreshore's bounty is so random, why I have eased an eighteenth-century clay pipe bowl out of the mud only to find a medieval coin beneath it, why Roman roof tiles lie next to Tudor bricks and Victorian bottles rub shoulders with shards of sixteenth-century stoneware jugs. The foreshore is a muddle of refuse and casual losses, and the broken and neglected barge beds have added generously to this swirling mess of history.

The Thames is England's longest archaeological landscape and thousands of the objects that fill our museums have come from its foreshore. Among them are numerous Bronze and Iron Age swords, shields and spears that were found along the stretch between Vauxhall and Teddington and include the famous Battersea Shield. It was dredged from the riverbed in 1857 during excavations for Battersea Bridge and remains one of the most beautiful objects ever to have been taken from the river. It is a long, rounded oblong sheet of bronze that would have been the facing of a wooden shield. It was made somewhere between 350 and 50 BC by an expert in their craft, who engraved and stippled intricate scrolling patterns around three roundels and a high-domed central boss. It is finished with twenty-seven framed studs of red glass 'enamel' in four different sizes.

Over the course of the nineteenth century the river was transformed. Embankments were built on both sides of it, Old London Bridge was torn down, new bridges and docks were built, and the channel was dredged to enable large ships to travel further upstream. The river began to relinquish its treasures. Rich collectors and antiquaries pounced on the objects that appeared in the dredgermen's buckets and beneath labourers' spades. Two men in particular, Thomas Layton and Charles Roach Smith, each built up enviable collections of exquisite river-found objects, which they bought from mudlarks, fishermen, watermen, dredgermen and workmen, often for little more than a bottle of beer.

Roach Smith was a chemist by trade and focused his attentions on the Roman objects being dredged out of the river at London Bridge. Layton, who lived at Brentford, spread his net far wider. He paid comparatively well for what he bought, and as a result he was well known among the river workers. As soon as anything of interest was found, word went round and Layton was contacted. His collection soon grew quite out of proportion. His house was stacked high with boxes of rare treasures that spilled out into his garden and filled thirty sheds. He became a recluse, gradually retreating into his own world in his odd house amid his hoarded possessions. Sometimes he lent pieces to learned societies, but mostly they stayed in boxes, hidden away and unrecorded. When he died in 1911, antiquaries came to assess his collection. They opened box after box of delights, among which they found twenty-eight Middle

Bronze Age rapiers, thirty-three Late Bronze Age swords, thirty-four spearheads and six bronze sickles, all of which had been found in the Thames.

But not all was as it seemed. In their haste to acquire booty from the river, some collectors fell foul of two cunning mudlarks called William Smith and Charles Eaton, who cleverly exploited the situation to make a few quid for themselves. Billy and Charley decided that they could make more money by manufacturing their own 'found' antiquities and began casting a range of faux-medieval objects in hand-cut plaster moulds. At the start of their enterprise they claimed to have found their trinkets at Shadwell, where the new dock was being excavated. For several years they passed them through a network of antique dealers who sold them to middle-class collectors, often with more money than knowledge, and even to some of the most eminent collectors of the time, among them Charles Roach Smith. But in 1861 they were rumbled by a sewer hunter who revealed their covert means of production to a member of the Society of Antiquaries.

Though their exposure restricted their market, Billy and Charley, who were never found guilty of anything, continued in business until Charley's death from consumption in 1870. Nothing more is known of Billy after this date. I like to think he retired on his profits, but it is more likely that he also succumbed to TB or met with a similarly miserable end in a workhouse. But the boys had the last laugh. Examples of 'Billy and Charleys' are now kept by the British Museum and the Museum of London where they are proudly displayed next to the objects they sought to emulate. On the open market examples are rare and much sought after, sometimes commanding an even higher price than the original equivalent.

It wasn't until the mid-twentieth century that people began to appreciate the ordinary treasures the Thames contains. And for this we have the late great Ivor Noël Hume to thank. The godfather of modern mudlarks, Noël Hume was a largely self-taught archaeologist who began work after the war excavating sites that had been exposed by the Blitz before reconstruction work on the city began. Hume tells the story of a fireman called Robin Green who, during the Second World War, fell into the water while fighting a blaze in a bombed-out warehouse and surfaced holding an eighteenth-century clay tobacco pipe. Green began visiting the foreshore, where he collected the objects that had to this point mostly been ignored – buttons, clay pipes, buckles and broken pottery. He amassed quite a collection, which he sold to the Guildhall Museum (a precursor to the Museum of London), which is where Hume worked.

Hume became an avid mudlark, or as he put it, 'a something for nothing collector', and spent eight years – 'the most stimulating and exciting hours of my life' – searching the foreshore before he left London for America in 1957 to become chief archaeologist at colonial Williamsburg. In 1955 he wrote the brilliant *Treasure in the Thames*, whose title says it all, and in 1974 he wrote an anecdotal book about the pleasures of studying and collecting everyday objects called *All the Best Rubbish*.

Hume was the first archaeologist to recognise the historical significance of objects found on the foreshore. Until he came along most archaeologists were dismissive of artefacts found out of context, perceiving them to have less historical value, but Hume was different and considered it his duty to rescue and appreciate objects for what they were in themselves and not just for where they came from. His ethos made him perfectly suited to the foreshore, because almost everything here is out of context.

Fine shingle and sand spreads down to the river in a gentle slope at Vauxhall, but this is not a stretch for the complacent. Dips and hollows hide thick mud and layers of gravel disguise treacherous sink patches that can suck you in, steal boots and hold legs tight. There are pinch points too – 'waists' of foreshore that fill back in quickly on the incoming tide, marooning the unwary. I've been caught out by one of these, further downstream, when I lost track of time and turned round to find that the river had cut me off. I escaped by wading knee-deep through icy water, but ten more minutes and the current would have been too strong to risk it. I've never had to call out the emergency services, but in that situation it would have been my only option. I'm more careful now. I keep a check on my escape routes and I watch the water carefully once it turns.

The unpredictable nature of the foreshore at Vauxhall means that I rarely visit alone. Sometimes I tag along with Mike, a foreshore archaeologist who has been visiting this stretch for many years and knows it well. His passion is pottery and we have spent long, convivial hours together combing the foreshore for unusual pieces to add to his collection. A gentle man with kind, bright blue eyes, he has a generous spirit formed by a life of hard knocks. History and a personal sense of place within time have gripped Mike since he was small. At the age of six or seven he was

told at school to go home and find out about his family history. He had known he was adopted from an early age, but
it wasn't until he was directly confronted by the past that
he realised he didn't have one. His obsession with history
grew from this, and a few years later the little boy without
a history found himself at the Tutankhamen exhibition at
the British Museum standing face-to-face with the funerary
mask of a boy not much older than himself. It was then
and there that he decided to become an archaeologist, but
it was some time before he realised his dream. After a few
false starts he eventually went to university, took his degree
and finally began work as a qualified archaeologist. Then
one day, in the mid-1990s, he was asked if he was interested
in helping to conduct an archaeological survey of the River
Thames and he was hooked straight away. He hasn't left
the river since.

Much of Mike's work has been to raise awareness of the
archaeological potential of the river and the value of the
foreshore, which until the 1990s was much overlooked. At
the time nobody paid attention to the artefacts that were
being found, except the mudlarks who were collecting and
selling them. Mike is committed to sharing the foreshore in
a more responsible way and encouraging people to use it to
explore their own history, but the river is more than a job
for him: being surrounded by so many fragments from the
past offers him a feeling of comfort and a sense of belonging
that fills the gap left in his own history.

It was Mike who took me back to prehistoric London
one low tide at Vauxhall. As the river retreated he
explained how it came into being and showed me where
the water had scoured the foreshore down to the firm

yellow-brown London clay, which was laid down on top of chalk around 55 million years ago, when London was under warm tropical seas. Around 40 million years ago the seas receded, land appeared and the river that was to become the Thames was born. At this time it was a tributary of the ancestor of the modern river Rhine in Germany and followed a course to the north of where it currently flows. Glacial advance 440,000 years ago pushed the river south to its current course, where it began to erode a path in the soft clay, leaving behind a series of gravel and sand terraces.

Encased in the clay and lying among the gravel on the foreshore are the fossilised remains of the creatures that inhabited those prehistoric seas. The pencil-like internal shells of belemnites, ancient extinct squid, that swam in shoals over 66 million years ago; bivalves the size and shape of cockles, frozen in stone; and 'devil's toenails', an extinct form of marine oyster that lived in the sediment of the seabed. At Warden Point on the Estuary, fossilised crabs, lobsters, shells, twigs and shark teeth fall from the low cliffs of London clay onto the beach where they can be collected by the handful, and occasionally smoothed pieces of yellow amber will wash ashore where the Estuary and North Sea mingle. Years ago, before people knew what fossils were, they were shrouded in folklore and assigned all kinds of quasi-religious and mystical associations. One of the most commonly found fossils in the south of England, and along the Thames foreshore, are echinoids. The colloquial name for echinoid is 'sea urchin', which comes from the old country name for hedgehog. But it is only their feather-light outer skeleton that survives fossilisation and transforms the delicate spiny creature into something smooth, strong and heavy.

When I was a child, my father's cousin had a farm on the chalky North Downs and every autumn we would follow the plough looking for these neat, bun-shaped stones, covered with intricate patterns of dots and lines. We understood their age and how they were formed, but they still held a fascination and a magical quality we found irresistible. They would have been familiar and yet mysterious to early prehistoric people digging for flints to turn into stone tools and they have been found in both Bronze and Iron Age burials, proving that they held special significance. Depending where you are in the country, they are known as 'fairy loaves', 'shepherd's crowns', 'pixie helmets', 'fairy hats', 'sugar loaves', 'chalk eggs' and 'eagle stones' for the apparent claw marks along their sides. They were kept by the hearth to ensure the house never ran out of bread and on windowsills to protect against lightning and to help predict the weather – they were said to sweat before a storm. They protected the owner from witchcraft and could cure and prevent disease, and in some areas they were kept in the dairy and the pantry to prevent the milk from turning sour. A sea urchin fossil lived in the dairy on the farm where I grew up. It was on a high dusty shelf and had been there, out of reach, for as long as I could remember. I'm not sure if someone had found it in a field and forgotten about it or if it had been left there on purpose, but as far as I know the milk never turned sour, even on thundery days.

Some foreshore fossils have come to London across oceans, arriving in the cargo and ballast of ships from all over the world. Close to a dump of fossilised coral limestone,

I once found a large, flat tooth, about two inches long. Every detail had been preserved in the smooth black stone including the characteristic lobed root that told me it was a shark's tooth. I queued at the Natural History Museum one wet miserable day to get it identified and was told it had once belonged to an *Isurus hastalis*, a giant white shark that became extinct around 3 million years ago. They can be found in many places around the world, but fossils like this are not known to come from the Thames area. Neither are the speckled chunks of fossilised *Lepidodendron* bark that are commonly found on the foreshore. Great forests of these tree-sized Carboniferous plants grew about 359 to 299 million years ago in the wetlands that covered the Earth's tropical land areas. The forests they grew in eventually became coal and the fossils probably arrived in London on coal barges from the north of England.

Flint came in the chalk that was used on the barge beds and it is also native to the foreshore. It formed many millions of years ago within chalk and comes from the natural layers of chalk that line the Thames basin. Areas of grey worn flint cobbles can be slippery and unstable to walk on; they twist ankles and slow progress along the foreshore. Newly eroded flint nodules strike tortured and eccentric shapes, natural modernist sculptures and miniature Henry Moores. Sometimes mistaken for ancient carvings, they are in fact Mother Nature's own handiwork. Flint is too hard and brittle to carve, but the gentle and persistent action of water can, over many millennia, drill holes through weaker points.

Flints with holes in them are easy to find on the foreshore and traditionally considered to be lucky. In England they are known as witch or hag stones, and were traditionally hung in doorways and windows as protection from evil. It was also thought they could cure and prevent sickness, guard from nightmares and provide a window into the fairy world. I used to collect them when I was small and lugged heavy bags of them home from the beach to thread with wire and make into giant necklaces. I collect them from the Thames now and still thread them into necklaces, which I hang on the fence and from the branches of trees in the garden. For luck, and as a reminder of the power and persistence of nature, I left a pile on the table at my wedding reception for guests to take away, and now I'm teaching my children to use them as spyglasses into magical realms.

Four hundred and forty-thousand years ago, the Thames flowed through a cold, treeless tundra inhabited by woolly rhino, mammoth, wolves, bear and early humans. As temperatures and sea levels rose and fell, other animals found their way across from continental Europe. Lions hunted giant deer along the banks of the Thames, hippos wallowed in its shallows, and by the Mesolithic period, ten thousand years ago, nomadic groups were hunting auroch, bison, wild horses and red deer on the grassy plains by the river and searching for berries and nuts in the dense woodlands nearby. They eventually settled along its wide, meandering course, fishing in the shallows and using dugout canoes to paddle between the many sand and gravel bars that dotted its waters.

Those early humans left behind a range of flint tools, including large oval handaxes and delicately worked small brown slivers with facets as smooth as glass that were struck off larger pieces. Worked flints are difficult to spot among the naturally occurring stones, but I have learned that the key to identifying them lies in the 'bulb of percussion' – a cone-shaped bulge that spreads out from the exact point where the flake is struck from the flint core. The tools these people produced would have had many uses. Small flakes may have been attached to a pole with resin and twine to make a harpoon for fishing, scrapers would have been used to clean hides and scrape meat from bones, and blades were multipurpose.

I searched for years on the foreshore before I found my first Mesolithic flint, a round mud-coloured stone that fits perfectly between my thumb and forefinger. Since then I've found several others in the same spot – my Thames-found collection is now of a reasonable size and includes small microliths, scrapers, blades and part of a broken spear-head – but the first one was the most special. You'd think picking a stone out from among other stones would be difficult, but it wasn't, it was obvious, it didn't fit into its background. I can't explain it any other way. It just didn't look as if it should be there – it looked 'interfered with' – and I knew exactly what it was the moment I picked it up. I'd found one at last and a mad, giddy, bursting-with-happiness feeling washed over me that had been waiting thirty-five years to get out. I was the first human to touch it in thousands and thousands of years. It was (and still is) the most ancient man- or woman-made object I'd found.

Along the waterline at Vauxhall are humps of what look like rich dark brown mud, which Mike told me was prehistoric peat, created around 3,750 years ago during a period that saw the water level rise and drown the scrub and forests that grew along the river's banks. Embedded in the humps are soft spongy roots, thin crumbling branches and perfectly preserved hazelnuts, delicate and blackened over time. I picked at the mud and looked carefully at its make-up. Tiny delicate plant fibres disintegrated between my pinched thumb and forefinger into a smooth chocolatey paste.

Hazel is the tree of knowledge and its forked branches are still used by some to find water and buried treasure. I have three delicate prehistoric hazelnuts from Vauxhall in my freezer and I don't dare risk defrosting and drying them in case they crumble away to nothing. It's incredible they've survived in such a perfect state. When I picked them up I expected them to dissolve into mush, but they were still hard, not as hard as a new nut, but hard enough to survive being transported home in a small plastic zippy bag. They were the oldest datable organic objects I'd ever found and I felt as if I had made an incredible discovery. But I was not the first to have noticed them. About a year after I found my little flood survivors, I came across a reference to something very similar in Pepys's diary. On Friday 22 September 1665 he wrote about a conversation with Henry Johnson, a ship-builder at Blackwall who had been digging a new dock there and 'did 12 foot under ground find perfect trees over-Covered with earth – nut trees, with the branches and the very nuts upon them – some of whose nuts he showed us – their shells black with age and their Kernell, upon opening, decayed; but their shell perfectly hard as ever'. I had made the same discovery as Pepys had 350 years ago and that felt almost as special as holding prehistoric hazelnuts in my hand.

The best evidence of prehistoric life on the Thames, however, lies almost twenty miles downstream from Vauxhall at Erith, right on the border of London with Kent. The foreshore at Erith has a reputation for unpredictability and

I had heard stories of people having to be rescued from the mud, so with this in mind Mike suggested I contact Jane, an environmental archaeologist and Inspector of Ancient Monuments who is tasked with protecting London's most iconic sites. Each year, on an early spring tide, Jane visits Erith to assess the site, and each year she reports fewer preserved prehistoric trees. They are slowly being claimed by the river: another disappearing riverine feature.

I joined her one miserably cold and wet day in January. A small, capable woman with an easy manner, she took the long walk from the station to the river at speed, a confident air of urgency about her. As we walked she explained her approach to the foreshore and its contents. 'People should know what's coming out of the river so that its importance is appreciated and understood,' she said. 'After all, it's not a discovery if you keep it to yourself.' I nodded enthusiastically. My thoughts exactly.

We approached the foreshore through one of the last remaining salt marshes in the area. The winter-browned reeds and grasses rustled and startled wading birds rose in front of us as we gingerly felt our way through them, wary of sudden deep patches of mud. Then, as we neared the river, the forest came into view, and it was mind-boggling. There were two levels. We jumped off a low sharp bank onto the upper shelf – there were tangled roots of ancient alder trees everywhere, still gripping the mud in tight knots where they had once grown – but the lower shelf, which is closer to the water, is the most spectacular. We took another sharp step down, sinking into smooth thick silt. All around me, as far as I could see on either side, remains of trees were lying in the mud.

We had stepped into a tree graveyard, though the fallen trees looked as if they had floated down the river and been washed up on the last tide, momentarily caught in the silt before being carried away on the next one. These trees had once been part of a dark, dense woodland that had edged the river 6,000 years ago (they've been radiocarbon dated to around 4000 BC) and they have been lying here since the water levels suddenly rose and swamped them. 'We've recorded oak, ash, elm and holly,' Jane said, pointing out each of the different species to me. The longest and largest were the yew trees, some of which must have been almost thirty feet long. They had a ball of gnarled roots on one end, which reminded me of the large pear tree next to the farmhouse that had been uprooted by the Great Storm of 1987, and they were wrapped in bark. According to Jane they were still hard inside, just waterlogged and not rotten at all. This brought to mind more of what I'd read in Pepys's diary when ancient wood was discovered at Blackwall further upstream: 'And a yew tree he showed us (upon which, he says, the very ivy was taken up whole about it), which upon cutting with an addes, we found to be rather harder than the living tree usually is. They say, very much, but I do not know how hard a yew tree naturally is.'

While Jane counted trees, I set off across the mud to search for signs of the people who may have lived and hunted among them. Worked flints and early pottery have been found around the fallen trees at Erith as well as in the peat beds at Vauxhall, though in the hour I spent looking all I found was a round stone that had been crazed and cracked by the heat of a fire. I rolled it around in my pocket and pondered on it. I'd been told that stones were used to heat water. Perhaps this one had helped keep a cold family warm 6,000 years ago.

My wellington boots were heavy and clagged with mud and as I walked, each step released the strong silty essence of the river. The aromas that lift off the foreshore vary along its length. I never know if the smell will delight or offend me, or what mental switches it will flick. Mud and clay form the base notes, while the top notes change with the location, the weather and the time of year. On hot days, the foreshore emits a dank, bestial stink – pungent alkaline bursts of warm algae, rotten wood and wet sand that fill my nose and rest on my tongue. It is a smell with flavour and substance, thick and chewable. In the winter months, a steely, mineral tang is caught on the icy winds that blow downriver and leaves a taste of frozen stone in my mouth. Storms call up the sea, lifting a faintly saline scent from the river that grows brackish as the clouds darken and thunder gathers. Summer rain ignites dry mud, releasing a chalky dampness into the air.

Sometimes, I catch rich wafts as I cross a bridge or walk past the entrance to one of the damp passageways that lead to the river's banks, but the full wealth of aromas can only really be appreciated from the foreshore itself. Sometimes the smell alone tells me where I am. At the tidal head, the river gives off the soft earthy scent of rotting leaves. On the Isle of Dogs, where the sand is dark with flakes of rust, the smell is hard and metallic. As the sun warms the thick strip of tar on the foreshore at Blackwall, the scent of sailing ships is conjured from the mud, while the oil-soaked sand at Woolwich releases traces of engines and machinery. At Erith and Vauxhall, when the tide is low, the fragrance of the foreshore is peaty and ancient. If time were odorous, it would smell like this.

I'd quite lost track of time when I heard Jane calling me from a distance. I looked up and saw that the river had turned. It was creeping steadily in towards us and we would have to begin our journey home. I slipped and skidded to where Jane was waiting on the upper shelf and found a place where I could clamber up, digging my boots into muddy footholds. From up here, I stopped to take one last look at the trees as they were covered by the water again.

The fog had begun to roll in, obscuring the Dartford Crossing, the last bridge on the Thames. It was the same fog that had settled on the river since the first primordial trickle began to cut a course through the London clay and the forests I had been looking at covered its banks. The Thames is famous for its fogs, which creep silently over the channel and smother the foreshore, a great white cloud of damp river breath, thick and consuming, filling ears and covering eyes, curling down throats and settling on lungs. Thames fogs can feel unbearably claustrophobic, too intimate and too invasive, but they also offer comfort and security, a soft white pocket in which to escape from the world.

When the fog is very thick and visibility is down to no more than a few yards, the discernible space is all that exists; there is no city, no traffic, and not another soul. The only reminders of the world outside are occasional muffled sounds, damp and distorted, coming from every direction and from nowhere: the cry of lost seagulls; muted shouts from men on riverside building sites, their hammers padded and soft; and passing boats, horns sounding in the distance, invisible engines growing louder as they pass then fade away, leaving waves in their wake that lap at the foreshore like a dog worrying a wound.

Time stands still in the fog. With all modern points of reference obscured, the river is ageless, static and ghostly. The spirits of the foreshore rise up in the mist, just out of sight. Through the swirling whiteness a medieval fisherman pegs his fish traps to the riverbed, a Victorian scavenger wanders barefoot through the mud, and a Georgian shipwright checks the hull of his newly built ship. On the river, invisible galleons and sailing barges glide past, wherries are carried swiftly downstream on the retreating tide, and a phantom paddle steamer pushes through the currents. Thames fogs are quite literally the mists of time. They are daydreams manifested, swirling visions of the past.

Trig Lane

The word treasure must surely be one of the most provocative in the
English language, for there can be few of us who have not at some
time in our lives dreamed of finding buried treasure.

Ivor Noël Hume, *Treasure in the Thames* (1956)

When people ask me where to start searching, I tell
them to study old maps. They are the equivalent of
treasure maps for mudlarks. At a glance they show where
the city began, the places it was busiest and most populated.
Where people worked and ships discharged their cargoes.
The sites of old bridges, river stairs, causeways, warehouses,
demolished palaces and great houses, quaysides, jetties and
boatyards. These are the places where the river hungrily
gobbled up the objects that were lost and discarded; where
the city's rubbish was dumped and where it was built into
the busy parts of the foreshore to level and stabilise it.

I look at old maps with a magpie's eyes, always thinking
of where to search next. Even when I'm looking at old
paintings, engravings and photographs of the river, I'm not
looking at the main subjects in the foreground, I'm looking
beyond them to the riverside for clues to what it once looked
like: the tumbledown dwellings and warehouses that edge
the waterside and the narrow alleys between them that lead

to rickety wooden river stairs, the fully laden barges and ships that sit on the mud. All of these are clues to where there might be treasure.

I like the panorama maps, which are usually drawn from the south side facing north to the city, where London began. Visscher's panoramic map, first published in Amsterdam in around 1616, is drawn from this angle. It measures six feet six inches and is the most detailed of all the early maps, which is astonishing since it is thought the Dutchman Claes Visscher never visited London and used old printed views for reference. Old St Paul's, without its steeple, looms large in the centre and smoke curls from some of the houses that line the river. Small boats fill the water to the west of Old London Bridge: wherries carrying passengers, barges laden with high loads of hay and vessels with sails bob about between them – perhaps they are fishing boats. To the east of the bridge there are galleons in full sail. Some look as if they are moored in the centre of the river, which Visscher drew far wider than it was. Old London Bridge is depicted in exacting detail, with its row of tall, grand-looking houses and even the heads of traitors displayed on wooden stakes above the south entrance, where a man stands ready to drive his cattle beneath them and across the bridge.

But the map I never tire of looking at is the Agas map, which was first printed about fifty-five years before Visscher's on eight sheets from woodcut blocks. Its style is far simpler, and yet its details are still wonderfully precise. The view is the same, from the south looking north, but the perspective is higher and the roads are drawn in and labelled with their names. They are lined with rows of jumbled houses with tiny doors, gabled roofs and windows and cargo is piled up on the quayside. In the shallow water where Cannon Street Bridge is today, there is a man with what looks like a hoe and two packhorses or donkeys. I don't know what he's doing, perhaps he's watering his beasts, or maybe he's searching the mud. Whatever he's doing, I've mudlarked his spot on many occasions. It's on my patch.

There are names on this map that I recognise from structures and places associated with the foreshore: a road called 'The Olde Swanne' that gave its name to a set of stairs, now little more than a few wooden posts and a vanishing causeway near London Bridge; 'Styllyarde', the fifteenth- and sixteenth-century trading base of the Hanseatic League, a group of powerful German traders, which has lent its name to a passage beneath Cannon Street Bridge; 'Thre Crans', now the name of the riverside path where there was once a large wharf; and 'Tryglane', an insignificant-looking street that led down from Thames Street (now Upper Thames Street) to a river landing place, now known as Trig Lane Stairs.

The lane itself – and the original stairs of course – is gone. Like so many other ancient lanes, alleys and streets that were demolished and forgotten through fire, war and redevelopment, old Trig Lane has been wiped from the map. The modern Trig Lane is a short dead-end road lined with modern office buildings that is easy to miss if you're not looking for it. It was created when the area was redeveloped and the old warehouses swept away in the 1970s and 80s, but the stairs are easy to see from the Millennium Bridge. They're not so easy to find from the river path though, and you need to look carefully for the short flight of steps that take you up to a gap in the river wall. Trig Lane Stairs lead down steeply from here. They are a good solid set of modern river stairs, at first concrete until they are clear of the wall and then they are made of wood. Where they reach the foreshore there are large old timber planks and beams embedded in the mud, which are thought to be where older stairs, possibly eighteenth-century ones, once rested.

Remains of medieval river stairs were discovered in the 1970s, when the Museum of London dug along the bank and across what was Trig Lane before it was redeveloped. Over generations the riverfront has crept into the river and the medieval riverfront was about fifty feet further inland from where it is today. Land levels in the City of London have also risen, by roughly a foot every century, which means nineteenth-century remains are about one foot underground and Roman remains about twenty feet. As they dug down through the centuries, the archaeologists found evidence from all periods of history, then at ten to twelve feet beneath the twentieth-century land surface they found an entire medieval quayside: the large oak timbers that formed the quayside itself and the foundations of dwellings that were built along it. This was where the people of Trig Lane lived and worked, including members of the Tryg family, fishmongers after whom the street was named in around 1422. Before then it was variously known as Fish Lane, Fishelane, Lane Called Fischwarf and Lane Towards le Fysshwharfe.

A lot of 'loose finds' were retrieved from the site. They were found in the 'fill' that was dumped behind successive river walls and used to reclaim land from the river. To me, the list is both transporting and very familiar: string, iron chains, bone knife handles, iron knives, wooden bowls, barrel remains, iron bucket handles, fragments of an iron cauldron, the leg of a copper skillet, fragments of stone mortars, remains of two plaited fibre mats, part of a copper lantern, an iron box, roof tiles and slates, iron nails, ceramic finials, part of a ceramic louvre, a piece of stone moulding, four pieces of lead window cames, three candleholders, a large iron door pivot and two iron keys. The largest category of finds was personal accessories and items of clothing: nearly 300 shoes from one dump alone, as well as shoe pattens, leather straps and girdles, scabbards, fragments of silk cloth and braid, a hair net, a wooden comb, a bronze ear pick, two gold rings with red stones, a plain gold ring, a bronze ring, fragments of two jet bracelets, a wooden bead, a copper alloy thimble, a stone spindle whorl, a stone mortar, a pewter spoon, a brass book clasp, two bone gaming counters, two bone tuning pegs from a musical instrument, dress fittings, a copper belt mount, buckles, and countless coins, jettons and tokens.

Over the years I have found at least half of these objects myself on the foreshore, many of them on the stretch between London Bridge and Trig Lane, which is usually where I finish up at the end of a tide. I always start mudlarking this stretch as close to London Bridge as I can and approach Trig Lane from the east, travelling upstream. If I start from Trig Lane it doesn't work as well, since I have to wait for the tide to let me through a pinch point before I can begin searching. Timing can be tricky and if I'm to give each spot my full attention I have to arrive just as the foreshore is starting to show by the river wall. The first area to surface is a low hump of rubble, conveniently situated at the bottom of a long ladder that's bolted to the river wall.

There are ladders like this at frequent intervals along both sides of the river and I avoid them whenever I can because they scare me, but sometimes the lure of a particularly elusive part of foreshore, or the need to maximise the time I have to search it, is too great to resist. And nothing plunges you into the past quite like a terrifying descent down a thin runged ladder, bolted to a thirty-foot wall.

I'm terrified of falling. Missing a rung, my hands slipping in the wet, a moment of silence then landing with a sickening thud on the rubble below, the tide claiming me as one of its treasures. I never look down and I prepare for my descent fastidiously. I tighten my rucksack, tie up the loose straps and tuck in my clothes, anything that might catch, tangle or trip. I wipe my hands again and again on my jeans, making sure they are dry before I inch across to the top, grip the cold metal and swing a leg out.

Some ladders are twisted and loose, rusted dangerously thin with missing rungs, or end too high. I only use the ones I'm sure about – with one exception. This particular ladder leads to an exclusive and otherwise inaccessible part of the foreshore. I'm not telling you where it is, of course, but suffice to say the finds are good because so few people can get there. I had been warned by another mudlark that the end of the ladder had rusted away and that it was eight feet short of the foreshore, so the first time I went I took a stepladder with me, which I lowered into place with a rope and tied off on the top rung. Although this worked quite well, I knew that carrying a stepladder with me to the river every time I went wasn't going to be practical, so I trawled the Internet for inventive alternatives. Eventually I found myself on a climbing website where I found something called an 'etrier' – 'a short ladder made of webbing that packs neatly into a small pouch no larger than a bag of sugar'. Teamed with a substantial climbing carabiner I can now get down to this special part of the foreshore whenever I like and it has become another of my regular 'patches'.

Climbing back up ladders, with the ground departing unseen behind me, is always easier than climbing down. As important as access routes are for getting onto the fore-shore, they are even more vital for getting off it again. The tide can turn quickly and it is easy to lose track of distance and time, so keeping a safe exit route in sight is essential.

The ladder that will take me down onto the foreshore today is safe, but very high. I grope for the first rung and shuffle my bottom round, only heaving myself on when I am sure I have a secure hold. Then I steady myself and take a few deep breaths before I start my slow descent, one rung at a time, hand over hand, foot over foot, every move carefully placed, each one another step away from the noise of the city, the screaming children, the looming deadline and next week's meetings. I drop below the high-tide mark. The wall is still damp from the retreating tide. About halfway down, the grey granite turns bright green with algae and the smell of fresh mud wafts up to meet me. I descend through a thin cloud of tiny flies that tickle my nose and buzz against my eyelashes then step off the last rung of the ladder onto a hump of rubble. My journey into another world is complete.

I quickly gear up as soon as I'm down there, impatient to start searching. I pull my filthy, permanently damp black knee pads out of my rucksack and strap them on. Then I snap on a pair of latex gloves, clip my finds bag around my waist, tuck my hair out of my eyes and I'm ready to start. There is a lot of rubble at the top of this part of the foreshore that sometimes catches larger finds. A few years ago, I stepped off the ladder almost on top of an eighteenth-century cosmetic set, which had caught between two bricks. It was a silver tube, about the length of my little finger, plain and battered as if someone had trodden on it centuries ago, but its lid wasn't damaged and it unscrewed easily. Inside, neatly packed by whoever had lost it, was a tiny spoon, for removing earwax, and a tooth scraper that looked like a miniature rake without the prongs. Both were cut from a thin sheet of silver and each had a pointed end, useful for picking dirt out from under fingernails and as a tooth-pick. By the seventeenth century people were aware of plaque, which they called 'scale', and were encouraged by their doctors to scrape their teeth frequently. Little cosmetic sets often included ear picks, tweezers, toothpicks and nail scrapers and were popular with the Romans through to the Victorians.

I walk back and forth along the waterline, dropping fur-ther down the foreshore as the tide falls and the bricks turn to shingle then sand. To the east, through London Bridge, I can see Tower Bridge in the distance and to the west of me is Cannon Street Railway Bridge. I spend plenty of time covering all my lucky spots and casting an eye over as much of the foreshore as I can. There's usually pottery to be found and sometimes the waves leave coins stuck to the sand as they retreat, but not today. I pick up a thick piece of terra-cotta and turn it in my hands. One side is roughly patterned with a series of grooves that look as if they were scraped or pressed into the clay when it was wet. There are patches of white mortar caught in the pattern and the other side is rough and plain. I know what it is because I've found them before and I have quite a collection of different patterns – straight lines, curved lines, parallel and crossed lines. It's a piece of hypocaust or box flue from a Roman central heating system.

England was supposed to be experiencing a warm phase at the time of the Romans, but anyone arriving from southern Europe would still have found our damp little island in the northern bounds of the Empire miserably cold, so those who could afford it built hypocaust systems into their homes to keep themselves warm. It was a clever and fairly simple solution: the ground floor was raised on little pillars that allowed hot air from a furnace to circulate and heat the room above. Sections of short open-ended square or rectangular pipes (box flues) were set into the walls and drew the hot air upwards and out of the roof, thus heating the rooms as it went. They were plastered over for aesthetic reasons, and the patterns on their outer surfaces provided a key for the wall plaster to adhere to. Even though they were never meant to be seen, designs were finger-drawn, combed or relief-patterned using a special roller, and were so varied and unique that it has been suggested they may have been the tile-maker's way of 'signing' or personalising his work.

I pocket the piece of hypocaust to add to my collection and turn to scan the river. The water is beginning to turn. If I'm going to do this stretch justice I need to start heading west now. Just before Cannon Street Bridge I pass over an area that's been filled in with shingle and hardcore and reinforced with huge nylon nets of stones, to stop the river from undermining the wall. When I first came here, I could walk across on the old surface, but over the years, the wake of passing boats that ate away at the foreshore where the revetments in front of it had collapsed and it had been softened and destabilised by mudlarks digging in the 1980s and 90s. The mudlarks left just a handful of hard compacted columns where they hadn't dug, but without support these crumbled too and all that remained, until it was filled in this year, was a curved bay of rubble with a small sandy beach.

It was sad to see, but I have to admit the finds were great. As the foreshore disappeared, it revealed the treasures it had been hiding for centuries: an old wooden drain made from a hollowed-out trunk of elm, prized for its resistance to rot and still in use beneath the streets of London well into the twentieth century; a silver shilling from the short reign (1553–58) of Mary Tudor; a round bone token for an eighteenth-century pleasure garden called Lambeth Wells; and a seventeenth-century pewter bodkin with the initials 'SE' scratched onto it. It is a flat, blunt needle, around seven inches long, with a large rectangular eye topped by a tiny spoon at the wider end. The little spoons had a multitude of uses, including extracting perfume from small glass bottles and even cleaning out boils. Like the tube of my little silver cosmetic set, it is bent and crushed, but the fact that there are initials scratched into it makes it special: it was someone's prized possession and it is a direct link to that individual. SE would have used her bodkin daily to lace her bodice together and even pin up her hair. She may have cleaned out her ears with it and used the earwax as a convenient and inexpensive alternative to beeswax, for drawing together fibres and lubricating thread. I have run my fingers over her initials many times and wondered who she was and how she came to lose her bodkin.

Under the bridge the foreshore is solid and flat, packed down hard with a kind of dark grey volcanic-looking rock, but even this is being nibbled at the edges. Where the Victorian revetments are broken and boards are missing, the river is starting to carve out hollows, revealing tantalising glimpses of what lies beneath, a sheer wall of spoil in which is embedded pottery shards, broken clay pipe stems, animal bones and oyster shells, the remains of countless ancient meals shovelled up and dumped onto the foreshore. There is a smell of rotten food and fermenting bins here, from the rusting rubbish barges that sit on a soft bed of white chalk on the other side of the bridge. I hold my breath as I walk past quickly, and then I'm at Three Cranes Wharf, named after the medieval wharf, which in turn had been named for the three large wooden treadmill cranes that hung over the water in front of it. They can be seen in miniature on the Agas map, but it's all gone now. Just one crane operates here today, accompanied by an irritating alarm as it lifts containers of smelly compressed waste over the riverside walk and into the barges behind me.

In front of me and as far as Queenhithe Dock the foreshore bristles with old scaffolding poles, wooden posts, car tyres and half-submerged traffic cones, which mark where members of the Society of Mudlarks have dug deep into the foreshore. I survey the battle-scarred terrain and see that they've been at work again recently. There's a low hump of grey mud, the remains of a spoil heap, standing just proud of the sand around it. It's been smoothed by several tides and is spotted with pebbles and pieces of pottery. Next to it is a shallow water-filled dip where the mud has settled in the hole they dug. All of this is worth searching for the smaller things they missed.

My best spoil heap find was from here: a chevron bead smaller than a pea that because of its rarity and collect-ability is worth more than its weight in gold. But I'm not interested in its value. I'd waited for years to find one and I'd never sell it. It is a miniature work of art, with alter-nating white, red and blue layers that were fused together and shaped with a special twelve-point star mould to give it a distinctive striped-star cross-section pattern. The tech-nique was invented by the Venetians around 1500 and is still used today. The very earliest chevron beads have seven layers, which I realised with growing excitement was what mine had, as I counted them under a magnifying glass at home. But for all its beauty, I knew it was probably made for more sinister purposes. Many chevron beads were produced for trade with West Africa. They were a cheap and efficient means of exploiting resources and were exchanged for gold, ivory, palm oil and slaves.

Today I pick a plain, flat, late eighteenth- or nineteenth-century button out of the mud. I find a lot of these, they're fairly generic, and probably came from waistcoats or jackets, washed down drains or pulled off the clothes of river workers. I pocket a couple of complete eighteenth-century pipe bowls – I'll wash the compacted mud out of them when I get home. The few pottery shards I pull from the mud are neither decorated nor particularly unusual, so I leave them where they are and move on to Tile Hill, which is under Southwark Bridge. Years of demolition and destruction has turned the foreshore orange in places, and beside the bridge the river has washed a mass of roof and floor tiles into a great mound of terracotta, delicately skirted by a drift of old animal bones. The dry bones are a lovely soft buff colour and they clatter beneath my feet as I walk over them, checking for knife handles and anything carved, decorated or out of the ordinary. Even discarded offcuts from bone working are interesting: pieces of flat bone, possibly a pig or sheep scapula, with a neat line of circles or semicircles where beads and buttons had been cut out of it.

I have spent many happy hours above the bones on Tile Hill, turning the tiles over one by one and searching for pieces of fourteenth-century floor tiles, called 'Penn' tiles after the village in Buckinghamshire where they were made. They would have covered the floors of churches and grand houses and are decorated with subtle white scrolls, geometric designs, flowers and fleur-de-lys; if you're lucky you might find the suggestion of a lion, a figure or a bird.

Roman and medieval roof tiles sometimes have a grey core due to lack of oxidisation in the clay during the firing process. Roman tiles are thick and distinguishable by their shape – flat tegula ones with turned-up edges and curved imbrex ones that fitted over them to make roofs watertight some 2,000 years ago. Medieval roof tiles were hung with wooden pegs and the round peg holes of old tiles are larger and more carefully executed than later ones, which are more roughly stabbed. After the Great Fire of 1666 the holes in tiles became smaller and were triangular, square or diamond in shape to accommodate metal nails instead. But the holy grail of Tile Hill is the rare pieces that have captured a moment in time, ordinary everyday events that were pressed into the soft clay of a freshly made tile. I have one with the perfect impression of woven cloth, perhaps the tile-maker's sleeve, and several with the prints of dogs and cats.

But I need to get a move on if I am to make it past the pinch point near Queenhithe Dock. The tide is coming in fast. It's already begun to fill one side of the tunnel that leads under the river path and I start to inch myself carefully along the sloping concrete on the side closest to the river wall. It's lethally slippery and I've seen a few people come a cropper here, so I walk sideways with my toes pointing up the incline and take it slowly. There's old rope and plastic bags caught in a multicoloured tangle on the metal posts inside the tunnel, water drips down from the roof and the advancing river splashes against the concrete lower down. I pop back out into the sunshine and jump down onto an old carpet that's been here, growing fuzzy with algae, for years; it's part of the foreshore now.

I walk slowly along this part, my eyes darting from one spot to another, looking for clean slivers of white silver, purity in the black mud. I spot one and bend down to pull it free, then wash it in a small pool of stranded river water nearby. It's a perfect piece of mother-of-pearl, almost as large as the palm of my hand, clean grey with a rainbow hue. But this is not a native river species. This is abalone, a marine creature found mostly in New Zealand, South Africa, Australia, North America and Japan. I had puzzled for years about how abalone had got here before eventually it came up in conversation with Mike. He told me about a shell warehouse that once stood on the quayside here where abalone, destined for furniture inlay, jewellery, buckles and buttons, was bought, sold and stored. Further research turned up some old photographs of the quayside taken in 1896. Suited men in bowler hats and straw boaters wander among numbered bins and boxes filled with shells as large as dinner plates. I imagine the rejects and floor sweepings ended up in the river, which is how they came to embellish the mud. They appeal to the magpie in me and I collect them, so I slip the shiny piece into my finds bag to take home.

I make it past the pinch point with a few feet of tide to spare and head towards Trig Lane. I could walk further west, as far as Blackfriars Bridge where, on very low tides, you can get right up to the large metal cover in the wall that's all that's left of London's famous buried river, the Fleet, but I rarely go that far. It's habit and routine that stays my journey at Trig Lane, and what little time I have left I'd rather spend searching here because it's often been lucky for me. This is probably because it's always been such a busy part of the river. Since medieval times Trig Lane was one of the frequent 'watergates', a landing place where people could board and alight from wherries and where they could wash, water their horses, do their laundry, collect water and use the public latrines. It's just the kind of place I look for on old maps because I know there will be treasure there – small items that were dropped and lost, ordinary objects that belonged to ordinary people going about their daily business: a simple brass shoe buckle, shaped like a small pair of spectacles, caught between the planks of a boat and torn off, and the decorated metal tag, or chape, from the end of a woman's thin leather girdle, finally broken free from thinning leather.

Most of what I have found at Trig Lane falls into this ordinary treasure category, but a few years ago I found a simple silver ring that qualified as real treasure trove. Under UK law, certain ownerless objects are defined as 'Treasure' and as such have to be reported to the local coroner since they belong not to the finder but the Crown, or other franchises such as the City of London. In order to qualify as Treasure a find needs to be over 300 years old and made of at least 10 per cent precious metal by weight; a group of two or more base metal coins over 300 years old; two or more base metal prehistoric objects from the same spot; prehistoric objects containing any amount of precious metal; and any material found alongside objects that qualify as Treasure (this would include bags, boxes, pots and loose gemstones). Local and national museums are given the chance to express an interest in buying the object, but if nobody wants it the Crown disclaims its interest and it is returned to the finder. If a museum wants to purchase the object there is an official inquiry to declare the item Treasure and its value is determined by an independent Treasure Valuation Committee. This is paid as a reward to the finder and the landowner (in the case of the Thames this is the PLA) who split it 50/50. The finder can also opt to donate it to the museum that wants it.

I was wading about in the shallows, having one last look at the end of a day's larking, when I found the ring. I've made some of my best finds just as I'm about to leave the foreshore, so I always put in a little bit of extra effort in the last few minutes, just in case. This time, a boat passed and I stepped back as the waves from its wake flooded the foreshore. As the river raked back over the shingle and prepared to send another wave crashing down onto the mud, I saw a small dark ring caught against the side of the Victorian revetment timbers. I had a second to act before it was washed away, so I nipped forward, snatched it up and leapt back up the foreshore, sustaining a welly full of water in the process. I could tell it was silver even though it was black with tarnish, but other than that it didn't look like anything special, and slightly disappointed I began to wonder whether it had been worth the cold, squelching walk home that lay ahead of me.

That week and the following one were busy, so it was some time before I got round to sorting and cleaning what I'd found that day, and it wasn't until I'd taken everything out of my finds bag that I remembered the little black ring, which was caught in a gritty seam at the bottom. I turned it in my fingers and held it up to the light. With my glasses on I could see more clearly and, on the inside, I could make out some letters. The style of the engraving made me think the ring could be quite old after all. I felt a twinge of excitement and grabbed a piece of paper and a pencil. Some letters were completely tarnished over, but I wrote down the ones I could read: 'H–PE X I –IV– IN'. It was like solving an anagram, with missing letters, which wasn't easy, but slowly I worked out what was missing and rearranged the words so that they made sense: 'I LIVE IN HOPE X'. A posy ring!

A posy ring is a ring inscribed with a short sentimental expression, or 'posy', from the Middle English word for poetry. They became popular around the fourteenth century and were given by either partner at any stage of the relationship and the inscriptions, both French and English, were usually concerning love, friendship and loyalty: 'God Made Us Two One'; 'In Thy Breast My Heart Doth Rest'; 'Love Never Dies Where Virtue Lies'; 'My Gift is Myself'.

Wearing the hidden motto next to the skin emphasised the intimacy of these messages. I slipped the ring onto my finger and instantly it felt too intimate, so I took it off again. Who had it belonged to? It was large enough to be a man's ring. Perhaps it had slipped from the finger of a sailor or waterman. Or maybe it had been dashed into the water in a fit of fury and passion, the sailor returned from his travels to find his intended in the arms of another, the hope he had lived for all the time he was away now lost along with the ring.

Knowing there was a chance the ring qualified as Treasure, I emailed the Finds Liaison Officer (FLO) at the Museum of London and made an appointment to take it in to show her. I take regular batches of foreshore finds to be recorded on the Portable Antiquities Scheme's database, a brilliant project that is not just a unique insight into our historical lost and found objects, but also a valuable resource to identify finds. I use the database all the time to help identify what I find and I'm a firm believer in contributing to it. In 2014, they recorded their millionth object, which shows just how much is being found in Britain's fields, coastlines and rivers.

Treasure can take several years to process, but I was lucky: the ring took just over a year and none of the museums wanted it. The British Museum already had one very similar in their collection, and it was this that the FLO used to date mine. English posy rings of the fourteenth and fifteenth centuries usually had their inscriptions written in French and on the outside of the ring. Mine had its inscription written in English on the inside, while the style of writing suggested it was from the sixteenth century, a time when the fashion for such love tokens was at its peak. It is one of my most treasured finds and, although it still feels strange wearing something that was once so personal to someone else, I sometimes wear it on a silver chain around my neck.

Most people's idea of treasure is gold and I'm always asked if I've found any. The short answer is yes, but not very much. Even the smallest piece of gold is easy to spot, as gold doesn't tarnish and it shines in the mud. You simply can't miss it. In all the years I've been mudlarking, though, all I've found is a broken tiepin, a modern wedding band, the butterfly from the back of an earring, a gold pen nib, a few chain links, tiny flakes and scraps of gold, three small plain gold beads and the most beautiful sixteenth-century Tudor lace end or aglet, which would once have decorated the shirt or jacket of a gentleman. It was my second piece of treasure trove and one I donated to the Museum of London. Despite being crushed almost flat, it is an inch of perfection, beautifully preserved and crafted with circles of twisted gold wire and a small filigree looped cage at one end with what is thought to be the remains of once vibrantly coloured enamel, which is now faded to the colour of the river. As soon as I saw it, the rich, soft butteriness of the gold told me it was old and pure while the craftsmanship suggested it was a high-status object. It dates from a time when only gentlemen were allowed to wear gold or silver decoration on their clothing, so it must have belonged to someone of great wealth and importance.

Hundreds of other tiny pieces of gold have been found where I found my lace aglet, including filigree beads, other lace ends and tiny shreds of intricate decoration from larger pieces of jewellery. One woman I've met spends most of her mudlarking time searching for it, picking through the sand quite literally grain by grain. When I last saw her, she had found almost 100 tiny pieces of gold, a diamond and a ruby. Every piece of the miniature hoard is remarkable and rare, exquisitely crafted, but incomplete or broken. This does not limit their possibilities though, quite the opposite, their condition and rarity makes them all the more interesting to me, and the stories behind them limited only by imagination. They might be pieces of scrap gold that were lost by a goldsmith. Perhaps he slipped on the wet planks as he scuttled down a wooden jetty to his waiting wherry and fell heavily, dropping the little leather bag of gold into the river as he landed. I imagine he plunged his hands into the cold murky water in his panic, but to no avail. No amount of desperate searching was going to help, the gold was gone.

But all that glitters on the foreshore is not necessarily gold. The gilding on one buckle I found had my heart racing until I picked it up. Even the smallest piece of real gold has a weighty feel to it and this did not have that. I have also been duped by what is known as 'nature's gilding': a chemical reaction that affects alloy metal containing tin and creates a gold-coloured layer. Fool's gold, iron pyrite, occurs naturally in London clay and sparkles through the mud in the sun. Other minerals can also be found at low tide, raw carnelian, amethyst and quartz, which may have arrived in London as ballast in trade ships.

Precious and semi-precious stones, fallen from brooches, rings, earrings and necklaces, wash up on rare occasions as well and these don't have to be declared as Treasure if they are found on their own. A fellow mudlark found a large uncut emerald and I know others who have found diamonds. In my time on the foreshore I have found a huge 8.2 carat Sri Lankan cut garnet, an amethyst cabochon, a smoky quartz and a large aquamarine. I have beads of pearl, jet, coral, crystal and amber, but the most mysterious are the raw uncut garnets that I have so far found in four locations along the Thames. They are the shape and colour of ripe pomegranate seeds, which is how garnets got their name. In Early French the fruit was called *pomme grenate*, meaning 'seedy apple'. *Grenate* came to mean 'red like a pomegranate' and was used by the French to refer to the red stones. When it was borrowed into English it became *garnet*. At one spot in particular, there are so many that they glow deep ruby red in the mud on sunny days.

The exact location of the garnets is a closely guarded secret and tales are told among mudlarks about how they got there. One chap spends hours on his knees collecting the stones with a pair of tweezers. He has amassed thousands, though he thinks that only 10 per cent of them are of jewellery quality (despite this, I know other mudlarks who have had them set into rings), and claims to have evidence that a sack of garnets fell off an East India ship in 1810, but there are plenty of other theories to rival it. Perhaps the small stones were in the floor sweepings of a jewellery shop that were dumped on the foreshore, rejects from a larger bag that would explain why so many are of such poor quality. They may have been washed down a drain and out into the river, or maybe someone stole a bag of them and dumped it in the Thames rather than risk getting caught with it. They could be older than nineteenth century, or, owing to their hardness, some think they may have been used more recently as an abrasive for industrial cleaning. I've also heard stories of sailors getting a commission for bringing garnets back from overseas. It is said they made holes in the sacks to let some of the stones trickle down onto the foreshore and returned on the low tide to collect their spoils from the mud. In truth, only the river knows how the glowing red seeds became embedded in its skin.

But my favourite kinds of treasures are pins, because there is nothing more ordinary than a pin. When I pick up a pin, I think of the hands that touched it, the pincushion it was pulled from the morning it was lost, the clothes it held together and the conversations that were had while it was being worn. So many lives have touched each pin: the pin-maker and his family who drew the wire to gauge, wound another piece around the top three times to make a tiny head, then polished and sharpened it on a piece of bone with grooves to hold it still; the Elizabethan haberdasher who sold it; and the ordinary person who bought and used it. Pins are not like precious jewels, they weren't loved or looked after, they were just part of everyday life.

Handmade pins date from around 1400 to the early nineteenth century, when pin-making was mechanised. They litter the foreshore in such great numbers because everyone used them, both men and women, from cradle to grave. They held swaddling in place and were used to make clothes and lace. They secured hats, veils, jewellery and ribbons; hundreds could be used in the complex folding and gathering of Elizabethan neck ruffs; they held clothes in place and in death secured shrouds around corpses. A warrant relating to Robert Careles, Elizabeth I's 'Pynner', shows that in 1565 he supplied 16,000 great farthingale pins at six shillings per thousand, 20,000 middle farthingale pins at four shillings per thousand, 20,000 great velvet pins at two shillings eight pence per thousand and 58,000 small velvet and head pins at twenty pence per thousand. Pins were not cheap, and the money allocated to ordinary women by their families or husbands to buy pins was not the trifling amount we now associate with the phrase 'pin money'. They looked after their pins carefully, having them sharpened to prolong their lives. But despite this it seems people still left a scattering of pins wherever they went.

I stick my best pins into velvet pincushions and have several hundred more in the printer's chest where I keep my river finds. Some are sturdy with large round heads, for pushing through thick woollen fabric; others are long and spindly, possibly for securing veils and headdresses. There are pins with decorated heads, very early medieval pins with a distinct collar under the head, and pins as fine as baby hair that may once have been used to secure delicate silk or for lace-making. I have pins that have been bent, either purposefully to fashion them into a hook or by accident on fabric that was too thick.

It took me a year or so to find my first one, but now I've got my eye in for them I see them everywhere. They often accumulate near old river stairs, like at Trig Lane, or where there was once a jetty or causeway, washing together in tangled metallic nests. In some areas the mud bristles with them and I search gingerly to avoid being pricked. If I find a good patch, I can lose myself for an hour or more, picking them out of the sand or mud, my mind completely occupied by the simple task of collecting.

But where pins lie in piles and are easy to find, handmade needles are rare. In all the time I have been mudlarking I have found just eight. They are made of brass and would have been kept in a needle holder, similar to the sixteenth-century one that was left for me by the tide near Trig Lane several years ago. The small pewter tube is around two inches long and decorated with delicate curling vines and leaves. The loops either side would have been for suspending it from a cord or ribbon and it would once have had a lid, which is missing. At some point it has been crushed flat at one end, perhaps trodden on after the ribbon broke and it fell to the ground.

I have found a few more thimbles than needles, enough for each of my fingers. Several have suffered the same fate as my needle holder, either crushed underfoot or flattened over the centuries by the weight of mud pressing down on them. Thimbles are an oddly sensual find. Spotting the pitted surface, picking it from the mud, cleaning it out and then slipping it on, being the first person to wear it since its original owner lost it, induces a heady mix of awe and excitement. For a second, time stands perfectly still, then the years tumble backwards and a brief window onto the past opens up, a glimpse of forgotten lives.

My Thames thimbles are plain, brass and utilitarian. Of those that haven't been squashed out of shape all but two fit me perfectly. The dimples of some have been punched by hand and are vaguely irregular, small and close together, suggesting they were used for ordinary needlework. Others have larger dimples and may have been owned by sail-makers, since sewing sails required larger needles and cor-respondingly larger dimples. Thimbles were very personal possessions and sometimes given as love tokens. I once found a perfectly preserved sixteenth-century one, probably made in Nuremberg in Germany, caught between two large pieces of broken masonry. I'd had it for some time before I noticed a small heart scratched into its base. Instantly it became more than just a sewing aid, it had a personal attachment and was now a token of affection, a prized belonging, a symbol of one person's love for another.

I spend the last half-hour of the tide at Trig Lane collecting more pins. As I crawl along on my hands and knees picking them from the mud, I spy a small silver disc caught in a hollow. It's completely smooth on one side, but there's a shadow of a monarch's bust on the other, with enough of an inscription to identify it as late seventeenth century, William III. I've found silver sixpences from the same era before and I know what size they are, yet this is larger and must be a shilling. That's it, that's the last good find I was waiting for; I can call it a day. It's been almost six hours since I began at London Bridge and my back won't bend any longer.

I climb Trig Lane Stairs with stiff legs, holding on to the steep steps as I go. Above me the most recently built Thames crossing, the Millennium Bridge, spans the river like the giant silver backbone of a whale. It is filled with people and some of them stop to watch me climb off the foreshore. On quieter parts of the river I can spin my daydreams out beyond the foreshore, but here it's a rude awakening. I push up through the gap in the wall and instantly crash back into the twenty-first century. I'm among the crowds, dodging bicycles and crossing busy roads, the sound of traffic and sirens smothering the voices of the past and jerking me back into reality.

BANKSIDE

If we are afraid to give way to our imagination, the river's treasures must inevitably remain dull and lifeless, for it is only in our minds that they can be transported from soulless museum cases back to their original settings.

Ivor Noël Hume, *Treasure in the Thames* (1956)

Before I leave the riverside at Trig Lane I look over to the south side of the river and assess the tide. The foreshore opposite is wider and shallower, so even if the water is quite high on the north side there's usually still time to carry on searching over there. I always try to fit in a quick recce at Bankside, convinced that the day I don't will be the day I miss the find of a lifetime. I climb another set of steep stairs, off the river path towards St Paul's Cathedral, and turn south, joining crowds of City workers and tourists on the Millennium Bridge.

I get a lot of funny looks as I walk along the bridge, and I can't say I'm surprised. I'm still wearing my dirty wellingtons, knee pads, blue latex gloves and a full suit of waterproofs smeared with mud: they haven't been washed in a while because I'm worried they'll lose their waterproofing. So yes, I do make an odd sight and I wonder if people look at me just as they used to stop and stare at Peggy Jones, a 'mud-lark' who worked the river just below me. Her story was published in 1820 in a magazine called *Kirby's Wonderful and Eccentric Museum; or Magazine of Remarkable Characters*. Her 'constant resort' was Blackfriars, where 'she was always to be seen, even before the tide was down, wading into the water, nearly up to the middle, and scraping together from the bottom, the coals which she felt with her feet'. She was 'apparently about forty years of age [a little younger than me], with red hair'. She wore short ragged petticoats, without shoes or stockings, and a heavy-duty apron folded up like a bag around her waist. A larger version of my waist bag, I suppose. The article reports that people passing over the bridge 'often stopped to contemplate with astonishment a female engaged in an occupation, apparently so painful and disagreeable'. Is that what people think when they see me?

Peggy sold her coals for eight pence a load, which she spent mostly on gin. I like gin, and I'm not averse to a tipple after a cold day on the foreshore, but poor old Peggy 'indulged to such a degree, that she would tumble about the streets with her load, to the no small amusement of mischievous boys and others'. The coal heavers took pity on her though, occasionally kicking a large piece of coal off the barges for her to collect, gruffly telling her to go away, and in February 1805 they were the ones who noticed when she suddenly disappeared. Nobody knows what became of Peggy Jones. Perhaps she went out too far and was taken by the currents or perhaps she simply passed away in her wretched lodging at Chick Lane, but I often think about her when I'm on her patch, and at least she hasn't completely vanished from history. If, like the people crossing

Blackfriars Bridge over 200 years ago, you want to stop and stare at poor Peggy Jones, take a moment to turn to the back of this book and you'll find her there.

There is no wall obscuring the river at Bankside, just a row of metal railings with a wooden bar along the top. Cleverly hidden in the railings, in front of Tate Modern, is an invisible gate that opens onto a wide set of concrete steps leading down to the foreshore. It is far more open here than it is on the north shore and is one of the easiest places to get down to the river. People mill around here, admiring the view – one of the river's most spectacular – skimming stones, sunbathing, chatting in pairs and idly picking up bits and pieces that catch their eye, but few venture much further east or west.

Because I'm usually here towards the end of the tide, I restrict myself to three spots. First I head west, under Blackfriars Bridge to Gabriel's Wharf. Then I double back, past the stairs I just came down near the Millennium Bridge, and head east towards Southwark Bridge, stopping at the bottom of the second set of stairs along this stretch. These are even wider than the first lot and descend gently from the low river wall in front of the Globe Theatre. There is a big drop onto the foreshore at the bottom, which is getting increasingly difficult to negotiate as the foreshore erodes away and leaves the stairs behind. The eastern stretch is a cul-de-sac that terminates at London Bridge and it can easily trap the unwary, so I have to work out if I have enough time to walk down to the bridge and back before the water cuts me off from my exit point. Piles of rubble from successive renovations and rebuilding make progress slow and uncomfortable, and the tangled legs of the Clipper jetty are a brown, slimy obstacle course. This is also a pinch point on the returning tide. Further along, an area of asperous volcanic-like rock stabs the soft soles of my boots and slashes my ankles. If I decide to go as far as London Bridge, even nature takes a turn at blocking my way, with drifts of shingle and large cobbles that crunch, slip and shift underfoot.

I go in the hope that where the rubble gives way or the stones have parted, the river will have scoured down to reveal its treasures, but in truth my efforts are rarely rewarded. In recent years these patches have become few and far between and even mudlarks seldom bother wandering this way, making this an oddly quiet stretch for such a central location. The feeling of isolation is compounded by the bridges that darken the foreshore and push the riverside path inland. But on my own down here and away from the crowds it is easier to imagine what it was like on this side of the Thames before the river was embanked and the city fingered its way south. In my mind, it once looked like the marshes at Erith. If I half close my eyes, I can picture a muted landscape of low scattered shrubs and scrubby grass, dotted with reed beds and stagnant boggy pools.

The Romans chose one of the small islands that dotted the river along this stretch for the south side of their bridge, which connected to their main settlement on the north shore. But it wasn't until the thirteenth century that the river here was embanked with a causeway to prevent it from flooding, which led roughly from Old London Bridge westwards. Over the centuries, the causeway grew into a solid bank along which houses and landing stages for boats were built, but unlike the north side, where land was reclaimed from the river by the ever expanding city, the riverside on the south shore stayed pretty much where it was and the south side of the river remained a virtually uninhabited marsh for centuries.

Until Westminster Bridge opened further upstream in 1750, only one bridge, London Bridge, linked the south shore with the City of London. This kept Bankside relatively remote and out of the jurisdiction of the City. Instead, it fell under the authority of the Bishops of Winchester whose London residence, Winchester Palace, was located close to the southern approach to Old London Bridge. The bishops tacitly permitted activities that were forbidden in the City and a string of inns and brothels grew up along the riverside road. By the middle of the fifteenth century, Bankside was where Londoners went to get drunk, enjoy a little cockfighting, bull- or bear-baiting and visit the ladies who worked in the 'stews'. There is still a thin alleyway on the north shore close to Queenhithe called Stew Lane, which leads down to the river in the direction of Bankside. Perhaps that was a known route for men crossing to the brothels. As they were rowed across the river, those who could read would have seen the names of the inns – the Beares Heade, the Gunne, the Crane and the Cardinals Hatte – painted on the whitewashed walls of the timber-framed buildings along the riverfront.

Cardinal Cap Alley, which runs between Bankside's oldest remaining riverside houses near the Globe Theatre, is the only reminder of these infamous inns – apart from the objects that wash up on the foreshore. It may have been a gentleman caller who lost the hooked tag I found here. Perhaps it had secured his cloak against the biting river wind, or it may have worked loose from a strap used to hook a whore's skirts out of the mud as she slipped and skidded down a causeway to a waiting wherry. It dates from between 1500 and 1650 and was half hidden in a patch of sand when I saw it. I spotted the decoration first, a pineapple or pinecone, and it is made from cast copper alloy that has acquired a rich patina during its time in the river.

A fair number of the objects I've found were probably lost by people travelling and working on the river. While the city's roads were muddy and its one bridge crowded, the Thames was fast and efficient and everyone in London used it to get around. The river on the Agas map is filled with wherries, some with tiny passengers in the back and the wherryman at the front pulling hard on a pair of oars. A wherry is waiting at Bankside, probably at Mason Stairs, which is almost exactly where the Millennium Bridge is today. There were said to be 3,000 watermen working on the tidal Thames at the end of the sixteenth century. This had risen to 8,000 by the start of the eighteenth century and 12,000 by the end of it. On Bankside, partway down an unassuming street and set into the wall of a modern building, are two stone slabs known as the Ferryman's Seat. It is thought to have ancient origins, but little else is actually known about it. The seat is narrow and the back slopes forward, which some say was to prevent the watermen falling asleep on the job. It's certainly very uncomfortable.

There were stairs and causeways all along the tidal Thames. At high tide, people stepped straight off the stairs and into boats; at low water, they negotiated slippery causeways down to the river. On John Rocque's map of 1746, there are eleven sets of river stairs between Old London Bridge and where Blackfriars Bridge is today, but over the years nearly all of them have been dismantled and the stones of many causeways reused or washed away by the river. The only set of older stairs left along the stretch at Bankside is just to the west of Southwark Bridge. The gate in the spiked iron railings at the top of them is permanently locked so you can't use them, but they are best seen from below anyway. At the top there's a short flight of narrow stone steps that widen where they leave the river wall and end on the foreshore at a broad, sett-paved causeway that runs thirty feet or so across the foreshore to the river. Where the causeway ends and the level drops, another five wooden steps lead down to the water's edge.

It's noisy down at Bankside. Trains rumble in and out of Blackfriars and Cannon Street stations and suitcase wheels zing loudly along the ridged metal path of the Millennium Bridge. Music drifts down from the buskers on the river path accompanied by the excited squeals of children chasing giant soap bubbles made by the 'Bubble Man'. It feels more exposed and less protected down here, and without a river wall to hide me from the modern world, people come to join in and ask questions. Even the foreshore itself is less protected here. Anyone with a permit can metal detect, scrape or dig up to 7.5 centimetres at Bankside, and they do. There were little holes heading west in a line where a detectorist had been before me last time I was here and someone had scraped away a large patch of shingle, right down to the mud beneath it.

It can be hard to tune in to the voices of the past when the present is so loud, but I'm a natural daydreamer and I'm practised at listening to them. Rummaging around in some old stuff recently – birthday cards from when I was five, embarrassing teenage love letters and photos of me in my punk phase – I found my old school reports. They were, in all honesty, dreadful, and had one overriding theme throughout: my ability to dream my way through class. The pages are filled with comments like 'inclined to be rather dreamy ... must be willing to concentrate fully ... would benefit from more active participation in class ... does not seem to realise that she must concentrate at all times ...'

I lived in a dreamland at home too, in a house where people had slept and eaten, loved, laughed and cried for over 500 years. I'd pull the strings on the old latched doors thinking of how many thousands of times it had been done before, and run my hands over the undulating plaster walls to feel the time that had passed around them. I could see goblin faces, flowers and birds in the shadows among the lumps and bumps of the old plaster. Had anyone else seen them too? Someone years before had scratched their initials into the plaster beneath the little wood-framed window in my bedroom and I wondered who they were. What was the view from my window like when they were alive? I played with the old Victorian kitchen range that was gently rusting away behind the lawnmower in the unused rooms at the back of the house, and spent long absorbed hours poking around in the garden bed near the front door. This had once been the kitchen midden, where centuries of fire sweepings, potato peelings and old cabbage leaves had enriched and lightened the heavy clay soil. I knew this place was special and that under the fruit bushes and between the thick clumps of bright orange self-seeded calendulas, I'd find evidence of the people who had cooked on the range and slept in my room.

So I was well primed for my riverside imaginings by the time I discovered the foreshore. I understood that there were stories hidden in the mud as there had been stories hidden in the bricks, beams and creaking floorboards of the farmhouse. I knew the ghosts of the past were waiting for me. All I had to do was look for them – and I'd perfected that skill in my childhood.

Sometimes the objects I find give me a helping hand. Scratched or stamped initials and names tell me something concrete about the people who once owned, made or used them. One cold bright morning I found a thin copper alloy token, about the size of a modern penny, caught against a large chunk of chalk that had once been part of a barge bed close to Old Billingsgate. On one side was a bulky ship with a domed cabin and the name ROBERT KINGSLAND around the edge. On the other side were the words AT SAVERS DOCK and three initials, K, R, E, in the centre. I knew it was a seventeenth-century trader's token. I'd seen them before in the dirty palms of fellow mudlarks, but I'd never found one myself and I couldn't wait to get it home to research it.

Seventeenth-century tokens are well documented online and it didn't take me long to discover who my trader was. Robert Kingsland was the landlord at Noah's Ark Tavern in St Saviour's Dock, just across the water and a little further east from where I'd found the token. The crude ship represented an ark and would have helped those who couldn't read to identify it. The trio of initials stood for Kingsland (K), Robert (R) and his wife (E). From this tiny disc I now had not only the name of a man who had lived 400 years ago, I also knew the name and location of his business and even his wife's initial. I had resurrected a long-forgotten Londoner. It almost felt intrusive, but I carried on searching and on the National Archives database I found the last will and testament of Robert Kingsland, Victualler of Saint Mary Magdalen, Bermondsey, Surrey. It was written on 24 April 1656 and is very difficult to read. The beautiful handwriting curls and loops across the page almost unintelligibly, but it solves the mystery of his wife's name. The E is for Elizabeth, to whom he bequeathed all his 'goods and chattells' and gave 'the lease of my house knowne by the name of the Noahs Arke in Saint Mary Magdalen of Bermondsey'.

Most early tokens were made of pewter or lead, which was cheap and easily worked, making it possible for ordinary people to produce their own coinage. They tended to echo the size of the coins of the time, with earlier tokens being the size of small silver medieval pennies. They were produced by, among others, the church, merchants and tavern keepers, and they had a multitude of uses. They were used to keep tally, perhaps of cargo being unloaded from boats, to exchange for goods and services, to administer the Poor Law, as passes, and most importantly instead of small change, which was generally in short supply in the seventeenth and eighteenth centuries.

Between 1648 and 1672 the authorities permitted the use of tokens as a temporary solution to the lack of halfpennies, pennies and farthings in circulation. This is when more professionally made copper and brass tokens, like Robert Kingsland's, were produced. He would have had between 500 and 1,000 of them made to use as change in the Noah's Ark. His tokens and others would have been accepted in taverns and shops in the surrounding area, provided the shopkeeper or landlord trusted the issuer, and kept in a tray under the counter until enough had been collected to return them to the original issuer in exchange for silver coins or exchanged through an intermediary called a 'Farthing Changer'. Since discovering Robert Kingsland, I have also found Ambrose Smith, landlord of the Fountain at Fenchurch Street, and his wife Anne; Richard Sewell, landlord of the Pink in Thames Street; I.A.A. from the Fleeing Horse in Charterhouse Lane; and I.A.C. from the Sword and Dagger in St Katharine's Lane. All real people and real places.

The government banned the use of tokens in 1672, but despite this people continued to make unofficial lead tokens in large quantities. They were usually struck or cast with crude images to help people identify the issuer. A bottle and glass were commonly used by tavern keepers and I have one token with the traditional sign of a candle-maker, a star and moon. Another of my tokens carries the image of a man in a wig with a prominent nose and chin. The reverse side may be a crown, or an owl if it's turned the other way up, so perhaps he was the landlord of the Crown or the Owl. Many of the later, eighteenth-century tokens are more simply decorated with a series of lines, cross-hatchings, stylised flowers, stars, tridents, crosses and dots. A personalised doodle was enough to identify the issuer of the token and the moulds for these simple designs could even be produced by the issuers themselves.

The name and life of another publican emerged from the foreshore when I was mudlarking on the Thames Estuary. It was stamped in a crescent into the wide curved shoulder of a brown stoneware flagon, covered with barnacles and bright green weed and home to a dun-coloured crab that slid out with the silt when I emptied it. Safely back on shore, I scraped away the white barnacle crust with my pocketknife to read the name underneath: 'W MAY, Kings Arms, Lower Thames Street'. I knew where that was. Lower Thames Street runs parallel to the river on the north shore, opposite Bankside. It was redeveloped after the war and it is now a busy road, lined with office buildings. I was intrigued. How had it ended up this far out? Had it been picked up or stolen by a sailor having a last drink in town and pitched off the side before he took to the high seas? It didn't look that old, so I reasoned it couldn't be that hard to track down W May.

I began my search the next day, tapping all the information I had into Google and up popped a London pub history website. This was going to be easy! Whoever ran the site had conveniently collated all the information for me: census reports, directories and insurance records. These were the people that lived and worked at the King's Arms, a list of names that conjured up characters from the past: whiskery men with swollen red noses; a buxom bar wench with an easy laugh; a severe woman in black who ran the pub and took in lodgers to make ends meet; and a thin young man, fresh from the countryside, collecting pots until his luck changed. Perhaps one of them had filled the bottle with wine or ale and given it to a rough-looking chap who was drowning his sorrows before leaving on the morning tide and who wandered away with it, back to his ship.

The exact location of the pub was 61 Lower Thames Street. It opened in 1775 and was demolished in 1920. The website listed the records of publicans dating back to 1807. The style of the bottle looked to me to date from the first half of the nineteenth century, so I searched those dates first. Benjamin Weller, a victualler, ran the Kings Arms until 1812 when Thomas Pope is listed as the publican. He presumably passed away, or perhaps ran off with the barmaid, and his wife Sarah is listed as running the pub in 1815 and 1819. There's no more information until 1832 when William Goodgame is listed as the licensee. Then, after him, is my man, William May, listed as the publican in Robson's Directory of 1835. But his reign over the Kings Arms was also short-lived and by 1839 he had gone, replaced by Thomas Smith. I had a date and I had a name, but that was all. I ran my eye further down the list. After 1851 the census gives far more information and since their lives couldn't have been far different to that of William May, I read on.

It made fascinating reading. Most of the publicans came from outside London – Northumberland, Yorkshire and Hampshire – which reflects the general population shift to large cities at the time. They lived with their extended families and employed young women as servants and barmaids and boys to collect the pots. What fascinated me more, though, were the lodgers, almost all of whom earned their living from the river. Sailors – Baccgalupo [sic] G Ballu from Geneva, Frederick Grant from Dorset, William Pinder from Lincolnshire, Cornelius Merxon from Norway, Richard Trevillick from Cornwall, Robert Beechener from Hull;

mariners – John Butler from Ireland and John Cohn from Guernsey; and a stevedore – James Sparrow White. These were not the anonymous figures who had eked out a living on the crowded and stinking Thames of the nineteenth century. They were flesh-and-blood men, from all over the country and around the world.

I've never been particularly lucky with my searches at Bankside. I usually arrive at the end of the tide, after other mudlarks have already gone over the good spots, and compared to the north shore there's less to find here, since before around the late eighteenth century it was less busy, with fewer barges and no riverside markets. Still, I've collected buttons, buckles, clasps and quite a lot of rose farthings, tiny copper coins barely large enough to cover the tip of my finger, which are found in such quantities on the foreshore that some mudlarks think they were used to pay wherry fares. These tiny coins were struck around the same time as the traders were making their own tokens, between 1636 and 1644, by private mints authorised by the king. They were intended to replace the silver farthings that had become too expensive to produce. The crowned rose on one side gave them their name, and instead of the head of Charles I on the other, there is a crown with crossed sceptres behind it. Their small size may have made them impractical but they were unpopular for other reasons too. People are said to have resented them for not being made of silver and distrusted them for not carrying the king's portrait. They were also heavily counterfeited, which led to the insertion of a triangular wedge of brass in an attempt to outfox the coiners. Several of my little rose farthings have lost their wedges, perhaps picked out by bored watermen or washed away by the river, leaving a jagged toothy gap in the edge.

But I must admit, erosion is making me luckier at Bankside these days. A barge bed is slowly being eaten away by the river. The compacted crust is cracking and dissolving, exposing the softer deposits beneath it. Impatient people dig into the dark gritty mud, which is speeding its demise, and each time I visit there seems to be less of it left. In past visits, I had found several Georgian pennies here and a Georgian shoe complete with buckle, so with half an hour to spare before a theatre performance at the Globe one summer, I decided to walk up and see if I could find anything. There, lying next to the eroding barge bed, as if it had just been dropped by a passer-by, was a chunky copper coin dated 1797 with the arrogant head of George III looking remarkably composed in the mud. It had been worth trashing my best shoes.

It wasn't the first of these huge coins I had found so I knew what it was: a cartwheel penny, a numismatic anomaly, named for its broad-rimmed edge and size. Cartwheel pennies were produced to restore the public's faith in royal coinage at a time when many of the low-value coins in circulation were worn and heavily counterfeited. The penny was pressed from an ounce of copper, equal at the time to the value of the coin and enough for the average person to buy a supply of candles to last a week. The two-pence weighed twice as much. Unsurprisingly, they were not popular coins and production ceased after just one year. They were more useful as weights and must have torn through many pockets and purses before they were replaced with a more practical alternative. I took my seat in the theatre that afternoon with a whiff of the river about me and a satisfying piece of history in my pocket.

A medieval brooch and a rare Celtic coin have been found at Bankside by other mudlarks, and I once passed a man who was inspecting part of a Viking comb he had just found at the water's edge, but I have never found anything much older than sixteenth century here, a time when the area was notorious for vice and entertainment. Bear Gardens, a small lane that leads down to the river at the end of which is the Ferryman's Seat, was named for the bear- and bull-baiting pits close by, where specially bred mastiffs were released to attack bears chained to stakes, ponies with monkeys tied to their saddles and young bulls. Bones from the paw of a bear have been found on the foreshore by a mudlark and at the end of one long day I spotted the tip of a horn sticking out of the mud. I gave it a wiggle and a hard pull, and a huge pair of cow horns broke through the surface. Our farm never had cows with horns. These days most modern cattle are bred polled (without horns), and the horns on those that do have them are nowhere near as big as the ones I found that day. It reminded me of the old breeds, like the aptly named longhorns. Perhaps it had gored a snarling mastiff and fought off several more before being pulled down and torn to pieces.

It is hardly surprising that the foreshore here is littered with shards of drinking vessels. Bungholes from medieval cisterns and large storage vessels are the easiest pieces to identify: thumb-width holes with a flat or crimped wall of thickened clay built up around it as reinforcement to prevent the stopper or spigot from cracking the pot when it was pushed in. They were mostly used for weak, or 'small', beer, which was drunk every day by people of every age and class as a safer alternative to drinking water. But it is the bearded faces on the necks of brown speckled stoneware jugs that I search out. The distinct fat-bellied bottles usually had a small looped handle on one side of their short necks and a bearded face moulded onto the other. The quality of craftsmanship varies widely. The earlier ones are often exquisitely detailed, with long flowing beards curling down in waves onto the wide belly of the pot. Crude masks feature on both early and late examples, but they became particularly pinched and ugly in later years, sometimes hardly discernible as faces at all.

In Germany, where they came from, they were known as Bartmann (bearded man) jugs and in England they were called Bellarmines, after a seventeenth-century Italian Jesuit, Cardinal Roberto Bellarmine. He was said to be staunchly anti-alcohol and on the wrong side of the divide at a time of great religious turmoil between Catholics and Protestants. It is commonly claimed that people smashed the bottles for the enjoyment of seeing his face in pieces. In reality, it is more likely the bearded faces were a representation of the Wild Man of the Woods, a mythical hairy being who was popular in folklore throughout northern Europe.

The first broken beardy man I found was beautifully sculpted, with heavy eyebrows, a smiling mouth and most of his beard. It had taken me some time to find him, but since then I've found scores of faces, part faces, eyes, mouths, noses and beards – though never a complete bottle. I can sometimes tell from the size and shape of the shard if it's going to be a neck and hold my breath in anticipation as I turn it over or pull it out of the mud. Each Bellarmine is unique: some faces are grotesque, sneering and angry, while others have cheerful, daft grins. My motley crew sit side by side in a cabinet at home, a line-up of broken misfits and odd bods. I like to think of them coming to life when the house is asleep, like a group of old men in a tavern, bragging and swapping tall tales.

The bodies of some German stoneware bottles can also be intricately decorated. I have a collection of shards with applied oak leaves, acorns, small portraits, flowers and the coats of arms of the various merchants who commissioned them and the towns and cities where they were made. Some are randomly splashed with cobalt blue on top of the brown salt glaze and I have one piece that is dated 1594, the year Shakespeare's *Comedy of Errors* was first performed. It makes me wonder if the bottle slipped from the hand of a theatregoer as he fell asleep, drunk, in the back of a wherry on his way home to the north side and his long-suffering wife.

Foreshore finds that can be attributed to a specific place or moment in history are particularly special to me and for this reason one of my most precious pieces is a Tudor money box that was found on the foreshore at Bankside in the 1980s. It was given to me by a mudlark who had been given it by another mudlark, and I will be its faithful custodian until I pass it on to the next person to continue its journey through time.

It is about the size of an orange, a perfect palm-sized fit, and made of a coarse, buff pottery with an uneven covering of rich speckled green glaze, characteristic of the time it was made. Pots, jugs and bowls that were decorated with this type of glaze were dipped quickly or splashed, leaving areas that were unglazed. The two small, unglazed circles on the side of my little money box might be where the potter's fingers held it while it was dipped or it could be where it rested between other money boxes in the kiln.

Fragments of similar money boxes were found during excavations at the site of the new Globe Theatre and I have my own collection of button-like moneybox finials from the foreshore at Bankside. It is thought they were used by 'gatherers' to collect entrance fees at the playhouses. 'Groundlings' stood in the uncovered yard in front of the stage and paid one penny, roughly one-twelfth of a worker's weekly salary. For an extra penny, you could stand in the covered galleries around the side and for a penny on top of that you could sit in the upper gallery. Only rich merchants and nobility could afford the sixpence for the Lord's Rooms, which were on a balcony at the back of the stage.

I wonder if the gatherer who once held my little pot had been busy with a whore and was late for work the day he used it, only just making the performance, which would have begun at 2 p.m. to make use of the afternoon light, and avoiding the wrath of his drunken employer. Perhaps he had snatched the empty box from a pile that had been delivered by the potter earlier that day before squeezing his way through the noisy crowd that had started to gather in front of the brightly painted stage. Much of the audience would already have been loud and drunk and as they pressed their small silver pennies into the slit in the side of the box, they would have blasted him with foul breath from the raw garlic they'd been chewing on.

His feet would have crunched on the thick layer of hazelnut shells dropped by previous audiences, which was mixed with cinders to give substance to the dirt floor onto which the rain fell through the open roof. The audience added to the stinking quagmire if they were unwilling or unable to urinate into the buckets, which were passed round during the performance and sold on to the dyers and tanners across the river afterwards. The apple, beer, wine and nut sellers may already have been circulating, and he would have held tight to the little box for fear of the pickpockets and rogues that preyed on the drunken crowd, which groaned with each new body that now squeezed in. By the time he closed the door there would have been barely an inch to spare. He would have returned the money box to the room behind the theatre, known to all as the box office, and left as his master began to smash the pots and count his profits.

Some of my most intimate and evocative foreshore finds are clay pipes, which are ubiquitous to the tidal Thames. Short pieces of broken stems and their little white bowls can be found on virtually every stretch of the river, from Teddington to the Estuary. Any visitor to the foreshore will notice them as soon as they look down. The first time I found one was the day I realised the potential of the Thames and it became more than just a place to walk off my angst; it was somewhere comforting, where I could surrender to the history beneath my feet and escape from the present. That small piece of clay pipe stem was a key to another world and an intimate connection to forgotten lives, a reminder that the human condition is a shared one passed down through the generations: we are not the first and will not be the last.

Tobacco was first brought back to England in the mid-sixteenth century by ships returning from the New World. To begin with it was rare and expensive and the bowls of the earliest clay pipes reflect this, being no larger than the tip of my little finger. Years later, people finding these tiny pipes thought that they had found the smoking apparatus of elves and pixies and they became known as fairy pipes. It soon developed into a craze, however, becoming both fashionable and commonplace – even Elizabeth I is said to have tried smoking, although in those days they referred to smoking as 'tobacco drinking'. But James I was not so keen and even wrote a treatise against it called *A Counterblaste to Tobacco*. In it he railed against smoking, calling it 'A custome lothsome to the eye, hatefull to the Nose, harmefull to the braine, dangerous to the Lungs, and in the blacke stinking fume thereof, neerest resembling the horrible Stigian smoke of the pit that is bottomeless'.

James I failed to turn the general public against smoking and instead it became even more popular. As demand grew, more tobacco was grown in the American colonies, the price of it fell and pipe bowls increased in size until by the eighteenth century they were roughly three times larger than the original 'fairy' pipes. London took to smoking with zeal. A Swiss traveller in 1599 noted: 'They carry the instrument on them, lighting up on all occasions: at the play, in taverns or elsewhere.' In 1614, a pamphleteer claimed that there were 7,000 tobacco houses, more than all the ale houses and taverns put together, where tobacco, snuff and smoking accessories, including pipes, were sold. Even allowing for some exaggeration, this shows how popular smoking had become in the capital.

Tiny Elizabethan pipe bowls are now rare and difficult to find. In all the years I've been mudlarking I've only found five very precious bowls, and all from one small area that's known for its Tudor finds. Later eighteenth- and nineteenth-century pipes are far more common and I've found hundreds of them, but unless they are exceptionally long I leave them where they are for others to find. By the time they surface on the foreshore the stems are usually broken and fairly short, but when they were new some of them may have been quite ridiculously long. In the mid-eighteenth century, pipes eighteen to twenty-four inches long called alderman straws were a fashionable, if impractical, choice. The nineteenth-century equivalents were nicknamed churchwarden pipes (some say it was because churchwardens liked to smoke them while they waited for church services to end), but the longest of all were known as a 'yard of clay'. Needless to say the fashion did not last. Complete alderman and churchwarden pipes are sometimes found preserved in the soft Thames mud, but as far as I know a complete 36-incher has yet to be found.

Most of the pipes are plain, but occasionally I'll spot a decorated bowl: the royal coat of arms, crowned and flanked by a unicorn and a lion; roses and thistles entwined to celebrate the union of England and Scotland; regimental coats of arms and those of livery companies, inns and taverns; Bacchus rolling indulgently around the pipe bowl; Aesop's fox reaching for some grapes; exotic-looking birds; the delicately moulded head of a Turkish man wearing a jewelled turban and sporting a luxuriantly curling moustache; an early seventeenth-century decorated Dutch pipe that looks like an overblown tulip.

Decoration lends extra character to pipes and can place them firmly in a point in time. The wigged and frock-coated gentleman depicted on a pipe I found recently was a clue to the individual who smoked it. The words on the pipe read 'PITT FOREVER', indicating that the man that smoked this pipe was a Whig and a supporter of William Pitt the Elder, who is credited with the birth of the British Empire 250 years ago. Perhaps the pipe smoker was a merchant and a beneficiary of Pitt's military campaigns in India, Canada, West Africa and the West Indies. Maybe he smoked it in a fashionable coffee house, where men gathered to discuss business and debate the issues of the day.

The earliest pipes were probably shaped by hand, before wooden moulds were introduced to speed up production and keep up with demand. One of the only seventeenth-century wooden pipe moulds in existence was found by a mudlark at Bankside. It is a mould for a very small pipe, the size of which has helped the Museum of London to date it to between 1580 and 1610. Metal moulds eventually replaced wood, and iron moulds became the standard right through to the twentieth century.

Each pipe was crafted in a process that often involved an entire family. Fine white clay was rolled into a thin sausage with a bulb at one end where the bowl would be formed. It was set aside to stiffen up a little before a thin metal wire was carefully inserted up the stem to form the air passage. The whole thing was then put into an oiled metal mould, which was clamped tight in a vice-like press, and a metal stopper was forced into the bowl end to compress the clay and form the bowl cavity. When the stopper was removed the wire in the stem was pushed in a little further to connect with the bowl cavity and excess clay was trimmed off the top of the mould with a knife. The mould was then opened, the pipe was lifted out on the wire, and it was set aside on a rack until it was dry enough to handle and the excess clay trimmed away. The whole process took just a few seconds, which is how so many could be made. Men usually did the moulding and women, most often their wives, finished the pipes, while children helped to prepare the clay and pack the finished pipes.

Between 1600 and 1700 the rims were usually smoothed and finished with a band of milling made up of a series of short lines, much like those on the edge of a coin, but after 1700, up to 1850, the rim was left with a plain cut surface that often showed the marks of the trimming knife. The best-quality pipes were burnished by rubbing them gently with a hard polished tool made of metal or stone (usually agate) before they were fired. This gave them an opulent smoothness and a soft shine that is still preserved on some of the pipes I find on the foreshore today.

The ends of many eighteenth- and nineteenth-century pipe stems were dipped in red wax to prevent them from sticking to the smoker's lips and freshly eroded pipe stems sometimes have an inch of this faded wax still clinging to the clay. At the other end of the stem, beneath the bowl, clay pipes also have what is known as a 'heel'. Either side of the small short heels of eighteenth-century pipes often have initials, or occasionally small symbols like suns, crowns and horseshoes. These are makers' marks. If they are viewed when the pipe is held facing away from you as if it is being smoked, the Christian name initial is on the left and the surname on the right. More rarely, seventeenth-century pipes have initials or monograms, often accompanied by stylised tobacco leaves, stamped into the flat heel of the pipe bowl, which can reveal a remarkable amount of detail about the men that made them – names, dates and even the addresses of their workshops. Smokers also left their mark – tooth marks on stems where the pipe was gripped between yellow stained teeth, bowls blackened inside with soot that some-times also licks up around the outside edge.

Given their fragility, it's incredible how many pipes sur-vive both the waves and the crushing mud of the foreshore. On very low tides, in one particular spot, it is difficult not to step on the eighteenth-century bowls that poke out of the mud and roll around at the water's edge. There may once have been a pipe kiln close by, or perhaps street waste containing thousands of discarded pipes was dumped in cartloads onto the foreshore. The reason that there are so many of them is that they were relatively cheap and made in hundreds of thousands. Most inns, taverns and coffee houses would have provided boxes of them for their customers to choose from, and some would have been sold ready-packed with tobacco. They were looked after and reused – stems were cleared of built-up tar in the hearth, sometimes bundled into special wire cages – but the stems broke easily and once they became 'nose warmers', too short to provide a cool smoke, they were thrown away. I find the number of pipes varies from tide to tide, though some mudlarks insist there are fewer pipes today and blame casual visitors for taking too many (I've been told that mudlarks have been saying this since the 1980s). Perhaps the river naturally rations its bounty, releasing them from the mud according to the tides. But once released from the protection of the mud, if the pipes are not collected, they will eventually break and wear away to nothing.

Searching for clay pipes is refreshingly simple. Their clean white clay bowls are easy to spot, and gently pulling on exposed pipe stems can yield some pleasant surprises – elegant long pipes that emerge from the mud with a satisfying slurp. Some people like to return their foreshore-found pipes to near pristine whiteness. They put them in the dishwasher or soak them in bleach, but this can be disastrous for the pipe, as the bleach soaks into the clay eventually rendering it down to little more than a pile of white flakes. I prefer to leave mine as they are with the rich patina they sometimes acquire in the mud and the distinct smell of river that wafts up from the boxes and trays I keep them in. I've stopped collecting all but the very old, unusual or well preserved, but I still get a kick out of spotting them in the mud. Even if I'm not going to take it home with me, I will pick one up just for the thrill of holding such a perfectly formed and skilfully made object. I don't smoke, but there's something so tactile about old clay pipes that they could almost convince me to take it up.

QUEENHITHE

The wealth which she rescues, half-digested, from the maw of
Father Thames, is of a various and rather equivocal description, and
consists of more items than we can here specify. We can, however,
from actual observation, testify to a portion of them: these are,
firewood in very small fragments, with now and then, by way of a
prize, a stave of an old cask; broken glass, and bottles either of glass
or stone unbroken; bones, principally of drowned animals, washed
into skeletons; ropes, and fragments of ropes, which will pick into
tow; old iron or lead, or metal of any sort which may have dropped
overboard from passing vessels; and last, but by no means least, coal
from the coal barges, which, as they are passing up and down all
day long, and all the year round, cannot fail of dropping a pretty
generous tribute to the toils of the tide-waitress.

Charles Manby Smith, 'The Tide Waitress',
*Curiosities of London Life or Phases, Physiological
and Social of the Great Metropolis* (1853)

There are parts of the foreshore that sing with the
voices of the past and have absorbed the richness of
life: people's toil, pain, hope, happiness and disappoint-
ment. Their ghostly essence is contained within the mud
and thrown onto the shore with every lapping wave. The
ancient dock of Queenhithe is one such place. It is the

remnant of a time when the riverside rippled with small inlets. As time passed, these have been filled in and built over, but Queenhithe was left, the only surviving ancient dock along the city's waterfront.

Queenhithe is located a little to the east of the Millennium Bridge on the north shore of the Thames and is tightly hemmed in on each side by ugly modern buildings: offices and apartments with dark windows that stare down on the ancient space. Now silted up, the dock is filled with shingle and rubble and a lake of deceptively deep mud at low tide. It slopes gently up from the river and traps the flotsam and jetsam of modern London life against its back wall. Bottles, balloons, balls, orange life-preserver rings, traffic cones and all manner of other plastic horrors pile up in a jumbled multicoloured mess. On one side, thick concrete columns support the red-brick building that juts out over part of the old dock, creating a dark, dank river cave lined with brown slime. At its mouth, the foreshore is skinned and naked, the shingle eroded away, exposing the mud to the mercy of the river, which removes a tiny bit more on every tide. As it erodes, the smooth mud gradually reveals the past that has been poured into it over centuries, spitting shards of pottery, buttons, pins, coins, old tallow candles and even a wooden barrel back into the land of the living.

Queenhithe, known as Aethelred's Hythe in the ninth century, is the grande dame of the tidal Thames. It appears on the earliest of maps and illustrations of the river and is a useful orientator along a foreshore that has changed dramatically over two millennia. It is likely to have existed as a harbour in Roman times, where imported goods from the Empire were unloaded to meet the tastes of the cosmo-politan and growing city. Wine came from Italy, Gaul and Germany, and olives, olive oil and a rich salty sauce called garum, which was made from fermented fish, was imported from southern Spain in large clay storage jars called amphorae, which sometimes wash up on the fore-shore reduced to coarse buff pottery shards.

The dock itself was created by the Saxons when they refounded the city in the ninth century under the reign of Alfred the Great. It became the centre of Saxon London, one of two large docks created at this time, the other being Billingsgate, which was filled in and built over in the nine-teenth century. The name 'Queenhythe' came from an old word for a landing place on the river (hythe) and Queen Matilda, wife of Henry I, who was granted duties on all the goods landed there in the early twelfth century. Much of London's food was brought through Queenhithe, and it was particularly associated with the transport and trade of salt, wood, grain and fish. Ships would have lined the quay-side and gathered at the mouth of the dock to wait their turn to load and unload. For a time Queenhithe also served as a port, taking people up and down the river and out to sea. It was one of London's busiest docks until the fifteenth century when ships began to favour Billingsgate, partly because it was downstream from Old London Bridge and easier to access. It was still a busy place in the nineteenth century, when warehouses and barge beds were built near and around Queenhithe, though by the 1960s even these had ceased to be used and the warehouses were demolished in the 1970s.

*

Queenhithe was identified as an important and potentially vulnerable area in the 1970s and designated a Scheduled Monument to ensure that it was never developed or built on and to protect it from diggers and treasure hunters who were turning it over like an allotment. It now has the same level of protection as Stonehenge and the entire dock is out of bounds to all mudlarks, even society members. It is illegal to remove anything from the Queenhithe Dock.

Often, of course, people visit the foreshore completely unaware of its historic importance. There are no signs along the river explaining it or the restrictions that are in place, and unless you've checked the PLA's website there is no way you'd know anything about them. Sadly, there are also those who are well aware of the restrictions that cover the foreshore as a whole and yet choose to ignore them. There will always be rogue mudlarks who dig a little bit deeper than they should; take objects from protected areas; and 'forget' to report what they find.

In the 1970s and 80s, professional treasure hunters dug up the foreshore and sold their spoils to dealers who stalked the river with fistfuls of cash, buying the objects straight from the ground. I've also been told how mudlarks kicked holes in the Victorian wooden revetments that protect the foreshore to let the river flow in and do their work for them. These days, online auction sites make it easier than ever to sell objects that are found on the foreshore, thus creating demand and tempting people to fill it. And it's not illegal. I have seen the most beautiful objects offered for sale on eBay – as well as a load of old rubbish: stones, bones and a Victorian butter-knife handle claiming to be early medieval.

Once an object is sold to the highest bidder though, it all too often loses its provenance and associated history, and while the Portable Antiquities Scheme has an agreement with eBay to monitor items that might be considered Treasure, there is still very little control over what is taken. Some people mudlark with carrier bags and buckets, taking as much as they can carry, whether they want it or not. I often wonder where it all ends up: forgotten in cupboards and drawers, dumped in the garden, or worse still, thrown out with the rubbish? Even ancient timbers that were still embedded in the foreshore have been dug up and removed, and I heard of one man who built a garden wall with the pieces of stone and masonry he collected. All of this is lost now, its connection with the river severed and forgotten.

But the biggest threat to the foreshore is erosion. While we can legislate to protect the foreshore from human activity, it's harder to protect it from the river itself. It is constantly building up and eroding, shingle covering sand and sand covering mud, scooping out hollows and gathering piles, drilling down through centuries of compacted mud and the city's ancient rubbish. It naturally deposits higher up and erodes at the low-water mark, with the rate of erosion increasing in the winter and spring, but even slight changes or additions to the river or foreshore have significant effects. Over the past twenty years or so more damage has been caused by the wake of increasing river traffic, which continually crashes onto the foreshore and sucks the surface back out with it, scouring away the top layer and digging out ancient features. It has a more rapid effect where the foreshore has been dug into by mudlarks and the mud is softer and less stable.

Along its entire length, the foreshore of the tidal Thames is a great moving mass. In the time it has taken me to write this book, it will have changed again. Subtle landmarks can wash away entirely, almost overnight, and the river moves surprisingly large objects at will, leaving much smaller and lighter things in the same place for months. For this reason, many mudlarks learn a relatively small patch, returning to it again and again, building up a mind map and watching as it transforms and rearranges over time.

I only take away what the river delivers to me, what's left on the surface, there on one tide and gone on the next. I choose not to scrape or dig to find what the river hasn't yet offered up. I collect what would otherwise be washed away or destroyed by the currents and tides. I also mudlark with the knowledge that one day its bounty will run out, so I don't take everything I find. Unless it's something I collect, it's unusual or an object I don't already have, I leave it for someone else to discover or for the river to reclaim. Although they're hard to resist, I stopped collecting ordinary shards of medieval pottery a long time ago because I have enough, and I recently returned a bagful of eighteenth-century clay pipes to where I found them. I think this pleases the river and maybe it improves my luck, but then again perhaps I'm wrong to leave so much stuff behind.

Some people say mudlarks shouldn't be helping them-selves to the treasures of the foreshore at all. But the flip side is that unless someone takes the objects, they will eventu-ally be carried off, broken down, worn away and dissolved. According to one foreshore archaeologist, the amount that is collected by mudlarks is fractional compared to the amount that is reclaimed by the river, and since the number of objects is finite, at some point in the future it will all be gone. So perhaps now is the time to save what we can.

The river exacts a heavy toll on artefacts that are free of the mud, tumbling, turning, scratching, smoothing and battering them, before it takes them away or destroys them. Metal, bone, pottery and stone objects are quite resilient, but even they are eventually worried away by the river. Much of what I find is scarred and damaged, but if I'm lucky enough to catch something as soon as it emerges from the mud it can look as if it was lost yesterday. Thames mud is a magical preserver. It is anaerobic, which means it lacks oxygen, and this is the main reason it produces such exceptional finds. Cocooned in a wet, oxygen-free environment, materials that would ordinarily perish – wood, leather, iron and fabric – can emerge perfectly preserved, held in suspended animation, kept exactly as they were when they fell into the river. Once they are exposed, it is a race against time to save them, but it is impossible to save everything.

I have watched willow hurdles laid down centuries ago to stabilise the mud, wooden barrels and what looked like the remains of a basket of elderberries slowly rise and wash away on the tides. The soft, waterlogged sticks of neatly woven wicker fish and eel traps, dating from between the fifteenth and nineteenth centuries, break down even more quickly, leaving just an outline like a drawing in the mud.

If wood is left to dry naturally it splits and cracks. The ageing process of hundreds of years condenses into days or sometimes hours. I have experimented with a number of methods of drying ancient wood, but in the end, I've found the simplest solution to be the best. First I clean the object gently with water before wrapping it tightly in cling film and putting it at the bottom of my freezer for as many years as I can bear to leave it. This effects a crude form of semi-freeze-drying so that when I take it out and dry it slowly in a cool dark cupboard, wrapped in a plastic bag pierced with holes, the wood dries very well. Just like mudlarking itself, patience, time and simplicity are the key to preservation.

If leather is left to dry naturally it curls and shrinks, and since I find quite a lot of it on the foreshore I've had plenty of opportunity to experiment with preserving it. I mostly find old shoes and shoe soles, although I recently found a leather hat which is at this moment sitting in a fridge in the conservation department of the Museum of London awaiting expert attention. But nobody seems to want the shoes and soles, which are left to me to try to preserve and I do this as well as I can because they are so special. Of all the objects I have found on the foreshore, leather shoes and shoe soles are among the most personal. Often the imprint of the last owner's foot is still clearly visible, the shapes of toes and heels pressed into the leather as soft shadows. In more complete shoes, the angle of wear on the heel, repair work and creases across the top of the shoe are as individual as fingerprints.

Old shoes are also a fascinating vehicle for social exploration, revealing snapshots of various times in history through their shapes, styles and the way they were made. Straight shoes, with soles that are neither left- nor right-footed, were common between 1500 and 1700, and long pointed soles come from shoes called poulaines that were fashionable in the late fourteenth and mid-fifteenth centuries. Thick soles with lines of rusty iron studs are usually from late nineteenth- and early twentieth-century hobnailed boots. My favourite, though, are the distinctive wide-toed soles of Tudor duck-billed or cow-mouth shoes. According to sumptuary law, which kept ostentatious show among the lower ranks in check, only men of wealth could wear these shoes, which were often slashed to reveal the brightly coloured stockings they wore with them. I have successfully dried the soles of Tudor cow-mouth shoes between sheets of newspaper, weighted flat to stop them from curling and twisting, but more complete shoes have proved to be beyond my amateur conservation techniques. I have tried drying the pieces slowly, but they shrank and became brittle. I spent weeks rubbing lanolin into one ancient shoe upper, only to end up with a sticky shrunken mess. My most successful experiment so far has been with the same cream I use on my leather sofa, which kept the toe of a shoe soft and supple as it dried out. But when I finally found a complete child's shoe, estimated to date from around the sixteenth century, I decided it needed to be dealt with properly.

Only the toe of the shoe was peeping out of the mud when I found it. I am used to finding pieces of old shoes, but they are usually just the sole or a section or two of the upper. This time, as I carefully moved the mud away from around it, I realised with growing excitement that it was complete. The thick, waxed thread that would once have held it together had rotted away, but it had been kept in shape by the mud and slid out wonderfully intact. In my hands lay a small, flat slip-on that looked about the right size for a child nowadays of around five years old. It was made of thick dark peaty brown cowhide and reminded me of the shoes

I had once seen people wearing and selling in Morocco; a simple workaday style that, like the wooden combs I find, has remained unchanged for centuries. When it was new, it was a popular style and many ordinary Londoners, adults and children, wore them. Perhaps it had been lost while someone was boarding a boat or was sucked off as he or she tried to walk through the thick mud. The owner had worn it right through at the big toe end, so maybe they had grown out of it or decided it was beyond repair. A podiatrist I showed it to suggested the hole was caused by a condition known as hammertoe, where toes are pushed down and the joint is forced up. To some, the hole might have been an imperfection, but to me it made it even more precious. The hole, the creases, the worn-out sole had been made by a forgotten child almost 600 years ago. I was enchanted.

I took the brown sodden lump home wrapped in plastic, which kept it damp, and I put it under the stairs where it was cool and dark. This is where it stayed for the best part of two years before I managed to track down someone willing to help me conserve it. My quest began at the Museum of London, but shoes are not uncommon finds in London; the museum has a lot in its collection and sadly not enough money to conserve them all. So I racked my brains for more ideas. Then I remembered reading an article about some similar shoes that had been found on the wreck of Henry VIII's warship, the *Mary Rose*. The *Mary Rose* sank in 1545 and was discovered in 1971 on the seabed near the entrance to Portsmouth Harbour. She was raised in 1982 and around 19,000 artefacts were recovered. Conservation is ongoing and their experience in waterlogged objects is second to none. I allowed myself cautious optimism.

I contacted the Mary Rose Trust and arranged to take my shoe to David, their head of conservation. In a small dark room at the back of the museum, he carefully removed the shoe from its wet tea towel. I cringed slightly, expecting to be berated for the condition I had kept it in, but he continued in silent contemplation, turning it over and peering carefully inside it. I had done a fairly good job, he told me, but he was sorry, they couldn't help. Funding, or the lack of it, had thwarted me once more. Still, there was a glimmer of hope. David had studied conservation at Cardiff University and he thought it might be worth contacting them to see if they could help.

I wrapped the shoe in its wet tea towel again, surrounded it in a cloud of bubble wrap and posted it to Wales where it was cleaned, measured, weighed, documented and assessed, before I was asked if I would like to go to Cardiff and see how it was coming along. The cleaning stage had been time-consuming since brushes of varying strengths, and eventually a microscope and tweezers, were needed to remove all the mud. The shoe was at the water-displacement stage and soaking in a bath of glycerol when I got there. This would provide a physical bond to support the degraded collagen fibres and give the shoe a degree of flexibility. Next, it would be shaped using inert packing supports and then placed in an ordinary freezer to freeze any remaining water molecules. Within a vacuum, the freeze dryer would then turn the solid water molecules into gas, without passing them through a liquid stage that could damage the surface of the shoe. Once freeze-drying was complete, the shoe would be stitched back together under a microscope and packed to keep its shape. This, then, was how freeze-drying worked.

Several months later a parcel arrived from Wales. The shoe was smaller than I remembered and, now that it had dried, the leather was a lighter brown, but the creases across the top, the worn-down heel and the hole in the toe were still there. I had worried that the process might remove some of the shoe's character and dull the past, but as I held it in my hand it felt just as magical, as if it had slipped off a child's foot yesterday. It has pride of place in my collection, in a display case of its own that keeps it free from dust and helps to regulate its environment – not too damp and not too dry.

In many ways, mudlarking is a quest in two parts: the hunt for the object and the journey to identify it and learn more about it. Soon after my first foreshore foray, I began to take home mysterious objects and spent the following week researching them before returning to the river for more. My research opened up a world of escapees and obsessives. However obscure the object, there seemed to be an expert in it. I found people who specialised in lead bag seals, Dutch clay pipes, pre-1800 buttons, bricks, lead tokens, seventeenth-century trade beads, Victorian lead soldiers, Roman coins, fossils and medieval floor tiles. There is a man in Wisconsin who strives to make the perfect medieval lace aglet and a woman who earns her living from making authentic Tudor clothing. Others immerse themselves completely and spend their weekends dressed up and reliving the past over and over again.

There are devotees of specific objects on the foreshore too. Graham has been mudlarking for over twenty years

Roman amphora stopper; Victorian sauce bottle stopper; Codd bottle 'marbles'; black vulcanite beer bottle stoppers.

My treasured pieces of Doves type that I found in the river at Hammersmith.

Medieval roof tiles, one still with its wooden peg and one with cat and dog paw prints; chunk of Roman mosaic floor; Penn floor tile, *c.*14th century; piece of Roman hypocaust.

Wooden comb, *c*.16th century; glass, coral and bone beads; book clasp, *c*.16th century; pleasure garden token and silver etui, both 18th century; thimble, *c*.16th century; pewter needle case, *c*.16th century; silver posey ring, *c*.16th century; medieval buckles.

Hag stone; Mesolithic worked flints; fossilised sea urchin; the mysterious Thames garnets.

A rare 17th-century chevron trade bead.

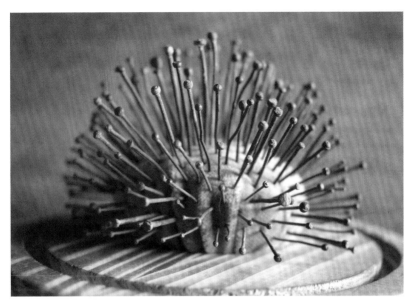

Handmade copper alloy pins, *c.*1400–1800.

Silver posey ring, *c.*16th century, with the inscription 'I LIVE IN HOPE'.

The bearded man from a late-16th-century Bellarmine.

Tudor moneybox and my collection of broken moneybox finials.

My most precious find: a Tudor child's shoe.

Clay pipes, *c.*1580–1900. As a general rule, the smaller the pipe bowl, the older the pipe.

Pocket sundial, late 16th to early 17th century.

Ivory scabbard chape that once belonged to a Roman auxiliary soldier.

Roman finds: bone game counters (one has been gnawed by a rat); bone die; broken bone hairpins; glass ring intaglio and melon bead.

The river's rich trove: silver, tin and copper coins dating from the Roman period to the 19th century; a giant cartwheel twopenny piece; a pirate coin dated 1654; tiny rose farthings, the King's shilling and a medieval long-cross penny; fakes, forgeries and coin weights; jetons for counting; pewter, lead and copper tokens for trade; coins as love tokens, bent, holed and engraved.

Broken pilgrim badge and ecclesiastic tokens, c.15th century.

Medieval riveted mail.

Late Georgian watch fob, depicting a boar standing on grass.

Ordnance mark under the head of an 18th-century coppering tack.

Eighteenth-century shoe pattern that would have kept someone's skirts clear of the thick filth that covered London's streets.

Lost toys: miniature pewter plate, dripping pan and a pipeclay cockerel, *c*.17th century; Frozen Charlottes, 19th century; a bone wizzer, medieval or earlier; a Victorian lead soldier.

Edwardian Lalique/Baccarat designed perfume bottle, with a dribble of scent inside.

Amy Johnson commemorative brooch.

and is obsessed with collecting pins. The first time I met him he was picking pins from the mud with a pair of tweezers. He wears three in the lapel of his muddy old suit jacket for luck. From counting out and weighing 1,000 of them, and then weighing his entire collection, he estimates that he has over 180,000 pins. Among them he has identified ninety-two different types. Johnny is another mudlark on a specific quest. He collects beads. It took him almost forty visits before he spied that first brightly coloured glass sphere lying in the gravel, and it sparked an obsession. Over the following two years he collected 598 beads in a rainbow of colours and a variety of shapes, sizes and materials, from tiny glass beads that may once have adorned the bodice of a dress to drilled semi-precious stones, someone's prized possessions. His bead collection must be approaching 1,000 by now.

I shudder to think of the treasures I have left behind simply because I didn't know what they were. Many years ago, on the foreshore near Bankside, I found what I now know to be a pewter syringe for administering mercury. Mercury was thought to be a cure for syphilis (a night with Venus meant a lifetime with Mercury), though its toxic effects far outweighed any benefits. It was administered in heated vapours, applied as a cream and injected directly into the nether regions. When I found the syringe, it was badly crushed and I looked at it carefully before deciding to leave it where it was because 'it didn't look very nice'. I still kick myself for that error.

After my early mistakes, I always take mystery objects home now, just in case. And sometimes, I get a nice surprise. A few years ago I found a small rectangular piece of ivory washed up in a drift of animal bones. Initially, I thought it was the back of a bone domino, but when I turned it over, instead of dots, there was a carved circular pit with radiating lines and the numbers 10, 11, 12, 1 and 2 delicately inscribed onto it. I showed it to a nearby mudlark, who confidently pronounced it to be part of a 1930s barometer, but that didn't seem quite right to me, so I bagged it up and took it home to research properly.

I mulled it over on the way back and for several days afterwards. I could tell it was probably ivory from the feel of it and the delicate grain it had that bone lacks, but I still had no idea what it was. Eventually I invited some friends over to see if they had any suggestions. Several bottles of wine later, the only thing we could think of was that it looked a bit like a miniature sundial. I grabbed my laptop and rather drunkenly typed in 'ivory sundial', not really hoping for much, yet there it was: a video of a near-identical example being excavated in a historic colonial settlement in Jamestown, America. We gathered round and watched as the archaeologist explained what she was doing, carefully digging and brushing away the dirt before lifting it up to the camera.

Now I knew what it was, finding out more was easy. My little broken timepiece was indeed a pocket sundial, probably made in Nuremberg in the late sixteenth or early seventeenth century. The circular pit would have held a glass-covered compass, used for alignment, and a string gnomon, tethered between a small iron pin and the lid (all now missing), would have cast a shadow that showed the time. It was an expensive trinket. Whoever had once owned it would have been a person of means, perhaps a visiting merchant or the captain of a ship. I'm sure it would have been proudly shown to friends, its little lid opened and turned until it caught the sun. It may have been taken on long voyages and angled towards the sun in the New World or the Orient. I have read quite a lot about such trinkets since then, learning that they may not have been intended to be precise timepieces after all, but kept as a memento mori, a reminder that life is vanity and death inevitable.

Even the most obvious objects can remain a mystery until they are properly identified and researched. The shards of two millennia litter much of the foreshore. It's clear they are broken pots, but the skill lies in identifying them. When I first started mudlarking I was indiscriminate. I'd come home with shards of pretty nineteenth-century china or bright, tightly designed bits of Georgian crockery, simply because they were easy to find. But as my knowledge grew, I became more selective and gradually developed an interest in older domestic pottery, thick artless shards of brown, yellow and green cooking pots, jugs, bowls and tankards. They weren't as pretty as the blue-and-white pottery or as sophisticated as porcelain, but I was attracted to their comfortable modesty, and the subtle natural colours of the clay and the glazes. Sometimes they were crudely decorated, but even the plain pieces were comforting to the hand and pleasing to the eye, and emanated a distinct sense of purpose and intimacy. History was made tangible and immediate where the potter's thumb or fingerprints were pressed into the clay, leaving impressions that perfectly fitted my own fingers.

The earliest medieval pottery I have found on the foreshore is known as shellyware, named for the large pieces of white shell embedded in the coarse brown clay. It dates from between the eleventh and the thirteenth centuries and is not very common. The pieces I have are small, undecorated and anonymous. They blend with the pebbles and rubble and are easy to miss. Redware, by contrast, is far more common. Heavy, utilitarian pieces were produced from this in vast quantities for use in London's kitchens and taverns from around the eleventh century right up to the twentieth. Earlier medieval redware can usually be distinguished by its coarser, sandy texture and the dark grey core that comes from firing at lower temperatures in less efficient kilns. Sometimes they were dipped or splashed with clear or green glazes, which were as practical as they were decorative, preventing liquids from seeping out through the absorbent clay. Of my larger medieval redware shards I have the wide flat rim of a bowl; part of a cup with a small handle, perfectly sized for my fingers and pinched either side by the potter to fix it in place; the hollow handles and short feet of cooking pots called pipkins; and the thick rims of vessels that are decorated with a line of thumbprints, an everlasting signature of the person who made it. I have a small ear-shaped handle from a porringer – a shallow bowl for 'pottage', the vegetable-based stew thickened with pulses and sometimes scraps of meat that was a staple food of the late-medieval period – speckled with rich green glaze on top and smoothed underneath by the potter's thumbs.

The potter may also have used very simple tools like the piece of flat bone I found that has a wide serrated edge at one end. I puzzled over it for a while until a friend of mine who pots in her spare time sent me a fifteenth-century

German illustration of a female potter at her wheel. She is wearing a loose sleeveless dress and her hair is covered with a turban-like wrap of cloth. A lump of clay sits on the floor beside her and her skirt is hitched up to her knees, revealing bare feet turning a wooden potter's wheel. She is putting the finishing touches to a tall jug or drinking vessel and in her hand is a comb-like object exactly like the one I had found on the Thames. According to my friend, they are still used for decorating and shaping pots while they are on the wheel. The barefooted German potter provided another visual reference for some more unusual shards in my collection. The base of the jug she is making is similar to the grey 'pie crust' pot bases I have found in the mud near Queenhithe. These roughly gathered clay skirts were attached to the tall jugs and drinking vessels that came to London from Raeren in Germany, brought along the Rhine in a trade ship, over the North Sea and up the Thames.

From around 1350 the fashion changed towards white clays, and the potteries on the Surrey/Hampshire border began producing vast quantities of pale domestic ware for the London market. It is difficult not to find pieces of borderware on the foreshore near Queenhithe. It is often coloured with a characteristic green glaze, which was created by filing ingots of copper, grinding the filings finely and adding them to the slip. The colour was enhanced with lead and a potter has told me that it is impossible to recreate its vibrancy without it. The pots were quickly dipped or splashed, leaving areas unglazed, and stacked into large kilns to fire. Shards of this green-glazed medieval pottery can be exquisitely beautiful and look surprisingly modern. The glaze was fired into a range of rich and vibrant speckled greens; I have one very special piece with burst air bubbles preserved in the glaze by the heat of the kiln.

Much of the borderware was undecorated, but some were scratched with lines and patterns and more decorative pieces had figures and scenes stuck onto them. I have two small green-glazed men that are thought to have broken off a fifteenth-century jug and a fourteenth-century chafing dish. The jug figure may have been a knight, though his helmet is missing, and the other figure may have been one of several that supported cooking pots over the hot coals contained in the chafing dish. They are simple, quirky little fellows with outstretched arms, prominent chins and noses and a simple slash for their mouths. I found them in the same area, several years apart, and both were lying face down in the mud, a lesson to me on the importance of turning pottery shards over before dismissing them.

Even the most innocuous-looking brown shard can reveal the heavily freckled salt-glaze of sixteenth- and seventeenth-century German stoneware; thick custard-coloured spirals, curls, lines and dots on gingerbread-like slipware; or the combed lines of decoration on yellow Staffordshire slipware that looks like the top of a Bakewell tart.

I have been bringing unusual objects home since I was a child – and I still feel the sharp pang of excitement at spotting something that's unusual or out of place. It could be something as simple as a dry snakeskin in the grass or a piece of quartz in the mud – covetable objects in their own right but which take on a magical quality when found out of context. It's this magic that I try to capture by collecting them.

I had a 'museum' for the things I brought home as a child: a dusty old chest of drawers in the barn next to the house. It had peeling veneer, ornate metal looped handles and three deep drawers, to each of which I assigned a different category of treasure. The top drawer was for natural finds – feathers, broken birds' eggs, dried leaves, desiccated butterflies and bumblebees, a rabbit foot, a young deer antler and the mummified head of a lime-green budgerigar the cat caught in the garden one summer. Human-made objects lived in the middle drawer – shards of blue-and-white Victorian china, clay pipe stems and glass bottle stoppers from the old midden in front of the house; a George V farthing I found on a molehill; some clay marbles from under the floorboards in the dining room; fishing flies given to me by a distant cousin; and anything else that didn't fit into the other two drawers. Weight decreed that fossils and unusual stones lived in the bottom drawer.

My mother had had a museum of her own when she was a child and would delight me with the story of the cat skull, the pride of her collection. She had found it by the side of the road in a state of partial decomposition and rather than wait for the maggots to do their job and risk losing it to another collector, she took it home and boiled it in her mother's best milk pan to remove the remaining flesh. I loved that story, but bedtime cocoa at my grandmother's house never tasted quite the same after I'd heard it.

Despite the number of years I have been visiting the foreshore, my collection is relatively condensed and well curated. Before we moved house, space was limited to a few shelves under the stairs so I learned to be selective. What I brought home lived in an assortment of boxes and zip-lock bags, wrapped in tissue paper, divided into categories and carefully catalogued. Once they were put away, they lived mostly undisturbed and neglected, too time-consuming and difficult to get out.

I've spread out in the new house, though, and my collection has been liberated. I have a muddy table in the corner of the garage, surrounded by bikes and assorted clutter, where I unpack and sort my finds and where I keep all my mudlarking, cleaning and preservation gear. There's a pickle jar of WD40 for soaking delicate iron objects, a box of latex gloves, wire brushes of varying gauges, ziplock bags in every size, my scrap lead box, a craft drill for buffing and removing rust, Neoprene gloves for the winter, a head torch for nightlarking and a pot of lanolin mixed with soot for rubbing into cleaned coins to enhance their details. There's a row of Victorian bottles lined along the windowsill that catches the morning sunshine and boxes of pottery shards (sorted by date and type). Bags of shoe soles and most of my clay pipes are stacked neatly on shelves under the bench. A section of the garden is dedicated to old bottles and Tudor bricks, and my hag stones hang on wires from a tree outside the kitchen. In the winter, when it's not full of tomatoes, I use the greenhouse to dry out driftwood, and I lay out iron finds to spray with WD40 or clear lacquer, which seals them and helps slow down the rust. I hang up larger objects like boat hooks from the roof of the greenhouse with string to paint them with Hammerite.

The shelves at the back of my office are gradually filling with bigger things: a complete Bellarmine that I swapped with a man in Australia for a clay pipe, my little green Tudor money box, two eighteenth-century free-blown wine bottles, a case gin bottle, a Codd bottle, a Georgian mustard pot and what I think might be an eighteenth-century chamber pot. I keep my coins in a wooden box in numbered trays with a complex grid reference system that corresponds to my written notes. My collection of cloth seals fits neatly into the small plastic wallets of coin collecting books. There are clay pipes displayed in box frames on the wall and my collection of Bellarmine faces stares at me from a glass cabinet next to my desk. Everything is recorded on tiny labels and in notebooks filled with codes that log the find spot, date found, age of the object and any other known details. I'm the only person who understands them. I like the added layer of secrecy, but if I dropped dead tomorrow it's true that nobody else would understand any of it so I really should write them out properly. One day. Maybe.

But most of what I have is small enough to fit in the handsome, ink-stained oak printer's chest, a chance find in a local junk shop, where it languished at the back for almost two years while I agonised over whether to buy it. It sits comfortingly near my desk – my own Cabinet of Curiosities and a grown-up version of my Chest of Drawers Museum. It has eighteen thin drawers, stained black inside with ink from the small pieces of metal type it once contained. I clean the drawers as I need them, carefully sanding away the ink stains and lining each small division with felt, a different colour according to my mood or the general theme of the finds it contains. Green suits my collection of worked bone objects; dark grey shows up glass well; it's easier to see tiny beads against orange; and one rainy day I threw caution to the wind and lined a whole tray in bright yellow. This is where I keep my unusual shards of more modern pottery. Three-quarters of the chest is now full, not just with my precious finds, but with the hours I have spent searching, my discarded problems and countless daydreams. The rest is waiting for future treasures.

LONDON BRIDGE

The bridge of London was overhead, the river at low tide, and
the only living being in sight – for it was but half-past six in the
morning – was as deplorable a specimen of woman-kind as ever
excited a man's compassion; a bedraggled, mud-be-spattered creature,
shoeless and stockingless; and on her head a battered old bonnet,
from out of the rents and rifts of which sprouted wisps of grey hair,
mud-smeared, as though, in her too eager pursuit of waifs and strays,
she had butted her bonnet against the hull of a stranded barge ... and
there she was ankle deep in the water and with her skirts dabbling in
it, washing the tenacious slime from her gleanings so as to give them
a marketable appearance.

James Greenwood, 'Gleaners of the Thames Bank',
Toilers in London, by One of the Crowd (1883)

I collect what others have lost; I never lose things myself.
Well, almost never, and when I do it really unsettles me.
I can become utterly consumed by a missing object. It will
play on my mind for days, sometimes weeks, as I run over
scenarios in my head hoping to jog my memory, looking for
clues. And I have always been good at finding things. As a
child, whenever anybody lost anything, they would ask me

to find it. I once found the tiny diamond that had fallen out of my grandmother's engagement ring glinting in the sun under the washing line. It was as if people's lost possessions found me: even a runaway tortoise in the top field. I called him Houdini and it was only a few weeks before he escaped from me too. The mystery of his disappearance was solved a year later when his bleached shell was revealed by the hay mower, a couple of fields away. Intrigued, I peered inside his remains and made a discovery that fascinated me: a tortoise's backbone is fused to the inside of its shell.

I have my mother to thank for nurturing my keen eye. On long walks, she tutored me in the art of looking. She pointed out birds' nests, mushrooms and caterpillars and taught me to look carefully at the details: the curl of lichen growing on a twig, the subtle patterns on a wet pebble, the veins etched in a leaf. I learned to empty my mind, slow down and lose myself in the minutiae of my surroundings. It's a skill I have taken with me into adulthood and I'm passing it on to my own children now. We watch ants marching to their nest, wait for snails to emerge from their shells and hunt for unusual pebbles and shells on the beach. I hope one day it will slow them down, teach them to take pleasure in small things and in a world that's spinning out of control, it will help keep them grounded.

It took me a lot of time, practice and patience before I started spotting objects lurking in the Thames mud. Mudlarks call this 'getting your eye in' and the mistake many people make is looking too hard. Mudlarking is a stubborn skill and the harder you look the less likely you are to be successful. The key to spotting objects on the foreshore is simply to relax and look through the surface.

Mother Nature rarely makes perfectly straight lines or circles, and as the eye becomes practised, imperfections and patterns start to stand out. The decoration and writing on a coin, for example, is easy for a trained eye to spot. It doesn't fit in with the organic shapes around it. Some people have a natural aptitude and spot things immediately, but most of us go through a more gradual evolution. I see this on the foreshore all the time, as new mudlarks proudly show me what they've picked up and ask if the rusty old welding rods and shards of drainpipe are worth keeping.

Almost everyone starts by picking up larger pieces – tiles, clay pipe stems or pottery shards – even if you have no idea of the history in your hands, these are obviously man-made. But to find the smaller things you need to get much closer and this has become my preferred method of searching. I kneel with my nose barely inches from the foreshore and immerse myself in it completely, filling every sense. I breathe in the muddy aroma of silt and algae and listen to the sound of water drying on the stones: a barely discernible fizz-pop as it evaporates and the lacquered shine turns to a powdering of fine grey silt. In this Lilliputian world I find minuscule shards of glass and pottery, flakes of rust, tiny blobs of dull grey lead, glass beads no larger than the head of a pin, and brightly coloured fragments of plastic, our disgraceful addition to the city's riverine history book.

Weather conditions, the dryness of the mud and light levels can all affect my ability to find things. The smallest variations in light can make all the difference. The best light is when the sun is either coming up or going down, not directly overhead. A bright January afternoon or early-autumn evening is perfect, when the sun is low in the sky and casts its light at an angle. The grey, leaden light that often comes before a storm is another very specific, but rare, light that favours mudlarking. It creates an intense 3D effect that can be disorientating, but which is perfect for picking out even the tiniest of objects.

But it wasn't until I went down to the foreshore for a night tide that I realised just how important light is and exactly where my eyes go when I'm mudlarking. Early on, I learned that the bright white glare and restricted circle created by a head torch doesn't suit my style of searching, but several years ago, with night tides lower than many mudlarks could remember, that didn't seem to matter. There was no way I was missing them.

For three nights in a row I caught the last train into London Bridge and waited under a street light for the water to recede. On the night it was due to fall to its lowest point, I found I wasn't alone. As I lurked in the shadows, others began to arrive; some I recognised, most I didn't. They came from all directions, one by one, gathering at the top of the river stairs until a handful of us were milling around, fiddling with head torches and strapping flashlights to metal detectors. We spoke in hushed tones, respectful of the unique moment we had been afforded. It's hard to explain the excitement of an exceptionally low tide: imagine Christmas Eve when you were about seven and you're almost there. It's a tummy-churning, heart-pounding, light-headed euphoria and an explosive happiness that's hard to contain.

I walked east along the water's edge to an area that had been particularly productive in recent weeks and began my search. Without the noise of the day to mask it, the river was surprisingly noisy. The gently lapping water carried with it the sounds of its bounty – shards of pottery and glass knocked together and clay pipe stems played a soft tune as the river pulled back and forth over them. My head torch cast a bright beam, illuminating a circle about three feet wide and concentrating my search. The darkness pressed in around me, blocking out the present and blanketing me in the city's history. The ghosts of the foreshore were all around.

I thought of the Great Fire of 1666 and how the flames would have danced on the water and lit the foreshore with an eerie orange glow. From where I was standing, I would have been able to see the houses along the old bridge burning and heard the panic as people crowded around the top of the river stairs, shouting and fighting, the wherrymen grinning as they hiked up their fares to take advantage of the situation. I recalled Pepys's description of the chaos that I'd read only a few days before: 'Everybody endeavouring to remove their goods, and flinging into the river or bringing them into lighters that layoff; poor people staying in their houses as long as till the very fire touched them, and then running into boats, or clambering from one pair of stairs by the water-side to another.' He described the river as 'full of lighters and boats taking in goods, and goods swimming in the water'. I looked out over the dark and imagined chests, boxes and furniture bobbing about between the heavily laden craft. How much had been dropped in the chaos and lay lost in the mud, waiting to wash up from the bottom of the river? Had any of my treasures once belonged to a terrified Londoner fleeing the flames?

That first night of the fire, Pepys stood and watched it from a boat on the river, close to where I was standing, before retiring to a pub on Bankside, opposite Three Cranes Wharf, to watch the city burn. As the fire spread along the waterfront, west from London Bridge, it reached the wharfside warehouses that were packed with hay, wood, tar, tallow and brandy. Had I been standing here just over 350 years ago, apart from losing my eyebrows, I would have seen pools of burning tallow floating on the water, fragments of burning buildings passing by on the tide, clouds of steam rising into the air where the burning tar met the water's edge, and a sky filled with thick black smoke and ash that fell like snow. There is a black layer in the foreshore that some say is cinders from the Great Fire. On occasion I've found blackened roof tiles and bricks at London Bridge. They might be rubble from the Fire, dumped into the river in the aftermath. Or they could just as easily be from one of the many other smaller fires that occurred over the centuries. There is no real way of knowing.

The Romans built the first known crossing over the Thames almost 2,000 years ago, around twenty yards downstream from where London Bridge is today. Many rickety wooden crossings followed. Some simply collapsed, fire and floods destroyed others, and invading Danes pulled down another. In the thirteenth century, a narrow stone bridge finally replaced the wooden constructions. It took thirty years to complete and lasted, in one form or another, for 600 years, becoming one of the wonders of the medieval world and the most famous bridge in history. Over the centuries it changed and evolved to suit the needs and demands of the city. At one point it had a wooden drawbridge to allow tall ships access upstream and stone gateways at either end that were locked to secure the city at night.

The old bridge was built with nineteen arches of varying widths and wide piers that sat on boat-shaped starlings, which created a virtual barrier across the river, impeding its flow and trapping the tide. Water wheels between the arches harnessed the river's power to pump water to nearby houses and grind corn. The bridge also created a lethal obstacle for the wherries passing underneath it, particularly in the hands of inexperienced or drunken wherrymen. Known as 'shooting the rapids', taken at the wrong angle a boat could easily turn and capsize or be dashed against the stone piers, and once in the water people had little chance of survival. Their heavy clothes dragged them down and the churning water quickly claimed their bodies and possessions, adding them to the river's rich trove.

The piers slowed the water to such an extent that in extreme winters, the river upstream from the bridge froze completely, sometimes for as long as two months. In the seventeenth century it froze twelve times and the first frost fair was held in the winter of 1607/8 between Westminster and London Bridge. With their livelihoods suspended, the wily and ever-resourceful watermen fitted wheels to their wherries so they could glide over the ice, hired out their boats as stages for entertainment and charged people for access to the frozen river. There were swings, bowling, bear- and bull-baiting, puppet shows, dances, ox roasts, horse-and-carriage races, and at the last frost fair in 1814 an elephant was led across the ice at Blackfriars Bridge. Booths were erected on the ice selling food, drinks and souvenirs. Imagine the objects that were dropped in pursuit of this revelry: coins, trifles and trinkets that fell into the slushy muck and drifted down to the riverbed when the ice finally melted. Rare bone skates have been pulled from the fore-shore along this stretch: bovine shin bones, shaped and smoothed to slide over the ice, which Londoners strapped to their feet, propelling themselves along the frozen river with long spiked poles.

Until recently, I dreaded the descent to the river at the north end of London Bridge. Cutting out of the crowds, I'd take a final breath of fresh air before going into an enclosed con-crete staircase in the bowels of the bridge where the stench of stale urine mixed with the chemical tang of industrial disinfectant to create an overpowering olfactory soup. It was a grimy, unpleasant and forbidding space that pricked my primitive sense of fear and sent me scuttling as fast as I could to the last turn where the river slapped up against the river wall. I'm very thankful for the new curvaceous stainless-steel staircase, which is bolted on to the outside of the bridge and has revolutionised my descent to the river path. I walk west along the path, passing under Cannon Street Bridge, until I get to the metal river stairs just the other side of it. Once on the foreshore, I walk back east towards London Bridge.

I begin by looking through the rubble that has washed up against the river wall. Many people forget to search the top part of the foreshore and concentrate instead on the water's edge, but I've found some good stuff here so I always give it a once-over before I move on. I peer between the bricks and stones, looking around them as much as I can without moving them: I'm in a protected area and I mustn't disturb as much as a pebble in my search. Kneeling down helps. It's a worm's-eye view that means I can look more closely into dips and crevices and underneath overhanging bits of rubble. I can also look across patches of sand for subtle contours that suggest something might be hidden just below the surface. This close up, the gravel is not just a grey-brown textured mass – every stone is different – and I scan it for anything that doesn't fit. If I hadn't been this close to the gravel several years ago, I would never have noticed the dark purple and white oval Roman ring intaglio lying in it. It is made of glass, designed to look like a special variety of two-layered onyx called nicolo, and carved with the figure of Bonus Eventus ('Good Outcome'). Nor would I have seen the edge of the blue-ridged Roman melon bead hidden in the same patch of stones.

Although the Roman quayside was much further inland, the most likely place to find Roman artefacts on the Thames foreshore still correlates with the location of the ancient city. The Romans' main settlement was on the north side of the river on two small hills – Ludgate Hill and Cornhill – with the Walbrook River running between them. The Walbrook brought clean water into the city and took away the waste, but over time it silted up and by the mid-fifteenth century parts of it had already been built over. The buildings sealed a waterlogged time capsule that is occasionally pierced during construction work, revealing Roman life perfectly preserved in minute detail: leather, wood, leaves, grass, seeds and even a small bird with its feathers still intact have all been found. But all that's left of the Walbrook now is an innocuous hole in the river wall covered by a heavy steel flap just west of Cannon Street Bridge. Water barely seeps out from around the edges and the shingle piled halfway up against it suggests it hasn't been fully active for some time.

Hundreds of Roman artefacts were brought up from the riverbed when the medieval bridge was dismantled in 1831 and centuries of accumulated silt were dredged to deepen and widen the channel. The ballast heavers and dredgermen hauled thousands of coins up in their buckets, as well as iron spearheads, tools, rings, brooches and pottery. They also found metal statuettes of Roman deities – Apollo, Jupiter and Ganymede – some of which appeared to have been deliberately mutilated. Small finds continued to appear for years from the dredged gravel that was taken upriver to the Old Surrey Canal where it was used to make a towpath between Hammersmith and Barnes, and at Putney.

Among the most impressive finds dredged up from London Bridge was a pair of castration clamps, beautifully decorated with the busts of deities and the heads of animals, and dedicated to the mother goddess Cybele. Roman London was filled with soldiers and merchants from all over the Empire, who had brought their own beliefs and religions with them. From the East came Mithras, the Persian god of light, to whom a huge temple was built on the bank of the Walbrook, and from Egypt and Asia came Isis and Cybele. One version of the story goes that Cybele fell in love with a beautiful youth called Attis, but he was unfaithful to her. Crazed with fury, she drove him insane as punishment and in his madness Attis cut off his own genitals and died. In honour of this, worship of Cybele was accompanied by wild orgies and castration. The eunuch priests perfumed their hair, dressed in women's clothes, and celebrated the mother goddess with frenzied dancing and acts of debauchery. The clamps found at London Bridge would have been used to help remove testicles by staunching the flow of blood. Perhaps the ceremony involved visiting the river, where the clamps were thrown in as an offering or were accidentally dropped. It is also possible they were disposed of by early Christians wanting to break from the Empire's more heathen ways.

My Roman finds might not quite compare with the castration clamps, but I've found a good selection of ordinary Roman life along the stretch of river between the Walbrook and London Bridge. Over the years I've collected many pieces of roof tile, mosaic flooring, pottery, coins, game counters, beads and hairpins. Some of the objects I've found may have been washed into the river down drains or along the Walbrook; they could have been dropped from boats or off the Roman bridge; or they might have arrived there in spoil brought from building works further inland to build up the foreshore in the eighteenth and nineteenth centuries.

In total, I currently have nineteen pieces of Roman hairpins, all made of bone. Some have delicate bobble finials at one end and I have the sharpened ends of others, but I haven't found a complete one yet. They are not easy to find. When they are wet, they look like dark brown sticks, only straighter and more regular in shape and size. Sometimes the only way to tell if they are hairpins or twigs is to push a fingernail into them. Wood is usually soft and gives, while bone, although almost 2,000 years old, is still very hard. As they dry, they turn to a warm honeyed brown and the subtle facets and lines made by the craftsman's tools become visible. Each slender pin would have been turned on a bow lathe and many must have broken in the process. Perhaps my finds are simply manufacturing spoil, but

I like to entertain more romantic notions: a Roman lady, dressing quickly after a morning at the baths and cursing softly under her breath as she looks for her missing hairpin, which has dropped into the drain at her feet.

Early on in my mudlarking career I found a perfect white cube in the gravel close to London Bridge. It was a bright day and the sun picked it out, glancing off the squared edge that made it so obviously not natural. Since finding one, I have got my eye in for them and I now have quite a collection of what I learned are Roman tesserae from the floors of Londinium's baths, public buildings and grander houses. They would have been set in mortar, sometimes in intricate patterns, polished smooth with rough stones and finished with beeswax. I also have an actual piece of a Roman floor: ten small squares of grey marble set in a chunk of rough, gritty mortar. The tesserae are satisfyingly smooth, worn by thousands of passing footsteps.

Roman game counters – bone discs about the size of a penny – are another lucky gravel find from the London Bridge area. They are impossible to miss if they are flat on, but trickier to see if they are embedded in the mud on their side. If this is the case it's just a matter of luck whether you find them or not, since you need to be looking in just the right place as the light catches the thin edge. Most of the counters I've found were lying face up. One of my favourites has two distinct wear points on the underside from the many times it had been put down and picked up; a hungry Roman rat has left toothy scrape marks all around the edge of another. But one of the plainest is the most interesting. It hides a secret on the underside, a faint Roman numeral X that someone scratched into it. I've seen similar

Roman counters from the foreshore with numerals on the back and have been told that they may have been illegal gambling chips. Gambling was considered harmful to the moral structure of the Empire and laws were enacted to restrict it. Betting on games of skill, such as chariot racing, was allowed, but gambling on games of chance, such as dice, was forbidden – perhaps my counter was disposed of before the owner was caught with it.

So many Roman artefacts have been found that some have suggested there was a shrine halfway across the bridge where people threw in coins and offerings for luck or safe passage. I found my first Roman coin on the foreshore here and have found every one since in the same small area. Coins can often emerge from the mud side on, like the game counters. They also stick to the bottom of posts and to the flat sides of rocks and rubble, which makes them hard to spot. Sometimes they are so tarnished and covered with cemented mud it is impossible to see they are coins at all, though the disc-like shape, size and flatness of them usually gives them away. If they have worked free of the mud and wash in on a wave or are left behind by the tide, they often stick to the surface of wet sand or lurk just below it, only visible to the well-practised eye as a small circle of raised sand.

My first Roman coin was a silver siliqua, minted under Honorius (393–423) in Mediolanum (modern-day Milan). I found it as I searched the water's edge, following the waves as they pulled back and forth over a wide patch of slick wet sand. As the wake from a boat sucked the water further out, the light caught on a low circle standing proud of the flat sand. I moved quickly, before the next wave crashed back in over it, gently brushing away barely a millimetre of sand with my finger and pulling out a nondescript disc, covered with centuries of thick black tarnish. Thick tarnish is a good sign, it means the coin has been protected from the smoothing, battering actions of the river.

At home I connected the coin to my home-made electrolysis kit – a mobile phone charger with two alligator clips wired onto the end, an old stainless-steel spoon and a bowl of bicarbonate of soda dissolved in water. Electrolysis is the most effective way I've found to remove heavy tarnish from silver, or rust and concreted mud on other metals, but it needs to be done with care. Too much 'zapping' and a delicate coin can dissolve away to nothing. I only use electrolysis where an object is solid and stable and so obscured it is impossible to see any distinguishing marks. Where coins or objects are delicate, or I'm not sure if they're silver, I use the spit-and-foil method – spitting on the object then wrapping it in foil and pressing it together. The spit acts as a medium for the foil to react with the silver; if the object is silver the reaction gives off a distinct smell of rotten eggs and in the process removes any light tarnish. Since I knew my Roman coin was silver, and it was quite substantial and heavily tarnished, I decided to risk electrolysis.

I dissolved some bicarbonate of soda in a bowl of warm water and attached one of the alligator clips to the coin and the other to the spoon. Then I immersed both in the bicarbonate solution and switched it on. The coin fizzed gently and gave off a pungent smell of rotten eggs – hydrogen sulphide, which is poisonous and flammable. I opened the door so that I didn't poison myself and watched as the years began to fall away, turning the water cloudy and black. Within minutes the coin was free of tarnish, but now it looked too bright and new. There was no contrast and the details were hard to see, so I set about artificially ageing it by holding it high over the flame of a candle so that it blackened with soot. This is called 'smoking'. According to one mudlark I know, the best candles for smoking are the old tallow candles that are sometimes found in the mud, but I make do with an IKEA tea light. When the coin was completely obscured and velvety black with soot, I rubbed it with lanolin, which replicated generations of greasy hands and fixed the soot into the tiny bumps and lines of the design, revealing Honorius in all his glorious detail.

Now the coin came to life. It was a living thing with a past and a story, a coin that had been carried to London in the purse of a soldier who had passed through Mediolanum on his way to the outer limits of the Empire. He may have used it to buy imported dates or wine to remind himself of home. Or perhaps he had thrown it into the water for luck and to honour the gods as he crossed the river on his way north to defend Hadrian's Wall against the barbarians.

I'm superstitious too. When I find a modern penny, I give it back to the river for luck and as payment for its treasures, though it is unlikely my offerings will survive as long. In 1992 the composition of 1p and 2p coins was changed from bronze to copper-plated steel, and 5p and 10p coins changed from cupronickel to nickel-plated steel in 2012. The modern coins I find are already bubbling and blistering with rust, anonymising the Queen and slowly dissolving in the river. Our generation's numismatic legacy will be negligible.

It was not just Roman artefacts that surfaced when Old London Bridge was being demolished. The accumulated silt had captured the treasures and sunken detritus of generations of Londoners, and among the objects most sought after by the Victorian collectors were the pewter medieval pilgrim badges that seemed to appear in some abundance on this particular part of the river.

I completely see why these rather crude metal trinkets were, and still are, so sought after. For me, the heavy-headed, spindly-limbed figures depicted on them epitomise the medieval period, and there is something almost magical about them. Perhaps they have absorbed some of the religious essence they represented. They were bought by pilgrims at religious shrines who pinned them to their coats, hats and bags to prove they had completed their pilgrimage and to take some of the power of the shrine back home with them. They were cheap, easy to make, and sold in thousands. From the number that have been retrieved from the Thames and found on the foreshore it is thought they may also have been thrown into the river in thanks for a safe return. A good number have been found bent in half in a similar way to Bronze Age swords that were ritually bent before being offered to the river, which adds credence to this theory.

The idea that there was some kind of shrine partway across the Roman bridge is pure speculation, since there is no historic record of one, but we do know there was a chapel in the middle of Old London Bridge, with stairs that led directly down to the river so that it could be easily accessed from the water. It was devoted to St Thomas Becket, the London-born archbishop who was murdered in Canterbury Cathedral in 1170. Becket was declared a martyr and sanctified three years later and his shrine at Canterbury became a popular focus for pilgrimage. London pilgrims often began and ended their journey at the little chapel on the bridge. Some went as far as Jerusalem, which could take several years, but many travelled to Canterbury in the south or to Walsingham in Norfolk in the north in search of protection, cure or absolution from a past sin.

Pilgrim badges still occasionally show up on the foreshore, almost exclusively in the London Bridge area, but they are a rare and lucky find and fifteen years on I am still searching for a complete one to add to my collection. It's become a bit of an obsession. I've said that I'll give up mudlarking once I find one, though I think that actually finding one might feed my obsession even more. Every time I visit London Bridge I go in the expectation that a Becket badge will be lying there waiting for me. One with a complex tableau of knights brandishing their swords at the unfortunate bishop would be nice.

In the end it's down to luck and I do at least have a treasured fragment of a fifteenth-century Our Lady of Willesden badge. The shrine in north-east London could be visited in a day, but it was quite an undertaking: the Willesden area was mainly woodland and bandit attacks were common. During the Reformation, in 1538, the Willesden image was dragged to Chelsea and burned on a great bonfire of other Catholic statues. Such idolatry was banned, and it was the beginning of the end of pilgrim badges.

The small pewter badges that the pilgrims brought back from Willesden had an image of the Virgin Mary wearing a crown and sitting within the horns of a crescent moon or boat. On her left arm is the Christ Child and in her right is a sceptre. I found the top half of one. It was lying face down and looked like just another anonymous piece of lead when I found it. But something made me turn it over and there, looking serenely back at me, were the two gentle, sleepy faces of Mary and Jesus. It may be broken, but it was my first pilgrim badge and it made me more determined than ever to find another. About nine months later, I did. This one was a round pewter 'mount', about as big as my fingernail, which dates from the fourteenth century. It has the initials 'iHc' – representing the Latin for 'Jesus the Saviour of Man' – cast into it in Gothic-style script. It is a cheap, generic badge and there is no way of knowing where it was bought, but someone once wore it as a proud symbol of their devotion.

Since finding the pilgrim mount, the only pilgrim-related objects I've found on the foreshore are the tiny pewter tokens that are thought by some to have been used as a form of currency to pay for food and lodgings along the pilgrim routes. It has also been suggested that they were ecclesiastic tokens, issued by the large and powerful monasteries that controlled much of life in London, and were redeemable for alms, the prayers of monks and as tokens for various services. They are surprisingly common – I've found eleven so far and mudlarks are always picking them off the foreshore. The earliest date from the thirteenth century, but most of mine come from the mid-fifteenth. They are like dark grey fish scales, so small that they balance perfectly on the end of my finger, and most are wafer-thin, which means they tend to stick to the surface of wet sand, making them easy to spot. One side is virtually the same on all of them, radiating lines around the edge and a cross in the centre with four dots between its arms. The other side varies. Some have initials, while others feature a variety of objects, including body parts, chalices, bells and keys.

I also find all manner of modern religious objects in the river. At Rotherhithe, at the bottom of a set of river stairs, I found an Islamic prayer asking for help with unrequited love. It was written on paper, folded up and tied to a stone with black and white thread to weigh it down. I wrapped it up again and left it where I'd found it, in a patch of large pebbles. A few years later, a little further east on the same stretch of the foreshore, I found what looked like a jar wrapped in black plastic. I shook it and something thudded up and down inside. All sorts of hideous objects sprang to mind. What if it was a body part? I knew a human foot had been found fairly close by a couple of years ago and I hesitated before slowly and cautiously unwrapping it. Inside was a glass jar and inside that was an onion. It seemed odd that someone had gone to such unusual lengths, so I photographed it and posted it on my Facebook page and was inundated with suggestions, the most popular being that it was a Wiccan 'spell jar'. This reminded me of what I had read about seventeenth-century Bellarmine jars, which were sometimes used to contain spells in a similar way and were often buried beneath the doorways of houses to protect those inside from bad spirits. In 1926, a mudlark searching the shore near Blackfriars Bridge found one of these 'witch bottles', although he didn't realise at the time what it was. He took it home, removed the clay bung and emptied out its contents: a liquid – most likely urine – rusty iron nails, hair, brass pins and a scrap of tattered felt cut into the shape of a heart and pierced by pins. This must be most mudlarks' dream find. It's certainly mine.

But by far the most common religious objects found in the river are Hindu. For the Hindu community, the Thames has become a substitute for the Ganges, representing vitality, purity, motherhood, fertility, life, forbearance, impermanence and a return to origins. The river is also an acceptable place to dispose of once-sacred objects that are worn, damaged or obsolete. I've found scores of statues and images of Hindu gods – Ganesh, Durga, Kali, Lakshmi and Shiva – caught between rocks, trapped in the mud and washed up on slipways with the plastic bottles and old footballs. I've found strings of prayer beads, small flat metal yantras to ward off evil, and lots of coconuts. Sometimes the coconuts are bound by a sacred red-and-yellow thread called a nada-chhadi or wrapped in cloth with rice or lentils. Just this year, a friend found one that had been cracked open and filled with rice, into which was pressed a small statue of Ganesh made from 1.9 ounces of solid gold. I find more Hindu objects on the foreshore to the east of central London, where there is a larger Hindu community, and the ghee or oil lamps called diyas increase in number in the autumn during Diwali, the Festival of Light. Some are painted bright colours, but others are plain and simple, handmade in India from terracotta. Their timeless appearance has raised the hopes of many new, and not so new, mudlarks with their remarkable resemblance to Roman pottery. While plastic statues fuel great debate as to whether they should be left because of their sacred attachments or removed as polluting litter, the lamps will eventually break down and return to the mud, a little bit of red Indian soil mixed in with the grey English mud.

That dark night at London Bridge, as the tide dropped lower and lower, my torch lit up treasures all around me: buttons, coins, buckles, and the fine shards of broken eighteenth-century tea bowls, many hand-painted with delicate flowers; thickets of pins, beads and tiny plain metal studs that would have decorated medieval leather belts and jerkins; more clay pipes than I had ever seen before. It was impossible not to step on them. I collected the longest and winced as others cracked and popped beneath my feet.

Every time I stopped to scrutinise the foreshore there seemed to be something new and different to collect. I found a worn Georgian farthing stuck flat to an old river-slimed post and a blackened wafer-thin Elizabethan penny lying at the bottom of a shallow water-filled dip. My torch reflected off the face of a late sixteenth-century jetton – the thin copper alloy tokens that were imported in bulk from Germany and used as reckoning counters, together with a chequered board to keep accounts. (The government's accounting department is still known as the exchequer, after these boards.) On one side was an imperial orb and on the other a circular design of crowns and fleur-de-lys with a rose in the middle, and the name of the maker Hans Krauwinckel around the edge. What I like best about jettons though are the words of doom and damnation that also run around the outside. Who could fail to be nudged into contemplation by ANFANG DENKS ENDT (At the Beginning Consider the End), or inspired to tighten the purse strings by reading HEVT RODT MORGEN TODIT (Today Red/

Alive, Tomorrow Dead). This one, rather appropriately, read GOTES GABEN SOL MAN LOB (One Should Praise God's Gifts).

I had already emptied my finds bag into my rucksack twice and was fiddling with its zip when the beam of my torch ran over something interesting: an open-ended oblong box, slightly thinner than a cigarette packet, with two comma-shaped perforations on either side and a scalloped edge. It's lucky I saw it – one more step in that direction and I would have crushed it. I bent down to pick it up. I could see it was carved from a single piece of what looked like bone or ivory, and something about it looked familiar. It was about the same shape and size as a scabbard chape – the protective fitting from the end of a sword sheath – but I'd only ever seen them in books and museums, and those had been made of metal, never ivory or bone.

I wrapped it carefully in a plastic bag and put it in my rucksack. It was past two o'clock in the morning and the tide was about to turn. I stayed for another hour, by which time I was exhausted and the tide had advanced well up the foreshore. There didn't seem much point in staying to search what I could easily get to in daylight hours and I reckoned the river had given just about all it was willing to give that night; it was time to catch a cab home.

The next day I took the scabbard chape (I was pretty sure that's what it was) out of its bag for a closer look. I cleaned it up and put it in a smaller bag, which I pricked all over with a pin so that it would dry out slowly and not crack. I put the bag on the top shelf of a kitchen cupboard and there it stayed for several months. By the time my next visit to the Finds Liaison Officer at the Museum of London rolled around, the scabbard chape was completely dry, so I wrapped it up again to take to show her.

It turned out my scabbard chape was Roman and dated from the late second to third century, when it would have been specially commissioned for the auxiliary army. It is one of only two complete examples found in the UK. (The other was found in Silchester in Hampshire.) Its original owner would have worn a simple mail or scale shirt over a tunic, leather or woollen trousers in cold weather, and a metal helmet. He would have carried an oval-shaped shield and a spear or long sword from which the chape had fallen. It is unlikely he was British. Auxiliary soldiers were usually stationed in provinces away from their homeland to make them easier to control. It reduced the chances of mutiny and hastened the process of Romanisation through marriage with local women.

I imagined a homesick soldier. Perhaps he was from Turkey, serving his time in Britain and hoping for Roman citizenship as an acknowledgement for his services to the Empire. As his unit marched through London, his scabbard chape worked loose and fell off. Somehow it found its way into the river where it was preserved in the mud for almost 2,000 years. If it hadn't been for such a low tide, if I hadn't gone out in the darkness that night and if the beam of my head torch hadn't pointed down in just the right place at just the right moment, I would never have found it.

TOWER BEACH

Education she has none, and she never had instruction worthy the
name. All her knowledge is to know the time of low water, and the
value of the wrecks and waifs which each recurring tide scatters all
too scantily over her peculiar domain.

Charles Manby Smith, 'The Tide Waitress',
*Curiosities of London Life or Phases, Physiological
and Social of the Great Metropolis* (1853)

Some people refer to the foreshore in front of the Tower
of London as a beach and it certainly looks like one.
But it's not easy to get to. It is the stretch of foreshore on
the north side of the river just to the west of Tower Bridge
that runs the entire length of the Tower complex. I walked
to it once, a number of years ago, along the foreshore from
Custom House, a little further west where there are easy
river stairs. I wasn't planning to mudlark, I just wanted
to have a look. That was on a particularly low tide and
involved a lot of clambering over slimy wooden posts and
wading through deep mud under jetties and piers, which
I don't like doing if I can avoid it. I recall collecting quite a
bit of small change as I scrambled through the muddy obstacle course, emerging onto a wide stretch of completely
empty yellow sand just beyond it.

I carried on towards Tower Bridge, past a wide stone staircase set into the river wall called Queen's Stairs, which were last used by a queen, Queen Mary, in 1938. They would have been the easiest and safest way down onto the beach, but these days they are kept locked. There's a tall gate halfway down that's crowned by a row of spiked railings, which makes it impossible for anyone to scale. Lack of use has turned the lower steps, where the river covers them at high tide, dark emerald green with algae.

From the foreshore you can see a wide bricked-in arch in the river wall with the words 'ENTRY TO THE TRAITOR'S GATE' stencilled above it in large white capital letters. The river entrance was bricked up in the middle of the nineteenth century and Traitor's Gate itself is on the other side of the wall. It was originally known as the Water Gate and was built in the late thirteenth century on the orders of Edward I to provide a convenient means to reach the Tower by barge. It acquired its present name in the sixteenth century, as the Tower evolved into a place of imprisonment, torture and beheading. Most famously, two of Henry VIII's wives, Anne Boleyn and Catherine Howard, came this way by barge before meeting their fate at the Tower. Anne's daughter, the future Elizabeth I, was luckier. She arrived at the Tower on Palm Sunday 1554, sick with fever, on the order of her half-sister, Queen Mary, who had accused her of plotting against her. Her barge had already shot the rapids under London Bridge on a low tide, which everyone knew was madness, and been grounded on a mudbank, before continuing to the Tower where, it is said, the tide was still too low to land. Some accounts claim that, knowing the fate of her mother, the twenty-year-old princess refused to enter through the gate and eventually waded ashore in heavy rain to Queen's Stairs. She remained in the Tower for two months before she was released for lack of evidence.

The half-moon of soft yellow sand that forms a gentle hill in front of the river wall and peters out to shingle towards the river, is all that remains of 'London's Riviera', 1,500 barge-loads of Essex sand that was spread over the fore-shore to create a public beach in 1934. This was the vision of the Reverend Philip Thomas Byard Clayton (otherwise known as 'Tubby'), the vicar of All Hallows by the Tower, who in the summer of 1931 came up with the idea of the foreshore as a city seaside, 'a genuine delight to the poor families who frequented Tower Hill'. King George V assured local children that they 'would have this tidal playground as their own for ever', and on 23 July 1934 the beach was opened to the public. *The Times* reported: 'the ladder was lowered, to the music of cheerful siren blasts from ships in the Thames'. Children swarmed onto the beach where unlimited lemonade and buns had been laid out on long trestle tables.

The beach was a great success. The ladder was lowered for up to six hours a day between April and September, depending on the tides, and there was a beach guard posted for safety. In the summer of 1935, around 100,000 people came to 'holiday' beside the Thames. Dockers' children, some of whom had never seen the sea despite living just forty miles away from it, built sandcastles and watched Punch & Judy shows. They paddled in the shallows, bought toffee apples, and hired rowing boats to go under the bridge and back again. The beach closed during the Second World War, but reopened afterwards and continued to be popular.

Photographs from the 1950s show men in shirtsleeves and braces relaxing in striped deckchairs, children in knitted bathing suits splashing in the water, and young women in summer dresses sitting on the sand eating sandwiches. It looks, to all intents and purposes, exactly like a day at the seaside. In 1971, however, concerns over pollution and safety and the cost of running it forced it to close. Today, most of the sand has washed away and the promise of 'free access for ever' has been broken.

The river wall is part of the Tower of London, which was designated a Scheduled Monument in 1900. The foreshore, which is one of the most historically important stretches on the tidal Thames, is owned by the Crown Estate, which has its own rules to protect it. Nobody is permitted to mudlark in front of the Tower of London without rare permission, though archaeologists are given occasional access to keep track of erosion and to monitor the foreshore. Several years ago, wire-mesh bags filled with large cobbled flints were brought in to protect the wall foundations and a new revetment was constructed. But the river is a persistent beast and it has prodded, probed and felt its way around them, transferring its attention to the unprotected foundations further along, which are now also being exposed and undermined.

The White Tower, so called because in 1240 it was painted white on the orders of Henry III, is what gives the Tower of London its name. It is also the most ancient building and last remaining castle on the tidal Thames. The rectangular stone keep was built by William the Conqueror towards the end of the eleventh century. With ramparts fifteen feet thick at the base and ninety-foot-high walls, it loomed over the wooden huts of the native population below, leaving them in little doubt as to where the power now lay. Being at the easterly end of the city and on the river, it was also built to protect London from invaders sailing upstream from the sea. The location was carefully chosen, making use of the old Roman wall to protect the keep's easterly and southerly walls. By 210, the Romans had enclosed an area of about 330 acres with a 2.2-mile-long wall thought to be twenty feet high in places and eight feet thick, and towards the end of the third century, they extended it along the riverfront. The Roman wall was still a feature of the city when the Normans arrived and it made perfect sense for them to use as much of it as they could.

The river brought people, troops, provisions and building materials to the Tower and provided water for those who lived and worked inside the enclosure. The river also filled the moat when it was connected to the Thames in the late thirteenth century. This added an impregnable ring around the complex, though over the years, as water levels in the Thames varied, it stopped draining properly and began to silt up, becoming little more than a disease-ridden, stinking bog. The moat was finally drained, cleared and filled with soil in the 1840s. I often wonder what they did with the silt they dredged out of it. It would have been packed with centuries of lost and discarded treasures. Did they dump it into the river in front of the castle, or was it taken somewhere else by barge or cart?

Over the centuries the Tower grew to a vast complex. It has been variously used as a royal residence, a prison, a menagerie, an armoury and a mint, and all of this is soaked into the foreshore in front of it. When I finally got to mudlark at Tower Beach and hold the objects that might have been made or used within the Tower, I could hear the trudge of soldiers marching in and out of the castle, and the orchestra of hammers, riveting mail and flattening discs of precious metals, that rose above the sounds of medieval London all around. The history I'd learned at school – a dusty stream of dates, battles, dead kings and queens – came to life.

One of the most direct links I found to the Tower on the foreshore were several small grey cups, shaped like shallow cones, which I later learned were called cupels and which may have been used at the Royal Mint to make coins. Cupels were made from finely ground bone ash, moistened with beer, water or egg, and pressed into a mould. They were used to extract precious metal at very high temperatures from samples of ore and to test the quality of scrap metal. Similar cupels were found during an archaeological dig in 1976 within the Tower complex at the site of a sixteenth-century furnace. Chemical analysis revealed they had been used to refine silver that was contaminated with copper. At the mint, once the metal had been extracted, it was cast into ingots, annealed (heat-treated) to soften it, and beaten or rolled into the thickness of a coin. Blank chips were cut from the flattened sheets of metal and were then placed between two engraved metal dies and struck with a hammer to produce a 'hammered' coin with a design on both sides.

Until 1662, when machines took over, every coin was produced by hand in this way. At the Tower, the mint workers were kept separate from other workers and guarded closely to make sure they didn't succumb to temptation. They worked in hot, dark workshops where the air was filled with poisonous fumes from the furnaces. While one man placed the blank disc on the bottom die, the other lined up the top die and struck it with a hammer. A mistimed placing or extraction risked losing a finger. When I look over the hammered coins I've found on the foreshore they lack the uniformity of later machine-made coins. Some have been struck off-centre, others poorly struck and ill-defined. I think of the moment the hammer came down on each one, how they fell to the floor of the minting room in the dirt and noise and heat, and I wonder about the men who made them.

I have found coins bearing the faces of kings, queens and emperors stretching back to Roman times: tiny, wafer-thin medieval pennies with quirky, naive portraits of strange-looking men; Elizabeth, the Tudor queen, with her high forehead and elaborate ruffed collar; the moustachioed Charles I; classically posed Hanoverian kings; and a youthful Queen Victoria, a single ringlet falling from the loose bun at the back of her head. Each coin represents a distinct moment in history and conjures images in my head of mundane as well as major events. Had it been in the purse of a man who succumbed to the Black Death; taken on voyages to new worlds; or used to buy a pie from a costermonger on a foggy East End street?

Coins have the power to fascinate and for some, the hunt for coins becomes an obsession. They spend their tidal time plugged into metal detectors, hoping that the next beep will be a Tudor shilling or a Roman denarius, and not just another scrap of old lead. I can't deny that the sight of these small metal discs emerging from the filth is exhilarating, but for me they can lack a certain mystery and uniqueness.

Assuming it is in good condition, a coin will willingly give up its secrets, instantly revealing what it is made of, the year it was struck and even where it was made. A coin is one of many, each one similar if not identical to the next. In most cases they don't surprise, confuse or challenge. They are safe and straightforward, easy to collect and categorise. What draws me in are coins that have been marked or changed by someone. I found a George III copper halfpenny one wet Sunday afternoon on the foreshore at Rotherhithe a little further east from the Tower. It has a crude 'X' scratched deeply across the king's face that might simply be an adaption to turn it into a tally token. It could also have been the work of a bored sailor or a symbolic act of an unemployed soldier, returned from the disastrous war in America and taking out his anger on the fat king's portrait.

It is thought that Anglo-Saxons pierced Roman coins to wear them as decoration, and in later centuries, in the absence of banks, those who didn't want to bury or hide their savings sewed coins into their clothes for safekeeping. In the nineteenth and twentieth centuries holed sixpences and threepenny pieces were worn as jewellery. The small pierced silver threepenny piece I found sitting on the mud at Hammersmith dates from 1918, the year the First World War ended. Perhaps its original owner had lost a loved one or fiancé and this was her way of keeping him close to her. Or maybe it could tell a happier tale – a baby born into a peaceful world or a son or brother returned safely from France. I wear it on my own charm bracelet now, carrying the essence of the person who lost it and taking it further on its journey through time.

Larger coins, shillings and half-crowns, were hung on watch chains as decoration and presumably slipped their loops and fell into the river, but my silver seventeenth-century

Charles I penny is too delicate and early for that. It's a thin sliver of metal, no bigger than a fingernail, that I found stuck on the wooden post of a revetment, as shiny as the day it was lost. The hole has been drilled carefully, just above the king's head, and it dates from the turbulent times when Parliament was demanding Charles denounce his God-given right to absolute rule. Had the hole been punched through the king's face it would tell a different story, an act of subversion carried out by a supporter of Oliver Cromwell's Commonwealth, but the fact that it so carefully avoids disfiguring the monarch suggests it could have been a secret talisman for a supporter of the king. Tied around someone's neck, he was worn close to someone's heart until the string broke or it was discovered, torn off and thrown into the river.

The coins that most spark my imagination are the worn silver ones that have been bent into a crude 'S' shape. These crooked sixpences are thought to be love tokens, shaped to hold love in their curves, and are heavy with tales of desire, loss and broken hearts. They became fashionable around the end of the seventeenth century. The sixpence, or occasionally lower-value copper coin, was bent by the young man in front of his intended before he presented it to her as a symbol of his affection. If she liked him, she would keep it. If she didn't, she would throw it away. Many must have been thrown into the river, because I have found a good handful of them on the foreshore.

Other love tokens lost or thrown into the Thames include engraved coins, which were popular throughout the eighteenth and nineteenth centuries. Pennies that were smoothed or worn down, and larger silver coins such as shillings and crowns, provided a perfect miniature canvas. Workmanship varies from the simplest scratching to beautiful engraving. Some coins were even set with semi-precious stones. Coins have been found with names, addresses, dates and short verses. Others, perhaps made by the less literate or more artistically inclined, are covered with patterns, flowers, leaves or simple drawings. The only engraved love token I've found on the Thames is a smooth copper penny with 'J Tweedy, 19 April 1864', scratched roughly into one side. I found it next to the river wall at Deptford, and as it sat in my hand, cold, wet and a little gritty from the foreshore, I wondered who J Tweedy was. Had the token been thrown into the water for luck or tossed away in despair?

I have only visited Tower Beach three times: once when I scrambled along the foreshore at low tide and twice on public open days. The open days began in 2001, to encourage public involvement and awareness of the fore-shore, and ended soon after permit rules were enforced in 2016, since it was too difficult to check permits and control the number of people attending the event. I'm in two minds about this. Although the open foreshore days gave ordinary mudlarks like me a chance to search a stretch that was usu-ally out of bounds, I only went twice because I didn't enjoy it very much. It's not my style of mudlarking. I like the fore-shore when it's quiet and I'm not motivated enough by the find to bother jostling with crowds of strangers for a piece of the pie.

On open foreshore days, the queue started well in advance of the unlocking of the gates. With just two and a half hours to search the shore at low tide before we had to leave again, there was no time to waste. I arrived early enough to be near the head of the crowd and stood among the other mudlarks. I recognised some of them, but even the ones I didn't know were conspicuous by their muddy knee pads. Families with children carrying buckets and spades evoked the beach days of the 1930s. Some people were prepared with welly boots and plastic bags for their spoils. The ones in sandals and 'good shoes' obviously hadn't a clue what they were getting themselves into, but they joined in anyway.

The line grew and we waited until the river had fallen to a safe level and a good amount of foreshore was exposed before a beefeater, one of the Tower's ceremonial guards, arrived with a key to unlock the gate. A buzz of excitement rippled through the crowd. We filed carefully down the slippery stone steps to the foreshore, collecting protective blue latex gloves from a smiling volunteer on the way. At the bottom, people fanned out in all directions. I had heard that the most productive part of the foreshore was closest to the bridge and I wanted to get to it before it filled up, so I headed east quickly, to where the end of the foreshore had been roped off with striped tape. Beyond it were the mudlarks known to the organisers, who were guarding it from the crowd. I was one of the lucky ones. I said hello and ducked underneath the tape to an area that was fractionally calmer.

I looked back at a foreshore filled with bodies, heads down, frantically rushing from spot to spot. Already people were scraping at the gravel to look underneath it. It was far less busy where I was, but even so I found it hard to focus. My concentration drifts with lots of people around me.

I start to look at what everyone else is doing instead of my own patch of foreshore; then I start worrying that someone might come and speak to me. But eventually I managed to block out the chaos around me and settled down to search.

I stayed until the foreshore behind me had started to clear of people and the tide began to brush away the piles and dips they'd made. I wished I could come back again the next day, without the crowds, when the mud had settled under a few tides and the objects that had been missed in the frenzy revealed themselves. I walked past the trestle tables, where exhausted sunburned experts were still identifying and explaining the heap of objects in front of them. It was mostly pottery, bricks, random pieces of metal, bones and shells, but there were sealed plastic bags in black trays that suggested more interesting objects had been found too. Perhaps they had some coins in there. They would be spirited away to the Museum of London to be recorded and examined more closely.

I was pleased with my own finds: two cupels; a little bone spoon, perhaps a nineteenth-century mustard spoon; the plain handle of a seventeenth-century pewter spoon; and the lock end of a broken seventeenth-century key, which I like to think might have once turned the heavy iron mechanism in a thick oak door at the Tower. I also had several tiny metal wire loops that I'd found trapped in the shingle and tangled up in patches of handmade pins. Some were linked together and most of them were closed by the tiniest of rivets. I knew what they were because I'd found them on other parts of the foreshore, but never as many as I found here. They are evidence of the medieval mail-makers who, like the coin-makers, toiled in dark workshops at the Tower in the Royal Armoury, where weapons and suits of plate armour were also made. They pulled wire to gauge, cut it to size and bent it into these neat rings, which they then looped together – four rings on every loop – and individually riveted. This created the metal mesh from which they made protective suits for knights, kings and soldiers.

Mail, not 'chain mail' as some mistakenly call it, was relatively easy to make, although time-consuming, and offered flexible protection from arrows, swords and spears. A knee-length mail shirt, known as a hauberk, was made up of 28,000–50,000 links, weighed up to thirty pounds and took around a hundred days to make. It was worn over quilted underclothes that would have absorbed the blows from weapons and protected the wearer from chafing, but it was expensive and most ordinary soldiers continued to go into battle in little more than padded leather jackets. Mail was worn throughout the medieval period; by the fourteenth century armour had developed into suits made from large plates of metal, with mail to cover the gaps. It offered good protection, but little resistance to projectiles fired from guns. From the sixteenth century, as firearms grew in popularity on the battlefield, mail and armour were shed and restricted to ceremonial use.

The mail links I have from Tower Beach are made of iron, but I also have links made of copper alloy. Both iron and copper alloy survive well in the mud, but once iron is free it quickly begins to rust and flake away. A tap of a hammer will remove the top loose layer of rust from large and solid iron objects, like padlocks and cannon balls. They can then sometimes be sanded down to sound metal and oiled to keep them rust-free. Some people use electrolysis and boil them for hours in wax to preserve them, but I've never tried that. With objects like chains and hand-forged nails, I clean as much of the rust off as I can and spray them with clear lacquer, which acts as a barrier against moisture. Iron mail is difficult to preserve, however, because it is so small and delicate. Once the rust takes hold it can crumble away to dust. To delay this, I soak the mail for several weeks in my pickle jar of WD40 oil and then store it in a 'dry box', a plastic food container with a bag of silica gel to keep the air inside moisture-free. This seems to work, but rust is persistent and I've been told by professional conservators that even they haven't found a failsafe way to stop it completely.

The Agas map of 1561 shows the castle with a full moat, the Queen's Stairs and the entrance to Traitor's Gate. And if you look very carefully you will see tiny cannons along the waterfront. It is not uncommon to find iron cannonballs embedded in the foreshore, particularly from the Tower eastwards and at Woolwich and Deptford, where Henry VIII established his naval dockyards. They were also used as ballast in ships, which may be why they are found on the foreshore at Rotherhithe where old ships were broken up and their ballast dumped. Cannon balls come in all sizes, according to the bore of the cannon they were made for, some far too heavy for me to move and others that are easy to pocket. Of those I've taken home, I've saved a few, but most have eventually burst open and peeled away in layers of rust.

Lead musket balls fare better. I've collected scores of them over the years and those I haven't given away (children love them) I keep in a glass jar on top of my printer's chest. I find them in the gravel and doming out of the mud. They are easy to find now, but it took me a few years to get my eye in for them and to spot the grey spheres disguised in the pebbles. If I'm in any doubt as to what they are when I spot them, the weight of the lead gives them away.

Like the cannon balls, the lead shot I've collected also varies greatly in size, from the smallest 'swan shot', which may have been used in early shotguns or blunderbusses, to large canister balls or grapeshot, which were packed into metal cans or tied tightly into bags and shot from cannons to inflict mass injuries. Unlike a modern bullet that pierces the flesh with a neat hole, musket balls tore into their targets, smashing bones and dragging filthy shreds of uniform into the wounds to infect and fester. My most treasured musket balls and nineteenth-century bullet-shaped Minié balls are those that are flattened on one side, having met their mark. Foreshore folklore tells of one musket ball found by a mudlark with a human tooth embedded in it, but I've never met anyone who's seen it.

Lead shot would have been made in huge quantities in the armoury at the Tower. The ones I've found on the foreshore may have been washed down drains or swept into the river with the rubbish. On other parts of the foreshore they may have been dropped by soldiers and sailors as they set off to and returned from war, rolling off ship decks and jetties. They may have cast their own shot on the quayside or on ships as they waited to leave, pouring the molten lead into small moulds, trimming the surplus and sprues, then filing them to a smooth ball. Not all of them were successful. I've found musket balls where the two halves are off-centre and a short set of three pistol balls that haven't been cut from the sprue. Whoever made them may have picked them up too soon, burned their fingers and dropped them into the river.

I've also found a few gunflints, which are difficult to find because they look so natural. I only saw them because their smooth flat sides caught the light and when I picked them up it was obvious the trapezoid shape was man-made. They're dark brown, almost black, which means it's likely they were made at Brandon in Suffolk. By 1800, Brandon was the sole supplier to the Board of Ordnance and by the height of the Napoleonic Wars it was supplying over one million musket flints a month. Brandon flints were the best, good for fifty shots before they had to be replaced, which was better than their rivals, but the flintknappers' life was hard. Their day started at 7 a.m. and ended at 8 p.m. In that time a man could produce 2,000 flints in a room so filled with dust that many died early of lung disease.

By the mid-nineteenth century bullets and rifles had mostly replaced muskets and lead balls. Live rifle rounds from both the First and Second World Wars still wash up on parts of the Thames foreshore, often close to the munitions factories at Silvertown and Woolwich where they were made. Some were dumped in the river, along with hand grenades and guns, by returning soldiers looking for a safe place to dispose of souvenirs and forgotten caches of ammunition. Unexploded bombs also lurk on the foreshore, cushioned by the water and the mud as they fell amid the noise and chaos of the Blitz almost eighty years ago.

I found my first and only ordnance early on in my mudlarking career. I was poking around on the south side of the river, almost opposite Tower Beach, where there's a lot of rock and rubble and not very much else. I'd been mudlarking all day and had decided to try my luck there before I went home. It was tough going across the slippery rocks and uncomfortable in my thin-soled wellies, really not worth the effort, and I had turned to retrace my footsteps back to the stairs when I noticed what looked like a large bullet about as thick as my arm lying innocently between two rocks. It looked interesting and I knew enough to know it was some kind of missile, but it didn't have the metal bit on the end so I reasoned it was probably harmless, picked it up, popped it in my rucksack and headed for the station.

At home, it sat in my shed for a couple of days before I remembered that one of my neighbours had an interest in planes, bombs and general war regalia so I took it round to show him. Once over the threshold I proudly pulled out my 'giant bullet' and he took a very big step away from me. On closer inspection he concluded that it was probably inert and most likely OK, but advised me to take it back to the river as quickly as I could, just in case. I did, and threw it out into the deepest part I could reach. Since then I don't touch so much as an old rifle round, which might seem like an overreaction, but they are still live and potentially dangerous, and since I'm certainly not going to take them home with me, I reckon they're better off left completely alone.

I've been told by fellow mudlark Dave, who spent years in the Army Bomb Disposal Squad, that old hand grenades can be extremely unstable. In 2015, police ordnance experts exploded a grenade that had been found by a mudlark on the foreshore near Greenwich. The explosion could be heard up to three miles away. When larger bombs are found, whole areas are evacuated while experts work to defuse them, often bringing the river and parts of London to a standstill. Because of the amount of unexploded ordnance in the river, the general rule on the foreshore is: if you don't know what it is, leave it alone, and if you do know what it is, leave it alone.

On a submerged sandbank off Sheerness in the Thames Estuary, an old ship has been nursing her cargo of explosives since she sank on 20 August 1944. Only her three rusted masts are visible above the water, with warning signs attached to them. The SS *Richard Montgomery* was an American cargo ship destined for France and loaded with 1,400 tons of explosives (13,700 different devices), when strong winds ran her aground and she broke up. She has been there ever since, too dangerous to empty, a ticking time bomb in the Thames. A government report in 1970 suggested a column of water and debris around 1,000 feet wide would be blasted almost two miles into the air if she ever exploded, creating a tsunami thirteen feet high and breaking every window on Sheerness. A more recent report in the *New Scientist* in 2004 said the force of the explosion would be roughly a twelfth of the size of the atomic bombs dropped on Hiroshima and Nagasaki. It is thought the chance of an explosion is remote, but in Sheerness she is known as the Doomsday Ship.

But beyond the bullets and bombs, the personal face of war is also buried in the foreshore; discarded and lost objects that tell otherwise forgotten stories. In 2015 a follower on my London Mudlark Facebook page posted a picture of a medal he had found close to Blackfriars Bridge. It was a World War I Victory Medal, with the winged figure of

Victory on one side and the name FA French and a service number, 19028, on the other. From these details the finder had already managed to track down the recipient: Francis Arthur French, born in 1899 in a village in Hertfordshire, and died, childless, near where he was born in 1958.

The trail had ended there, but his post was shared by an amateur historian to a Facebook page for the village that Private French had grown up in and incredibly it was seen by a distant cousin called Kristian. Kristian was able to fill in the gaps and even provide a photograph, which shows a well-built young man, immaculately dressed in the distinctive dark blue uniform and peakless cap of the Royal Marines. He is looking directly into the camera, his mouth set hard in a straight line.

Private French was born into a poor labouring family and joined up shortly before his seventeenth birthday in 1916. He was too young for overseas service and instead was sent to Ireland to guard Dublin Harbour. Aged eighteen and finally eligible to serve overseas he joined HMS *Morea*, an armed merchant cruiser. He would have been on board to witness the disaster of the HMS *Llandovery Castle*, a Canadian hospital ship torpedoed off southern Ireland in June 1918. Two hundred and thirty-four doctors, nurses, members of the Canadian Army Medical Corps, soldiers and seamen died in what was Canada's deadliest naval disaster of the war. Some were machine-gunned in the water and the German U-boat responsible ran down all the lifeboats but one. Only twenty-four people, the occupants of this single life raft, survived.

A senior officer aboard the *Morea*, Captain Kenneth Cummins, vividly described the horror: 'We were in the

Bristol Channel, quite well out to sea and suddenly we began going through corpses. The Germans had sunk a Hospital Ship, *The Llandovery Castle*, and we were sailing through floating bodies. We were not allowed to stop, we had to go straight through. It was quite horrific, my reaction was to vomit over the side ... It was something we could never have imagined, particularly the nurses, seeing these bodies of women and nurses, floating in the ocean, having been there some time. Huge aprons and skirts in billows, which looked almost like sails because they dried in the hot sun.'

I can only guess at the lasting effect such a sight would have had on nineteen-year-old Private French, but he stayed in the marines and travelled the world, living for a time in Bermuda before returning to England in 1942 to serve in the Second World War. In the first four months he was back, he served on HMS *President*, a training ship moored just upriver from Blackfriars Bridge and armed with anti-aircraft guns to protect St Paul's Cathedral nearby. It was also used as a floating base for the French Resistance, who planned subversion and sabotage missions from deep inside her hull. It is then that he must have lost his medal, perhaps in the chaos of an air raid.

The same year that Private French's medal was found at Blackfriars, a Victoria Cross, Britain's highest honour for bravery, was discovered in the mud further upstream by a metal detectorist. It is one of only 1,358 Victoria Cross medals to be awarded since 1857 for 'gallantry in the face of the enemy'. Being potentially valuable and historically significant, it was passed to the Museum of London, who tested it for authenticity and began the search for its original owner. The metal was compared to metal of the cannon from which almost all VCs are made. It passed the test, it was genuine, but the only clue to its recipient was the date of the battle engraved on the back: 5 November 1854, the day the Battle of Inkerman took place during the Crimean War. The lower ribbon suspension bar, on which his name would have been engraved, was missing.

Research by the Museum of London and the National Army Museum eventually concluded that it had most likely been awarded to Private John Byrne of the 68th (Durham) Light Infantry. Byrne was born in Kilkenny in Ireland and enlisted in 1850 at the age of seventeen. He was by no means a perfect soldier, though, and in November 1853 he was sent to prison for an unknown crime. He was released in August 1854 to sail with his regiment to the Crimea, where he shone under battle conditions. The *London Gazette* of 24 February 1857 reported: 'At the Battle of Inkerman, when the Regiment was ordered to retire, Private John Byrne went back towards the enemy, and, at risk of his own life, brought in a wounded soldier, under fire. On the 11th May 1855, he bravely engaged in a hand to hand contest with one of the enemy on the parapet of the work he was defending, prevented the entrance of the enemy, killed his antagonist, and captured his arms.' His regiment went on to fight the Maoris in New Zealand, where he was awarded the Distinguished Conduct Medal, and in 1872, after twenty-one years in the army, he took his discharge at Cork.

Byrne's discharge papers offer us the only known description of him, as five feet seven inches with grey eyes, brown hair and a fresh complexion. By 1878 records show he was working as a labourer for the Ordnance Survey in

Wales, where, on 10 July 1878, he accused one of his work colleagues of disrespecting the Victoria Cross. An argument broke out and Byrne shot the man, John Watts, in the arm with his revolver, before fleeing. Several hours later, when the police arrived at his house, he put the barrel of the gun in his mouth and pulled the trigger.

At the inquest into his death at the Crown Inn in Newport, Monmouthshire, in July 1879, Watts denied the insult. Evidence of Byrne's fragile health was given by a Lieutenant Barklie who claimed that Byrne had spent time in what was then known as a lunatic asylum in the Straits Settlements – now Malaysia and Singapore. Barklie also said he enquired after Byrne's Victoria Cross. Newspaper reports of the inquest that ran in July 1879, stated: 'When Byrne came to Bristol for his pension Lieutenant Barklie asked him if he knew why he had not had his Victoria Cross, and Byrne seemed rather embarrassed so the question was not pressed.'

Byrne was destitute after he left the army and possibly in poor mental health. There is no evidence that he went to London and even if there was we will never know if or why he threw his medal in the Thames. It may even have been stolen and ended up in the river many years later. Private John Byrne VC was initially buried in an unmarked grave near Newport, but a headstone was erected for him in 1985 in recognition of his valour.

ROTHERHITHE

Mudlarks are boys who roam about the sides of the river at low tide, to pick up coals, bits of iron, rope, bones, and copper nails that fall while a ship is being repaired ... The copper nails fetch four-pence per pounds but they are very difficult to find, for the mudlark is not allowed to go near a vessel that is being coppered (for fear of their stealing the copper), and it is only when a ship has left the docks that the nails are to be had. They often pick up tools – such as saws, hammers, etc. – in the mud; these they either give to the seamen for biscuits and beef, or sell to the shops for a few halfpence.

Henry Mayhew, *Letters to the Morning Chronicle*
(1849–50)

There is still a set of rotten wooden river stairs at Cuckold's Point on the tip of Rotherhithe Peninsula, where the river pushes north-east in a wide loop that stretches over two miles from Bermondsey to Deptford. It leads to a stone-paved causeway, where the ferry once departed for the north side of the river, and has been known as Horn Stairs since 1562, when a pair of ram's horns, an ancient symbol of a cuckold, was tied to the top of a pole and erected there, perhaps a reminder to sailors of what their wives had been up to while they were away. The stairs marked the start point of the notoriously riotous

Horn Fair, where people gathered before processing east through Deptford and Greenwich to Charlton Hill. They also marked the turn in the river where it begins to make its way upstream into the Pool of London.

The original Pool of London is the naturally deep channel east of the Tower that runs alongside Old Billingsgate Market. It is a powerful, brooding part of the Thames, which has accommodated seagoing vessels since the Romans and swallowed centuries of the city's history. Seemingly disconnected from what flows into and out of it, some days it is thick and dark like treacle, with a flat, mirrored finish; on others, flocks of seagulls ride high choppy waves. It is unique both in character and in importance. In 1581, under Royal Act, Elizabeth I established legal quays on the north side for cargo to be assessed by customs officers and taxed. A century later, it was handling 80 per cent of the country's exports and 69 per cent of its imports. As trade increased and ships became larger and more numerous, so-called sufferance wharves and docks spread east, and the Pool of London grew. The original section became the 'Upper Pool' and the new stretch between Bermondsey and Limehouse was referred to as the 'Lower Pool'.

Until the end of the seventeenth century, maps of London mostly ignored the river east of the Tower of London, but John Rocque's map of 1746 shows how important this stretch had become. His map takes in the whole of the Pool of London, both Upper and Lower, all the way out to Cuckold's Point, which is marked on the map between two timber yards. It is busy on both sides of the river, with stairs, wharves and docks, but the peninsula itself is empty and deserted. The great docks of the nineteenth century had yet to be built and the area was still inhospitable marshland, unsuitable for farming. A road snakes around the edge of the peninsula and the riverbank is lined with shipwrights and timber yards. To illustrate how busy it was with ships that had come from all over the world, Rocque has drawn the river east of the Tower with tiny galleons in full sail and tall-masted seagoing vessels.

Until the early nineteenth century, there was only one large dock where ships could unload their cargoes. Howland Wet Dock, renamed Greenland Dock at the end of the eighteenth century, is London's oldest riverside wet dock. It could receive up to 120 large merchant ships at a time, while the rest waited in the Pool for their turn to offload. Some waited for riverside berths, while others were unloaded midstream by lighters, small barges that ferried goods to the riverside, thus making the ships 'lighter'. In 1726, in *A Tour Through the Whole Island of Great Britain*, Daniel Defoe 'found about 2000 Sail of all Sorts, not reckoning Barges, Lighters, or Pleasure-boats, and Yachts; but of Vessels that really go to Sea' in the Pool. By the early 1800s, colliers bringing coal to fuel the rapidly industrialising city swelled the number of vessels on the Thames even further. In 1835, the daily number of colliers awaiting a berth was between forty and three hundred.

The river was so densely packed with boats of all types, it was said to be possible to walk from one side to the other on their decks. It had become a vast floating city, filled with bored, restless men – and whatever they dropped overboard, the river hungrily gobbled up. Broken clay pipes, dark green shards of rum and wine bottles, smashed bowls and plates and piles of chopped mutton bones wash up every day on the foreshore at Rotherhithe. I've found the soles of shoes and the buckles that once held them together, boots squashed flat by the weight of the mud, coins, buttons, pieces of broken watch chains and several pewter cufflinks set with coloured glass stones.

I usually leave Rotherhithe with something interesting. One freezing cold afternoon, as I headed for the stairs and the pub to warm up, I spotted something square emerging from a patch of smooth grey mud. Luckily it was coming out face first and my eye caught on its engraved decoration. Sideways on and I would have missed it completely. I held my breath. It looked like a watch fob, set with a carved intaglio. I hoped I was right. I knelt down and gently picked it out with my fingernail. It left a small indent in the otherwise perfect mud, a cast of its striped patterned back. I could see where the loop that had once attached it to a chunky watch chain had broken off and reasoned that this was probably how it got lost. I wondered how many years it had lain there, whether it had been washed around by the tide before it settled or if it had fallen right where I was standing almost 200 years before.

Holding it tightly in my frozen fingers, I walked down to the edge of the river and began to wash the mud off: my hands were so cold, the water actually felt warm. When it was clean, I took a good look at it. It was a clear, square, flat-sided stone, a little smaller than a stamp, in a low copper alloy setting. I tilted it to catch the light. It was easier to see the engraving because it was still wet – a shield with a tiny boar inside it, standing on some curly grass. From the style of the setting I guessed it was eighteenth or early nineteenth century and some trawling around antique jewellery websites later that evening confirmed my suspicion.

What a beauty! Someone had once made their mark with this, pressing it into blobs of hot sealing wax to authenticate important documents. Imagine the ship's captain or merchant's irritation when he went to seal his next letter or document, only to find it missing!

Sometimes other personal items wash up: tobacco and snuff tins, pewter and bone spoons, dominoes and dice. I have a little spotted rectangle of yellowing bone, a domino, and a tiny handmade lead die that may have been knocked out of a musket or pistol ball by a sailor using whatever was to hand. Dominoes were brought to Europe from China by sailors in the eighteenth century and may have arrived in England with French prisoners from the Napoleonic Wars, who carved sets from cow bones to exchange for food while they were being held on board the prison hulks moored on the Thames.

It was probably a sailor or an ordinary river worker who once owned the heavy nineteenth-century folding knife I found there. Perhaps he was far from home, whittling a toy for the new baby he had yet to see, when the knife slipped from his hand into the river. The blade was open when it fell and it was little more than a rusted stump when I found it. I have scores of old bone, ivory and horn knife handles from the Thames, but this one is special. The original owner must have valued his knife as he had crudely carved his mark, 'XX', into the rough staghorn handle. Personalised finds like this are rare and highly treasured by most mudlarks; they add a human dimension to the object and another layer to its story.

A sailor would likely have played the Jew's harp I found sticking out of the mud, legs first, in a pile of old ship nails.

The Jew's harp (thought by some to be a corruption of jaw harp or even juice harp) is an ancient instrument with an undefined past: some say it was brought to England from the Middle East at the time of the Crusades. But it was the perfect instrument for sailors – small, cheap, portable and virtually unbreakable – and they are found in reasonable numbers and varying conditions on the foreshore. It was only chance that I pulled on it that day and out came a small, round-headed copper alloy frame. The thin metal tongue that would have produced a twang when played had rusted away, but other than that it was in excellent condition. I finally found another earlier this year at Trig Lane and this one even has its little tongue. I probably shouldn't have risked it, but the temptation was too great. It seemed sound enough, so I decided to pluck it gently with one finger, just once, and it let out a single, magical, flat-toned note, the first noise it had made in over 300 years.

Trains rumble through the tunnel beneath the foreshore at Rotherhithe, but above ground it is quiet and deserted. The sky is huge and empty and past the bridges that tie it down further west the river has grown wider and more free. For the first time there is a feeling of openness and expanse. I can walk and mudlark in peace for hours on end here, sometimes without seeing a single person. But it's not a lonely place. The silence over Rotherhithe is strangely suspended, as if the past is merely on hold and not entirely gone.

The bones of old ships, river-slimed and rotting, lie exposed on top of the mud and emerge from the shingle and sand: large slabs and chunks of oak and elm, carved and shaped, grooved and bored with holes for the wooden pegs that once held them together like a huge wooden jigsaw puzzle. Some have large nails, bolts and hooks driven into them and notches cut out where other pieces of timber would once have slid into place, precision-fit partners now lost for ever. There are wide planks and rudders, keel pieces, deck beams and thick post-like windlasses with square holes to take the stout poles that were used to turn them. Most were left there for a purpose, reused as moorings or supports for beached ships; some parts were merely abandoned where they had fallen.

Even the briefest visit to the foreshore at Rotherhithe will reveal something of its seagoing past. Millions of ship nails from the many vessels that were broken up and built here are scattered everywhere, among them countless copper alloy tacks that were used to nail sheets of shining copper onto ship hulls to protect them from shipworm. The first experiments in coppering hulls were made in 1761 and were so successful that the navy set about coppering its entire fleet. It gave them the edge over their adversaries, making their boats faster and allowing them to stay in the water for longer.

When the ships were finally broken up at Rotherhithe and the copper was removed to recycle, the valueless nails were dropped in the mud. Most are fairly unremarkable, though some have marks from the tools that were used to extract them and around three in every hundred has a mark in the shape of a three-lined arrow cast into the shaft or the underside of the head. This is the Broad Arrow mark, sometimes referred to as the 'crow's foot', which is the sign for the Office of Ordnance, a department created by Henry VIII to supply guns, ammunition, stores and equipment to the navy. In 1597 it was renamed the Board of Ordnance and the Broad Arrow symbol was adopted to indicate government property. By throwing a handful of marked nails into every sack or box, the authorities deterred thieves and prevented the nails from being used for non-government purposes.

Over the years it has been used to mark a great variety of objects: mast-quality, Crown-owned trees were cut with the mark in the seventeenth century, and in the nineteenth century British jail and transportee uniforms were covered with the little arrows to mark out those wearing them. It was used all over the Empire and the colonies in a variety of styles on everything from spoons and cannon balls to milestones and postboxes. Once you've seen it you will start to see it everywhere and it is still being used by the War Department and the Ministry of Defence. Coppering tacks were worthless to the original mudlarks, but if I am in the mood and I need to empty my mind completely, I'll spend a few hours picking through them, looking for crow's foot nails. Sometimes I won't find any. But once I found three in less than ten minutes.

There are nails for every purpose here. Some have flattened 'spade' ends to slip between the grain of the wood without splitting it. There are clumps of rusty iron nails, a pile of coppering tacks fused together in the shape of the sack that once contained them and heavy handmade iron 'rosehead' nails with heads knocked into tiny pyramids by four final strikes of the blacksmith's hammer. Warm-coloured copper nails that missed the recycling sack and were overlooked by Victorian mudlarks occasionally surface bright and shiny in the mud. They were used below deck where the gunpowder was stored because they didn't spark. They also had the added advantage of not rusting. Some look as if they have never been used, while others, wrenched from beams and timbers, are tortured, curled and twisted.

Other random ship parts lie in the mud: sail grommets (copper and brass rings of all sizes that were used to reinforce holes in canvas sails), and wooden wheels and pulleys that were once part of the rigging. Deadeyes, round blocks of wood with three holes to take the rope and keep rigging taut, sometimes push their haunted faces to the surface, and I once found a wooden belaying pin, further testament to the preserving nature of the Thames mud. It is the size and shape of a police truncheon and would have been one of many, lined up like thin starved soldiers around the deck of a sailing ship to secure loose rigging lines. Even old rope, possibly rigging, spills out of the Rotherhithe foreshore, separating and fanning out across the mud like thick tawny hair.

The shipbuilders too left evidence of themselves and their work in the foreshore. In some places the mud is light, almost fluffy, with saturated wood shavings, planed and chiselled from the lumps of wood that were shaped into beams, futtocks and rudders. Their old leather boots, low at the heel and worn through in the sole, flap about on the sand and the heads of old brooms bristle to the surface. Sometimes a simple precious tool washes out of the mud, a potentially disastrous loss for the poor hard-working man who relied on it. Caulking irons, the heavy blunt chisels that were used for pushing twisted lengths of oakum between the seams of boat decks and hulls, are common, which suggests that many men were employed in caulking new ships and replacing it in old vessels. A rarer find are the eighteenth-century ship dividers that I pulled out of a thicket of ship nails a couple of years ago. They are plain, iron, and fused open as if lost while measuring out the plans for a new ship or mapping a route to a faraway place.

Many of the exposed timbers at Rotherhithe are thought to be from eighteenth-century naval ships that once defended Britain against the French during the Napoleonic Wars. They were sold and broken up in the early to mid-nineteenth century, when the huge fleet was an expense that was no longer needed. Of the twenty-seven ships that fought at the Battle of Trafalgar, twelve were built on the Thames: nine in London, two at Gravesend and one at Sheerness. Several of them ended their days broken up on the foreshore at Rotherhithe. The most famous of them was the ninety-eight-gun HMS *Temeraire*, which was painted by Turner in 1838, a shadow of her former glory, being towed up the Thames by a steam tug to be reduced to scrap.

As the ships were pulled apart, dismantled and cannibalised, everything was taken to reuse or sell. At a time when a copper penny was worth the value of the metal it was made from, copper nails and hull sheathing were particularly valuable. Bands of nineteenth-century mudlarks worked the Rotherhithe foreshore searching for copper scrap, which could make the difference between a decent meal or surviving on roadside leavings. Ships' timbers were reused as beams in houses and to make furniture, chopped up for firewood and made into wooden blocks to pave the streets. Timbers from the *Temeraire* were used to make furniture and fittings for St Mary's Church at Rotherhithe, and a piece of it was turned into a wooden leg for a sailor who had fought in the Battle of Trafalgar. Even old rope was sent into prisons and workhouses to be picked apart and turned into oakum for caulking.

I have been told that ships sometimes made repairs with whalebones while they were at sea when wood was scarce, and there is a whalebone disguised among a line of old wooden posts at Rotherhithe. I had been walking past it for years before I learned it was there and I decided to make a special trip to find it. Even then it was hard to work out exactly which one it was, since it was the same size and shape as the other posts and the river had turned it the same sludgy brown. It was only when I started to look closely that I saw the honeycomb of tiny holes telling me it was bone and not wood.

Other whalebones have been found at Rotherhithe: long plank-sized bones, scored and marked by the whalers' knives; a giant vertebra; and a mystifying bone with a large nail hammered into it. Last year I found a section of whalebone as wide as my thigh lying on the mudflats on the eastern arm of the peninsula, where the thick treacherous mud protects and preserves long clay pipes and fragile old bottles. Like some of the other whalebones embedded in the foreshore that are shaped and drilled, it has a hole bored right through the middle. Maybe it had been used to repair a whaling ship that docked at Greenland Dock, which has its entrance near to where I found it. This was the main port for London's Atlantic whaling fleet. The fleet hunted the cold waters around Greenland and brought the great beasts back to Rotherhithe, where they were rendered into barrels of oil in boiling houses that belched foul-smelling smoke into the damp river air.

The remains of lost whales have also been found buried in the foreshore. In 2010, the partial skeleton of a fifty-five-foot North Atlantic Wright whale was found at Greenwich. Its head was missing, presumably taken for the oil it contained, and the rest of it was found deep beneath the mud. It is thought it had become stranded or was harpooned after becoming lost in the Estuary, and then dragged back to Greenwich where it was butchered on the foreshore more than 200 years ago.

Lost whales have been documented in the Thames since medieval times. In 1658 John Evelyn described how a whale, '58 foote: 16 in height', was pursued between Greenwich and Deptford and how 'after a long Conflict it was killed with the harpooning irons, & struck in ye head, out of which spouted blood and water, by two tunnells like smoake from a chimney; & after a horrid grone it ran quite on shore & died'. In 1783, a twenty-one-foot bottle-nosed whale was captured close to London Bridge, and in 2006 a whale reached as far upstream as Westminster. She had been lost in the river for at least three days and was weak and sick, and though she was lifted by crane onto a barge and carried back downstream, she died before she reached the open sea. Her bones were treated in much the same way as those of her ancestors, stripped and drained of their oil, but this time they were laid out with care in a glass case and displayed by the Natural History Museum.

The appearance of a whale in central London was a reminder that London Bridge is less than eighty miles upstream from the North Sea and the river a highway not just for shipping but for nature too. Flocks of gulls follow the water inland and seaweed floats in on each tide, a constant reminder of the river's saline destination. Seals have been seen as far upstream as Richmond; I have spotted their furtive little faces bobbing in the water around the Isle of Dogs and once had to give a wide berth to a large seal that had hauled itself up onto the foreshore at Gabriel's Wharf to warm its blubbery body in the early-morning sun. One quiet evening at Queenhithe I saw a porpoise, or possibly a dolphin, rise twice in the middle of the river. Prawns, miles from their usual saline habitat, make suicidal leaps from the waves onto the foreshore in central London, sparkling and crystal clear in the sunshine with long whiskers and black bead eyes. I rescue them when I can from the keen eyes of crows and gulls, snatching them off the foreshore and feeling their hard muscular bodies flick against the palm of my hand.

The Thames is also home to rarities like the short-snouted seahorse – I've seen one washed up as far inland as Bankside – and stowaway invaders that are slowly taking over parts of the river. Zebra mussels were first found in the Rotherhithe Docks in 1824. They spread through the canals that linked their native home in the Black Sea and the Caspian Sea to the rest of Europe and arrived in London clinging to imported timber and in the ballast water of the ships that delivered it. They are now firmly established along the tidal Thames and congregate in vast numbers, as many as 100,000 per square yard. They smother native species, clog up pipes and drains, and are almost impossible to control. The estimated 10,000 yellow-tailed scorpions that live in the cracks and crevices of the walls at Sheerness Docks are less invasive. They are thought to have arrived in the eighteenth century, on ships carrying cargoes of Italian stone, and are now the largest known wild colony of scorpions in the UK.

I've also seen Chinese mitten crabs, waving their furry claws and scuttling away across the mud. They came to

London as larvae in the ballast of Oriental ships in the 1930s. Pollution prevented them from establishing quickly, but as soon as the Thames began to clean up the population exploded. In Asia they are an expensive delicacy, steamed and eaten with soy sauce, but in the Thames they are a threat and a menace, killing native species and weakening the riverbanks with their burrows.

Many species of fish – dace, smelt, bass and flounder – migrate up the river using the flood tide to push them upstream, sometimes as far as Teddington, where they feed and grow before travelling back down the river to the Estuary or out to sea. But the most enigmatic and mysterious fish in the Thames is the European eel. For centuries their origins were shrouded in myth and folklore. It was commonly thought that they simply emerged from the mud or even grew from horsehair suspended in water, but in the early 1900s a Danish researcher finally learned the truth of their fantastical life cycle. He tracked their migration to the Sargasso Sea, close to the West Indies and home to the Bermuda Triangle, where eels lay their eggs. The larvae drift on currents back towards Europe, arriving as transparent glass eels. Once they enter the river their colour darkens and they transform into miniature forms of the adult, called elvers. They migrate upstream, through central London and past the weir and locks at the tidal head. They even leave the water to travel short distances overland until they find somewhere suitable and transform again, this time into yellow eels. They live and grow in this state for up to twenty years until they sense the urge to return to the Sargasso, changing one last time into silver eels and often leaving under the mystical darkness of a new moon.

At certain times of the year dead elvers drape like bootlaces over the shingle. The arrival of elvers once turned the edges of the river black and triggered an 'eel fair', sending people rushing to the river with anything they could use to collect them in, but sadly elvers no longer return in such numbers. Although eels were one of the first fish to recolonise the Thames in the 1960s, after the river had been declared biologically dead in 1957, their numbers have been steadily falling and nobody seems to know why. They are now classified by conservationists as 'Critically Endangered', but despite this I have seen them curled tightly around the taut lines of fishermen, who cast their rods illegally and in secret beneath London Bridge, and I have watched as they writhe and twist around the necks of cormorants in a desperate struggle for survival. I often see early fatalities of the migration washed up on the foreshore and have many times rescued tiny gasping elvers from the shingle. I send each one on its way in the hope that it will one day return to the Sargasso Sea.

The foreshore too is home to tiny pieces of faraway places. I have the shell of a huge Pacific-dwelling barnacle and tiny non-native cowrie shells from as far as Australia. They had fallen from hulls or arrived as ballast in the bellies of trade ships, shovelled off beaches into holds to weigh the ships down in the water and prevent them from tipping in stormy seas. The amount of ballast was adjusted according to the weight of the cargo and whatever was available locally was used. When the ships arrived in London, or were broken up or repaired, the ballast was dumped on the foreshore and became part of the rich tapestry of the Thames. I have found a lot of coral on the foreshore, and according to the Natural History Museum most of it once grew in the warm seas of the Caribbean. There's a huge lump of it, about the width of a car wheel, at Rotherhithe, and I also know where there are secret stashes of raw carnelian and large chunks of amethyst and quartz the size of my fist.

Ships also filled up with London ballast: riverbed gravel, dredged up by big-boned, muscular men known as ballast-getters, who tied pieces of sail around their feet and legs to prevent the gravel from falling into their shoes as they worked. In this way London's flint, bricks, rubble and even broken pottery were spread across the world and mixed into foreshores and beaches thousands of miles away. Flint from the riverbed of the Thames has been found in New Zealand, Australia and Canada, where it was used by indigenous people to make tools and arrowheads. Broken English pottery has been found scattered over beaches in Bermuda, and it is quite possible that the silver Edward VI shilling, dated 1551–3, which was found by a metal detectorist on a beach on Vancouver Island in 2014, arrived in ballast dredged up from the Thames and not, as has been speculated, from a secret voyage made by Francis Drake.

As I step over the ship timbers and crunch through the nails, I wonder if any of them were once part of the *Mayflower*, which set sail from Rotherhithe in July 1620 on the first leg of her voyage to found the first permanent colony in New England. She returned in May the next year and by 1624 she was described as being 'in ruins'. Although there is no factual evidence to support the myths, rumours suggest the *Mayflower* was broken up on the Rotherhithe foreshore in front of the pub that was rebuilt in 1958 and renamed in her honour. The Mayflower pub is still one of the only places in the UK where American postage stamps are sold, a leftover from the days when it was licensed to sell British stamps to mariners for their letters home.

I have found other possible evidence of New World settlers at Blackwall on the opposite shore further east from Rotherhithe. The Virginia Settlers were sent by the Virginia Company, a commercial trading company with a charter from James I, to establish an English colony in the New World. They left England from the river stairs at Blackwall and the voyage took them just over four months. On 14 May 1607, they landed at the site that was to become the first permanent English settlement in America: Jamestown. They had taken with them everything they needed to begin a new life in an unknown land and over the following decades supplies were sent out to them from London.

In the mud at Blackwall I've picked up seventeenth-century clay tobacco pipes and shards of delft, German stoneware and early blue-and-white hand-painted Chinese porcelain, all of which are a perfect match for the shards of costrels, dishes and bowls that have been found beneath the soil at Jamestown in America. One morning I found what looked like a coarse pink clay bangle, half submerged at the edge of the water. It's actually the lip of a Spanish olive jar, just like the ones that have been found at Jamestown and which are mentioned in the Virginia Company Records of June 1623, when Robert Bennett acknowledged the arrival of '750 jarse of oylle' from Spain. They were also used as containers for bullets, capers, beans, chickpeas, lard, tar, wine and olives in brine.

I have found trade beads on many different parts of the foreshore – like the white, red and blue layered chevron bead I found at Three Cranes Wharf – and at Blackwall I have found the same long, drawn-tube beads that were taken to Jamestown. They were probably made in Venice, or possibly Bohemia in the present-day Czech Republic, by pulling a cylinder of molten glass into a long thin tube and cutting it up into beads of varying lengths. In this way vast numbers could be made relatively quickly. The ones I have are mostly plain yellow, green or blue, but I also have treasured candy-cane-striped beads. Tiny seed beads wash up on the foreshore as well, often among the handmade dress pins. They were also made by drawing and cutting long tubes of glass and were traded with American Indians in bulk from the mid-nineteenth century. They are so small that they would have easily fallen through the tiniest rip in a sack and dropped between the wooden boards of quays and jetties as they were being loaded onto ships.

The settlers in Virginia began to cultivate tobacco soon after they established their colony in Jamestown. Their tobacco was sent back to England on the ships that brought them their supplies and it soon formed the basis of the colony's economy. But as the American tobacco plantations flourished, the English tin industry collapsed. In an effort to bolster it, tin money – farthings and halfpennies – were minted between 1684 and 1692, but people didn't trust money that was made from what they saw as worthless metal. They were also easily counterfeited, so they were quickly withdrawn. I have several of these twisted, pocked and bubbling tin coins. They have been affected by tin pest, a disease of the metal caused by an allotropic reaction in the cold mud that turns the normally white metal powdery and grey. A tin coin in good condition from the Thames is a rare and elusive find.

In August 1688 several tin-mine owners put in a request to expand the project to include the 'American Plantations'. Minting presses and tools from Skinners' Hall in the City were used to produce patterns for the coin and they were sent to the Royal Mint for approval. There is some doubt as to whether this was ever given and no evidence that these plantation tokens were circulated in America, but during the final months of James II's reign, before he fled to France and abdicated, some plantation tokens must have been minted.

I have two American plantation tokens, both of which I found within a few feet of each other (I'm not saying where), and several years apart. Despite the tin pest, it is possible to see the four crowned shields of England, Scotland, France and Ireland on one side and James II resplendent on horseback on the other. Perhaps some of the coins leaked into circulation and were discarded when people discovered their worthlessness. Or maybe a whole bag was stolen in the confusion of the king's deposal and eventually dumped into the river when the thief decided they weren't worth risking the hangman's noose for, which would explain why so many tokens have been found in one place. I know of several mudlarks who have found them in the same spot.

I find Georgian halfpennies all along the foreshore of the Lower Pool, most of them smoothed almost blank from a million transactions, the king's face worn away and

Britannia rubbed out. I can tell what they are only by the size and thickness of the disc. Sometimes just a shadow of the design hints at which of the Hanoverians I'm holding. They are so common and so badly worn that some mudlarks ignore them completely, throw them back into the river or leave them where they are, but I collect them for the history they hold and I have quite a handful to jingle and stack. It is said they come from the old custom of 'buying the wind', when sailors tossed a coin into the river before setting sail to guarantee luck and a fair wind on their journey.

Much has changed along the river, but the wind has not. It is a biting, whipping wind that blows along its length from west to east, leaving the water at the Isle of Dogs to race between the tall buildings of Canary Wharf before emerging onto the river again at Blackwall, and gathering pace until it is a powerful force that blasts the wide flat expanse of the Estuary. The wind on the tip of the Rotherhithe Peninsula is especially strong. It slices through jackets and squeezes under scarves, pulling hair and slapping cheeks. The waves it conjures pound the foreshore and dance across the river's surface like tiny demons, lifting brackish spray into the air to settle on my lips. It is the same wind that once caught the sails of great sailing ships and rattled their rigging. It blew trade into the city and sent ships to new worlds. Sometimes, out on the peninsula, when I close my eyes and strain into the wind, I'm sure I can hear their canvas sails snapping and their ropes creaking.

WAPPING

You asked me who were Light Horsemen?—that's a name for one set
of people who live by plunder:— that lighter will have a good slice
of her cargo out to-night; for those who cut her adrift, know what's
on board of her. Then we have the Heavy Horsemen,—they do their
work in the daytime, when they go on board as lumpers to clear
the ships. And then we've the Coopers and Bumboat men, and the
Ratcatchers and the Scuffle Hunters, and the River Pirates; and, last
of all, we have the Mudlarkers: all different professions, Jack; never
interfering with each other, and all living by their wits.

Frederick Marryat, *Poor Jack* (1840)

Wapping is the stretch of foreshore directly opposite
the Mayflower pub at Rotherhithe. It is part of the
north side of the Lower Pool that extends eastwards through
Shadwell to Limehouse. When the Romans arrived, it was
low-lying marshland with gravel terraces and small islands
that stood proud of the spreading water, but by medieval
times tidal mills had been built along the water's edge to
harness the river's power to grind London's corn. Slowly
the land was reclaimed and turned over to pasture, and as
the world opened up and the Pool of London spread east,
Wapping grew too. By the time John Rocque drew his map
in 1746, it was a busy riverside community of dockers,

sailors, slop sellers, taverns and brothels, a place of closely packed cottages, wharves, warehouses, yards and narrow alleyways leading down to the river. On the north side of the river, from the Tower to Limehouse Hole where the Lower Pool ends and Rocque's map ends, there is barely a patch of open riverside space.

The map shows far more river stairs on the Wapping side than at Rotherhithe, with wonderful names like Frying Pan Stairs, Execution Dock Stairs, Pelican Stairs and Kidney Stairs. Some of them lead up from the river to taverns, where sailors, fishermen and lightermen came straight off the water to drink. By the mid-eighteenth century there were thirty-six taverns on the stretch of road that ran behind the yards and buildings alongside the riverfront. Their names reflected the occupations of the men who drank in them: the Ship and Pilot, Ship and Star, Ship and Punchbowl, Union Flag and Punchbowl, the Gun, North American Sailor, Golden Anchor, Anchor and Hope, the Ship, Ship and Whale, and the Three Mariners.

Today, there are just two of the original old pubs left along the riverside at Wapping – the Prospect of Whitby and the Town of Ramsgate – and nearly all of the old warehouses have been converted to apartments. Private developers have done their best to block public access to the river and the streets are eerily deserted, but of all the places I visit on the tidal Thames, Wapping is the most evocative. The narrow passageways that survive are cobbled time tunnels, unchanged for centuries; dark, cold and windy, musty and damp with river air, they smell and feel like the past. In places they lead to equally ancient stairs, rotten wood and stone steps worn by millions of feet into a series of sagging crescents. And with the outside world kept at bay behind the tall brick walls that line the river, I can easily lose myself in another world altogether.

Wapping is usually quiet and I can almost guarantee I will be left alone to mudlark, which is one reason I like it; but I also have a deeper and more personal pull to this part of the foreshore. This is where my people first came to the river when, around the middle of the nineteenth century, my great-great-great-grandfather James, a fisherman, boatbuilder and crofter, left the Shetland Isles for work. I knew the bare bones of the story from my grandmother, who told me how her grandfather had worked in the boatyards at Blackwall and that her mother, Kate, had been born within the sound of Bow Church Bells, a true cockney (not that she ever wanted people to know much about it after she moved upriver to Teddington to 'better herself'). I filled in the rest by searching through old photographs and birth, marriage and death certificates, visiting the streets where they had lived and searching for houses that had been flattened by the Luftwaffe or pulled down in slum clearances.

For James to have moved to such a place for a 'better life', suggested that life on Shetland was even worse. Indeed, his flight from the island coincided with two historic disasters. First, the Clearances, when crofters were thrown off the land they rented to make way for more intensive sheep farming; and then a famine, after potato blight struck. According to the records, James lost a wife and two daughters in Shetland, so it may have been grief or hunger, or both, that drove him south. For a time he worked in the dockyards in Sunderland, where he remarried and my great-great-grandfather John was born in 1855. Soon after, they moved to London, where in the 1860s the Thames had the greatest concentration of iron shipbuilders in the world. John's brother James was born in Limehouse in 1857. Four more children followed and by the 1871 census they were living in Poplar, alongside the Limehouse Cut, a short canal that connected the lower reaches of the River Lee to the Thames at Limehouse. James is listed as a shipwright and fifteen-year-old John as a 'Rivit Carrier', presumably in the same shipyard as his father. By the time he got married, John had become a boilermaker, a skill that reflected the change in shipbuilding that came about in his father's life. While James's skills lay in building sailing ships made of wood, John worked on the metal ships that replaced them.

Sometimes as I come down the river stairs at Wapping and Limehouse I stop and look at their worn curves. I pick out a mark or imperfection in the stone and think about the feet that have passed over it and how the riverfront has changed over the years. My riverside ancestors must have used the same stairs as I do along this stretch and walked down the causeways on the foreshore that are now broken up and vanishing. I am treading in their footsteps and it makes the foreshore here feel like it belongs to me. I can't help wondering if they ate off the broken plates I find embedded in the mud, or if any of the rivets I find on the Isle of Dogs and at Blackwall were once in young John's bucket. Did James smoke the pipe I found yesterday, as he sat on the quayside watching the ships pass by, or did he drop it as he chased the mudlarks away from the hull of one of his newly built ships?

The wooden fid I found washed up on the foreshore at Limehouse has become one of my most treasured finds. Not because of its age or rarity, but because of the family links I have imagined and attached to it. It's a tool that James might have used and would certainly have been familiar with. It's about as long as my forearm and as wide as a broom handle with one end sharpened and the other neatly rounded off and decorated with a simple line around the top. Fids were used by sailors, riggers and rope-makers to create spaces through which the rope could be woven together, or 'spliced'. It has the comfortable feel of a well-loved tool; perfectly balanced, weighty, smoothed by use and with a slight depression on one side that fits my thumb perfectly. The small dimple on top of the blunt end is where it was held in the lathe while it was being turned and the pointed end has been roughly sharpened with a knife. Perhaps after years of loyal service it became blunt and worn and was sharpened to extend its life. It's made from lignum vitae, one of the heaviest types of wood in the world, which sinks rather than floats in water, but its density is offset by the oils it contains, making it the perfect material for use at sea.

The most poignant objects for me, though, are toys. I can't help but wonder if they were once part of the games my great-great-great-uncles and -aunts played, but even without a direct personal link, lost toys are powerfully resonant. They have been sucked down into the mud and suspended in time as their young owners grew up. Entombed in the foreshore are forgotten and dismembered china dolls; Meccano wheels from the 1960s, just like the ones that lurked in the dust beneath my brother's beds; the tangled wreckage of an old toy tram; an army of lead soldiers separated from their mounts, legs, arms and heads missing, their once smart uniforms scoured away, and a fearless kilted Highlander, fixed bayonet snapped, red jacket worn to faded pink patches, separated from his regiment.

Some toys are simple and timeless: clay marbles that have changed so little over thousands of years that they are impossible to date, and their more glamorous modern glass counterparts, swirled with bright colours, sometimes chipped, often dulled from being washed around with the shingle. I once found a pig tarsal bone with two holes drilled through it for a cord that had turned it into a 'whizzer' or 'buzzer', and a little whistle, whittled from a broken pipe stem.

Tiny frozen Charlottes are the simplest and smallest of dolls, and Kate would probably have had one. I have a collection of six from the Thames – one of them is not much more than an inch high. They are pale, naked children, moulded in unglazed bisque porcelain and sparingly coloured or painted. Most were made in Germany and were popular throughout northern Europe and America in the late nineteenth and early twentieth centuries. They could be bought cheaply at fairs and the smaller ones were baked into cakes or puddings as lucky charms. Their name is less prosaic than it seems though, and has a macabre association with a popular American folk ballad, 'Fair Charlotte', which was based on the poem 'A Corpse Going to a Ball'. In it, a young lady called Charlotte refuses to spoil her pretty dress by wearing a warm coat and freezes to death on her sleigh ride to a ball.

Along the river I have found nineteenth-century dolls' house furniture – two broken, tiny white china ewers and a small tin bath with no base, all in the same spot – and an early twentieth-century doll-sized teacup that's missing its handle. Pewter toys are precious finds and can date back to medieval times. I have half a seventeenth-century plate, the back of a toy watch and a beautifully preserved toy dripping pan of the same date that is a perfect copy of those that were placed under the spit to catch the fat that dripped from roasting meat. Tiny toy cooking pots, frying pans, plates, jugs, cups and bowls as well as muskets, cannons, carriages, anchors, chairs and candlesticks have all been found by mudlarks on the Thames and are a delightful insight into childhoods of the past.

I usually start my visits to the Wapping foreshore at New Crane Stairs, next to New Crane Wharf, taking in a deep, polluted twenty-first-century breath before cutting off the main road and walking back in time, down a long dark passageway to my other world. It emerges onto a beach of fine, sugar-soft yellow sand, where pigeons peck contentedly at the waterline and heavy black cormorants sit on wooden posts just offshore, spreading their wings to dry and stretching the S-shaped kinks from their necks. If the sand is still smooth and unmarked there is a chance I will be blissfully alone, if only for a short time as this beach is popular with other mudlarks as well as dog walkers.

Most river stairs are slippery, but New Crane Stairs are perilous, as I found to my cost one cold wet day about ten years ago. Each step is deceptively unique in depth and height and the lower section is covered with slimy green algae. Despite the crude cross-hatchings incised into the surface of some of the steps, I lost my footing here, fell heavily, and bumped unceremoniously down the last few steps on my bottom. Luckily nobody was there to witness it and I limped away with little more than a bruised backside, but it taught me a painful lesson and instilled a near-pathological fear of wet river stairs that I have yet to shrug off.

Sometimes, I'll start my visits further west and come down Wapping Old Stairs. There has been a landing here for many centuries, and the current stairs date to around the nineteenth century when it was one of the busiest points on the river. I once found an eighteenth-century shoe patten partially submerged in the mud here. It's a cloverleaf-shaped iron hoop that would have been nailed to a wooden sole with leather cuffs to strap it onto the bottom of a shoe. They were used by women of all classes to keep their shoes clear of London's muck and this one is worn thinner on the right at the back, which shows it had been worn on someone's right foot. This is what makes it so intimate and special and what helps me to conjure a picture of the woman who lost it. In my mind she's rather rotund, red in the face and tottering down the busy causeway at Wapping Old Stairs to a waiting wherry. Her iron pattens are ringing on the stones like the hooves of a newly shod pony when suddenly there's a scrape, a faint crack, a yelp and she's come crashing to the ground amid the sludge. In the confusion that follows, her right shoe is pulled off, and together with its patten is lost in the mud.

Wapping Old Stairs are next to an old riverside pub, the Town of Ramsgate, once called the Red Cow (allegedly after a red-haired barmaid) and renamed for the fishing boats from Ramsgate that moored there to avoid the taxes they would have had to pay for mooring further upstream, closer to Billingsgate fish market. In the eighteenth century the pub's cellars were used as a holding cell for the men and boys who were pressed into service aboard navy ships by the press gangs that prowled the inns and taverns in the area, preying on the drunk, homeless and vulnerable from whom they could earn a reward. Impressment into service on land and at sea was legally sanctioned, but the press gangs' tactics were ruthless. They knocked men unconscious and dragged away those who had passed out from drink, slipping the king's payment of a shilling into their pockets unseen. Sometimes they dropped the shilling into some poor wretch's mug of beer and it was only as he drained the dregs that he realised his fate. The practice of accepting a shilling in advance payment for joining the services dated back to the English Civil War, but it became synonymous with the press gangs of the eighteenth century, when England was heavily engaged in war on several fronts.

I have yet to find a silver shilling on the Wapping foreshore, but I have one George III shilling that I found on the foreshore at Greenwich. Old hammered shillings are satisfyingly large and treasure-like, but by the eighteenth century they had been reduced in size in accordance with the value of silver, and my shilling from this period is far smaller and altogether less impressive. I imagine it being pressed into the dirty calloused palm of a drunken man, such a small and insignificant object to exchange for a life of hardship, oppression and fear.

The cellars of the Town of Ramsgate are also rumoured to have held convicts – men, women and children bound for transport ships that would take them to the colonies to serve out their sentences. Britain had been using transportation to 'colonies beyond the seas' as punishment since the early seventeenth century, when criminals were sent to the American colonies to provide labour. After American independence in 1776, and following James Cook's expedition to south-eastern Australia, the British authorities began to transport convicts to New South Wales. The first convicts left England for Australia in 1787 aboard a group of eleven ships known as the First Fleet. A total of around 160,000 men, women and children were transported. I had been reading about transportation ships after finding three beautifully preserved eighteenth-century wine bottles out on the Estuary, far from any settlement, where prison hulks had been moored in the eighteenth and nineteenth centuries. Thames prison hulks held, among others, those awaiting transportation to the colonies and I grew curious. The more I read the more I began to wonder if one of them might have been related to me.

The one good thing about having a name that nobody can spell is that it's easy to research. I'm related, however distantly, to just about every Maiklem in the world, and we all originate from a fairly small area just outside Glasgow. I found websites with lists of the ships that transported people to Australia and I decided to tap my very unique name into the search bar. Much to my surprise, up came a result: Robert Maiklem, departed from London on 22 July 1831 on board the *Strathfieldsay* and arrived in Van Diemen's Land (Tasmania) on 15 November the same year. I was beside myself with excitement. A link!

Every detail of every convict transported was recorded: their crimes, occupations, physical appearance and even their conduct in the colonies. Robert Maiklem appears in Description Lists, Conduct Records and Assignment Lists, in elegant copperplate writing. From them I learned that he was five feet four inches, with a 'low brow', light red hair, hazel eyes and a fair complexion with freckles. He had a wife and two children and was a ploughman. He was thirty years old when he was found guilty of forgery and sentenced in Glasgow to fourteen years' hard labour on the other side of the world in Van Diemen's Land. He was transported with 224 other men: highway robbers, housebreakers, pickpockets, arsonists, embezzlers and thieves. One man had stolen a basket of eggs, another some cheese – crimes that we would now consider little more than petty misdemeanours.

Robert Maiklem, prisoner number 4602, was brought down from Glasgow and briefly held on the prison hulk *Justitia* – originally a teak-built East India ship, launched in Calcutta in 1799 under the name *Admiral Rainier*, and hulked in 1824. The hulks were moored alongside areas such as Woolwich Marshes and the Estuary, where few people lived. Many prisoners were held on the hulks for the whole of their sentences. Others, like Robert, were confined while awaiting transportation. Conditions on board were appalling. Twenty years before Robert found himself at Woolwich on board the *Justitia*, James Hardy Vaux, a pickpocket, thief and fellow forger, described his own experience on the *Retribution*, a prison hulk also moored at Woolwich. 'Of all the shocking scenes I had ever beheld, this was the most distressing. There were confined in this floating dungeon nearly six hundred men, most of them double-ironed; and the reader may conceive the horrible effects arising from the continual rattling of chains, the filth and vermin naturally produced by such a crowd of miserable inhabitants, the oaths and execrations constantly heard among them; and above all, from the shocking necessity of associating and communicating more or less with so depraved a set of beings.' Men slept shackled in irons and were crowded beneath decks so low they couldn't stand up; they were often barely clothed or shod; food was scarce and rotten and drinking water was drawn directly from the river. Cholera, dysentery and typhus were rife and around 30 per cent of prisoners died.

But Robert Maiklem survived the hulk and the four-month journey to Tasmania. By 1842, he had served his sentence and as a free man he was given permission to marry. But that's where the trail runs dry. I can't find any evidence that he had children with his new wife and I haven't found any living Maiklems in Tasmania either. But perhaps he left something of himself in the river. Some of those imprisoned on board the hulks engraved 'leaden hearts', simple mementos for the loved ones they left behind. They used copper pennies, which were plentiful at the time and easy to smuggle in pockets and coat hems, and polished out Britannia and the monarch's head, both symbols of their incarceration. On them they recorded names, sentences and dates: in many cases their only personal testament to their pitiful end. Of the many engraved coins that have been found on the Thames foreshore it is entirely possible that some were engraved by those awaiting transportation. And maybe one of them was engraved by Robert Maiklem. I look for him when I search the mud at Woolwich and wonder about the things I find that fit with the dates that he was there. Did he chew on this bone? Did this button fall off his coat? The *Justitia* was sold in 1855 and eventually broken up. Perhaps some of the nails at Rotherhithe were part of it.

In some ways Robert was lucky. At least he hadn't been hanged. In the eighteenth century, the crime of forgery more often than not led to the gallows, and for those who had committed piracy and treachery on the high seas there was a special gallows on the foreshore at Wapping. Exactly where on the foreshore is uncertain, but it is likely to have been at a place marked on Rocque's map as Execution Dock.

Between 1735 and the last foreshore hangings in 1830, seventy-eight men were hanged at Wapping. They were tried by the High Court of Admiralty and detained at the notorious Marshalsea Prison in Southwark, on the south bank of the Thames near London Bridge. On the day of their execution, they were taken by open cart along streets lined with jeering crowds to Wapping. The procession was led by the Admiralty Marshall who carried a silver oar as a symbol of his authority, and the prisoner was flanked by the hangman and a chaplain. In Wapping High Street they made one final stop, at the Turk's Head Inn, for a last quart of ale to steady the prisoner's nerves and prepare him for what was to come.

The gallows on the foreshore was erected at low tide and, to ensure a brutal death, the condemned were hanged on a short rope that denied them the swift end of a broken neck. As they slowly choked, their arms and legs thrashed about in a macabre dance known as the 'hempen jig'. Once they were still, their bodies were taken down and bound by an iron chain to a wooden post for three tides to pass over them. The bloated corpses of the worst offenders were then covered with pitch, enclosed in an iron cage and hung from gibbets at Cuckold's Point, Blackwall, Woolwich and Tilbury. The crew of any ship arriving in London would be in no doubt as to how crimes at sea were dealt with in England.

The most notorious pirate executed at Wapping was Captain Kidd, who was hanged in 1701. He had been commissioned by the Admiralty to suppress pirates in the Indian Ocean, but turned pirate himself and is said to have buried his treasure somewhere in the Caribbean. He was finally caught in New York and brought back to London for trial. By the time he reached the scaffold he was completely inebriated, which may have spared him the full horror of what happened next. The first noose snapped, he fell into the mud and the whole dreadful process had to be repeated. Then, after the obligatory three tides, his body was tarred and left in a gibbet at Tilbury where the crows picked his bones clean. They were left there for several years.

Among the great crowds watching the hangings was one of the most hated men of the seventeenth century, Judge Jeffreys, who took prime position on a small balcony in the Prospect of Whitby pub, which was known as the Devil's Tavern. Here he watched the hangings of the men he had condemned to death in court. Everyone else crammed into the riverside taverns and sat on the decks of ships moored out on the river to watch the spectacle unfold. With this in mind, I generally reach Execution Dock convinced that I'm going to find something special, but I've only ever found one thing with a connection to these gruesome times: a chunky, irregularly shaped copper coin that I spotted late one summer evening in a shallow water-filled dip, behind what I imagine was once part of an old revetment. It was getting dark and in the half-light it looked like just another Georgian halfpenny, perhaps a bit bashed about by a bored sailor. So I popped it in my bag and didn't think much more about it until a few days later when I was cleaning my finds and noticed it was covered with stamps and counterstamps. One of them was a date, 1654, which by coincidence was the year that Captain Kidd was born.

The coin turned out to be a maravedis, which was struck from irregular discs between crude dies mostly for use in the Spanish colonies. The gold and silver coins that were produced in the same way are also known as cobs, or more romantically as 'pirate money'. They are the original treasure coins, silver pieces of eight and gold doubloons, that were made from rough chunks of precious metal hammered flat and clipped by hand to the correct weight. So who's to say my humble copper coin hadn't fallen out of the pocket of a pirate, or at least that of a visiting sailor who may have picked it up in South America or the Caribbean where pirates most famously ambushed their quarry?

Execution Dock is around fifty yards to the east of the Thames River Police station, a distinctive mainly Edwardian building whose origins date back to the eighteenth century. It stands flush with the river wall and has five white-painted bay windows and an apex roof topped with a fluttering Union Jack flag. A walkway that the officers refer to as 'The Brow' leads down to a floating pontoon to which at least one fluorescent striped police boat is always tethered. There is a set of river stairs to the side of the police station that has seen better days. Most of the steps have rotted away and there's no way you could use them to get on and off the foreshore any more. They end on a wide cobbled area that covers half of the foreshore in front of the station, where the old patrol boats were hauled up.

The River Thames Police have been patrolling the river since 2 July 1798 and it is the oldest continually serving police force in the world. It was formed by a Scottish magistrate called Patrick Colquhoun, together with a former sailor and merchant seaman called John Harriott, to deal with 'the *many thousand* individuals, male and female, prowling about in this Metropolis, who principally support themselves by various depredations on the Public' and to protect the thousands of tons of cargo that sat on lighters and ships at anchor in the overcrowded Pool. In 1792 imports into England amounted to £17,898,000 and exports to £23,674,000. Of this, around £500,000 (£35–40 million in today's money) of cargo was being stolen.

Part of the problem was a lack of security. Despite the value of the cargo, the ships were poorly guarded – scores of rusty eighteenth- and nineteenth-century padlocks are found by mudlarks, many cut and broken. But the system by which ships were unloaded also allowed for the tacit appropriation of goods in lieu of wages. Much of the missing cargo disappeared into the deep pockets of the lumpers, the men who unloaded the ships. They were badly paid, if they were paid at all, and this unofficial 'payment' was an accepted and necessary perk of their job.

Alongside the lumpers, there was an army of specialist thieves and general crooks. Colquhoun estimated that around 10,850 people were involved in theft on the Thames. Light- and heavy-horsemen stole almost exclusively from the West India ships. Light-horsemen, also known as night plunderers, were gangs of corrupt watermen who connived with the watchmen nominally tasked with guarding the cargo. They rowed back and forth to the ships, filling black sacks with plunder, which they hid in the bottom of their boats. The heavy-horsemen were criminal-minded lumpers. As well as assisting the light-horsemen at night, they also went aboard in broad daylight to fill the large pockets of their under-waistcoats, long bags, pouches and socks that they tied to their legs under their trousers.

Game watermen conveyed the stolen goods to shore and game lightermen stole from the cargoes of sugar, coffee and spices that they were legitimately tasked with rowing to the quays. Scuffle-hunters worked the quays and warehouses, hanging around on the pretence of finding labour and all the while helping themselves and hiding plunder beneath their long aprons. River pirates, thought to be mostly ex-soldiers or ex-sailors, stole parts of the ship itself, including the anchors. Even the rat-catchers were on the make, first infesting the ship with rodents to drive the crew ashore and then stealing at will as they exterminated the vermin.

For a price, shipmates, watchmen and revenue officers colluded with them all by turning a blind eye. The illicit bounty was taken to the copemen, who were the wholesale dealers, receivers of stolen goods and chief facilitators of all illegal activity on the river. They visited newly arrived ships to broker contracts with the shipmates and revenue officers, provided the black sacks and the bladders that were used to steal rum from barrels, and moved the goods onwards into the black market. Wapping itself was flooded with illegally acquired goods, with twelve 'factories' receiving them and selling them on throughout the city.

At the bottom of this pile of miscreants were the mudlarks, the lowest class of criminal, mere auxiliaries to the lumpers. They lurked around the ship hulls at low tide, searching for rope, coal and old bits of wood, and collecting the bladders of rum and small bags of sugar, coffee, pimento and ginger that were dropped overboard by the lumpers. In *The Routledge Dictionary of Historical Slang*, the first definition of 'mudlark' is thief, and comes from Colquhoun himself, who recorded the 'nefarious practices' and 'aquatic depredations' of all these fantastically named gangs in his 1796 book *A Treatise on the Police of the Metropolis: Containing a detail of the various crimes and misdemeanours by which public and private property and security are at present injured and endangered and suggesting remedies for their prevention.*

Henry Mayhew estimated there to be around 280 mudlarks – mostly children and old women – working the foreshore of the Lower Pool, on both sides of the river, in the mid-1880s. He described them as 'most deplorable in their appearance' and 'dull and apparently stupid'. Their bodies were foul with grime and their meagre, tattered clothing soaked and stiff with river mud. 'They never speak but with a stolid look of wretchedness they plash their way through the mire, their bodies bent down while they peer anxiously about.' He wrote of a group of child mudlarks, none over the age of twelve, that he came across at a set of river stairs, soon after the children had left the foreshore: 'The muddy slush was dripping from their clothes and utensils, and forming a puddle in which they stood ... Some carried baskets filled with the produce of their morning's work, and others old tin kettles with iron handles. Some, for want of these articles, had old hats filled with the bones and coals they had picked up; and others, more needy still, had actually taken the caps from their own heads, and filled them with what they had happened to find.'

In the eighteenth century, the most valuable cargo was the rum, coffee, sugar and spices that came in on the West India ships. By 1800 about a quarter of Britain's income came from West Indian imports. Colquhoun and Harriott persuaded the West India Merchants to put up £4,200, on the understanding that only West India ships were protected, and at 5 a.m. on 2 July 1798 the West India Merchants and Planters Marine Police Institution went out on their first patrol. It was a roaring success. In the first year the West India Merchants saved over £100,000 in stolen goods, several lives were rescued, and the government saved vast amounts of tax revenue. The West India Merchants bought a building on the river at Wapping from which the new police force could operate and this is where the Thames River Police has remained. The foreshore in front of the building regularly yields evidence of their long history. When the river was recently dredged just offshore to build a new pontoon, dozens of early police radios and handcuffs were pulled up, together with old mugs and spoons from thousands of cups of tea. Modern mudlarks have found old shackle-style handcuffs and one of only two known examples of very early River Police uniform buttons. The other was found on a sunken prison ship in Bermuda. Perhaps it had been lost by an officer who had taken a new job transporting prisoners, or maybe it had fallen off while he was herding the condemned onto a prison hulk in London.

I've found more counterfeit eighteenth-century coins around the River Police headquarters at Wapping than anywhere else on the foreshore, which makes me wonder if confiscated property was dumped there. But forgeries are not unusual among the scores of eighteenth-century halfpennies that wash up on the foreshore and are an indication of the sheer number of counterfeit coins in circulation at the time. Most halfpenny forgeries were made of copper mixed with lead or tin, which was cheaper and easier to work with. They are thin, light, brassy-looking and crudely designed, quite obviously not the real deal. Some coiners cunningly cast their coins to look worn and used, but others seemed to make little effort to create a realistic lookalike, with the king cast off-centre and deformed versions of Britannia on the reverse.

Evasion tokens were produced by forgers to exploit a loophole in the law that made the copying of coins an imprisonable offence. The law only applied if the forgeries were an exact copy of a regal coin, so evasion coins were made to look like regal coins with subtle but deliberate changes. Sometimes the legends read as nonsense, other times they are a cheeky dig at the establishment. The one I have dates from 1788, too early to have been made by Prisoner Maiklem, but it is the year the first transportation ships arrived in Australia carrying men like him who had been convicted of forgery. Instead of 'BRITANNIA', my evasion coin reads 'BRITONS RULE'.

Counterfeiters of gold and silver coins were often skilled craftsmen – button-makers, locksmiths, clockmakers and goldsmiths. Small-scale counterfeiting of half-crowns and sixpences could be achieved with a simple carved chalk mould, some scrap pewter and a small crucible. Clay pipes were perfect for this job, with the stem providing a useful spout to pour the molten pewter into the mould. My only Victorian forgery is a tin sixpence, which is badly infected with tin pest, but my handsomely crafted brass George III sixpence has stood the test of time well. All it's missing is the thin layer of silvering that would have passed it off as solid silver.

Coin debasement was another of the coiners' tricks. Clipping – shaving small amounts of metal from the edges of coins until enough had been collected to melt down into a bar or to make counterfeit coins – has been done for thousands of years, probably ever since the first coins were struck. A Roman coiner clipped my fifth-century silver siliqua and I have Elizabethan and medieval pennies where the words that once ran around the edge have been shaved away completely. To guard against accepting underweight clipped gold coins they were weighed on small scales with tiny brass or copper weights, known as coin weights, which corresponded to the unclipped weight of the coin. I have a few of these satisfyingly neat little square weights, one for a sixteenth-century Rose Ryall gold coin with a galley ship on one side and a small hand, the symbol for Antwerp (where it was made), on the other.

Over the centuries various measures were taken to prevent people from clipping coins. A long cross design, the arms of which reached to the edge of the coin, was introduced to silver pennies in 1247. If the cross was interfered with the coin was deemed illegal. In the seventeenth century a square copper plug was punched through the middle of tin halfpennies and farthings to make them harder to forge and the huge cartwheel pennies and twopennies that were minted in 1797 had sunken writing around their wide edges, also designed to foil the forger. After 1662 all coins were produced by machines, which made them uniform in shape and harder to clip. Then, as an extra precaution, Isaac Newton, who was master of the Royal Mint between 1699 and 1727, introduced a reeded edge – small lines that ran across the edge of the coin – which made clipping impossible and is still on some of our coins today.

The harsh penalties that were meted out to coiners and those trying to pass off forged coins may have encouraged people to get rid of forgeries, and the simplest and most reliable way to do that was to chuck them in the river. The river is still a useful repository and continues to swallow up crimes and misdemeanours. In the centre of town, stolen wallets, bags and purses, usually relieved of their cash and cards, are dumped off bridges. Further east, stolen bikes and motorcycles lie stranded and abandoned in the mud. And there always seem to be mobile phones, laptops, cut bike locks and once even the bolt croppers lying on the foreshore under the park at Shadwell, between Wapping and Limehouse. A fellow mudlark once found eight passports lying on the foreshore and last year I found a big black bin bag full of marijuana plants. Over the years I have come across an arsenal of offensive weapons too – a knuckleduster, lots of vicious-looking knives, a samurai sword and the loaded chamber of a revolver with the barrel and handle roughly sawn off and the serial number filed away.

People often ask me if I feel safe on the river and the answer is generally yes. It's open and exposed on the foreshore. There are no dark corners for people to hide behind and I can always see what's coming. If there are people around, they are usually busy with their own business and it feels safer than on the streets. The most trouble I ever get is from drunks and teenagers showing off on the river path above. They've thrown water bottles, cigarettes and beer glasses at me, but I know it's extremely unlikely they'll actually come down and get their feet dirty. I carry a personal alarm though, just in case, and I have the number of the River Police in my phone so I can dial it quickly in an emergency.

I've only ever needed to call the River Police out once. I was mudlarking very early one morning, close to London Bridge, at a spot with only one access route in and out. I was so engrossed in what I was doing that the first I knew of my approaching company was the sound of sliding rubble behind me. Two men had followed me onto the foreshore and were making their way unsteadily towards me. One was waving a half-finished bottle of vodka in the air as he steadied himself over the rough terrain. They shouted to each other loudly in Russian. Here we go, I thought. I was irritated that they had stolen my peace and quiet and taken me from my thoughts. But my irritation grew into intense annoyance as they got closer, and then I realised that they had me trapped.

I don't get scared very often. So that day, as well as being angry with the loud drunk Russians, I was also angry with myself for being scared. The seriously drunk one slumped down on a large piece of broken concrete to watch the proceedings and yelled what sounded like encouragement to his friend who came and stood next to me. I moved. He came and stood next to me again. They yelled to each other some more and I moved again. Again he followed me. It was a game of cat and mouse and I was running out of foreshore. I reached for my personal alarm, for all the good it would have done at that time in the morning with no one around, and with my other hand I phoned the police.

It took a moment for my aggressor to comprehend the flashing blue light and the men in uniform shouting at him from the police boat that arrived within minutes at the shoreline, and then he turned and fled. His friend simply lay back in the mud and laughed. The police scraped him up and led him off. The other was caught by the river stairs. An officer asked me if I wanted to press charges, but I said no. The tide was coming in. All I wanted was my peace and quiet back so I could make the most of the time I had left on the foreshore.

GREENWICH

It's down by Greenwich I used to go out. The swells sometimes
would pitch us coppers out o' the inn winders and laugh to see us
duckin' our 'eads and our 'ands, an' tumblin' one another over in the
slush, scramblin' arter them.

Richard Rowe, 'A Brood of Mudlarks',
Episodes in an Obscure Life (1871)

Greenwich was my home for thirteen years. I moved into
a little Victorian cottage, a two-up two-down affair,
nothing fancy, in 2002. It was a five-minute walk from
the river, just across the water from where my great-great-
grandfather had worked and my great-grandmother was
born, and five miles upstream from where Robert Maiklem
had been held on a prison hulk, though of course I didn't
know any of that at the time.

All I knew was that I wanted to get out of Hackney and
away from its noisy, dirty streets, and it was in Greenwich
one hot late-summer's day that it suddenly became clear
to me that this was where I should move to. I'd sweated
my way to the top of the hill in Greenwich Park, and was
sitting in the long dry grass catching my breath, just under
the Royal Observatory where time begins at the Prime
Meridian. At 12.55 a large red metal ball on top of the

Observatory climbs halfway up a long pole, at 12.58 it rises to the top of the pole, and at precisely 13.00 it falls. Since 1833 the ball has served as an accurate time check for anyone close enough to see it and for the sea captains waiting to set sail from the river below. Where better to start a new life? From the top of the hill, I could see the old and the new layered over each other, Wren's Royal Naval College underlining the towers of Canary Wharf in the distance, and – just – the long, lazy loop of the river meandering its way around the Isle of Dogs. There was green space, the air was fresher here and the river was like a barrier against the city. The smell of the hot dry grass reminded me of haymaking on the farm, and as I looked out across the view, it felt like home.

I had been walking along the river path a lot that year, trying to escape the mess of my unhappy relationship, marching against the wind and staring out across the khaki water. And now it was on my doorstep, the river became my regular escape, my healer and my therapist. Whenever I could, I walked east towards Woolwich, past the cement and aggregate works that filled the air with dust at Victoria Deep Dock, and around the deserted peninsula where the empty Millennium Dome was mouldering among the growing weeds. Sometimes all I needed was a half-hour hit, long enough to feel the fresh breeze off the river and to clear my head. And since I lived so close to the water it was easy. I'd walk down to the railings and watch the Clippers roar in and out of Greenwich Pier, depositing crowds of tourists and commuters, or sit on a bench in front of the Naval College, which is now part of Trinity Laban Conservatoire of Music and Dance, and listen to the students practising.

If the tide was low I gingerly descended the slippery steps to be closer to the water. I mooched up and down the line where it played against the stones and gravel, leaping back every time a Clipper sent waves crashing into the shore.

Gradually my walks became less frantic. My relationship finally came to an unpleasant end and I began to slow down, remembering what my mother had taught me all those years ago on our long, absorbing rambles together, losing ourselves in the details of our surroundings. I spent less time on the river path and more on the foreshore, peering into the mud and kicking over pottery. Eventually I realised I was walking on 'stuff': pipe stems, holey stones and pottery seemed to be everywhere. I made mental notes of where there seemed to be more of it and returned to those spots again and again. Since I worked from home, it was easy to time my visits with low tide and I went whenever I could, sometimes twice a day in the summer when the days were long. To begin with, I would get to the shore at low tide, but I soon learned that I had two to three hours either side of it to play with and my visits grew longer. I developed a routine and for several years this was the only part of the river I visited.

A double set of grand stone steps sweeps down to the foreshore at Greenwich in an inverted 'V' in front of the Naval College. I generally walked east first, slipping and sliding through the smooth flint cobbles to a long line of jumbled animal bones that ended just before the Trafalgar pub, which rises out of the river wall and whose large bay windows look out over the foreshore. In the nineteenth century, toffs threw pennies out of these windows for the amusement of watching the mudlarks scrabble about in the mud for them. Sometimes the children would perform tricks and wade out into dangerously deep mud to encourage their audience to throw more. Beyond the Trafalgar, but before the power station, the foreshore is more industrial, filled with nails, rust, smelly tar, abandoned paintbrushes and patches of poured concrete. The local rowing club has a slipway here and early-morning rowers would look up from their preparations to watch me crunch and wobble past.

Further on there are more bones and lots of modern junk – shoes, phones, toys, and once, rather disconcertingly, some false teeth and a pair of glasses on the same tide. When I reached the fat slimy legs of the pier, I'd turn and go back so that I could get to the western end of my stretch at the lowest point of the tide, walking back past the stone steps, avoiding the deceptive patch of deep rusty gravel that still appears at very low tide and which once swamped my boots. The foreshore was muddier at the western end, with grey patches of erosion, old wooden posts, masonry and bricks and pottery galore. Sometimes I saw other people doing what I was doing here, but it never occurred to me that it had an actual name. I was just happily fossicking, forgetting my troubles and enjoying the peace and quiet.

Then one day I read a newspaper article that described what I was doing as 'mudlarking', by which time, I suppose you could say I was a fully-fledged mudlark. I'd ditched the Tupperware container I'd been taking with me in favour of a bum bag that left my hands free. My favourite wellingtons were kept stationed by the door and I'd started taking a rather cumbersome foam kneeler so that I could search the mud more closely. I had watched my small stretch of the river shift and change over several years and learned how the currents and tides scoured its banks and deposited its treasures. I now knew what freshly eroded mud looked like and that this was where I could find newly exposed objects. I had learned that pins washed together and that smaller metal things joined them, that there were fruitful spots along the back wall worth searching and that worked bone and ivory could be found among the animal bones. I'd also gathered quite a collection of vulcanite bottle stoppers from the place where modern junk washed up by the power station pier and worked out that most of what I was finding at the western end of my patch was medieval and Tudor. My collection was growing.

I got married in 2008 and instantly created a foreshore widow. I would sneak off to the river whenever I could and in all weathers, leaving a trail of muddy footprints through the house and filling the windowsills and back garden with pipes and pottery. My ever-patient wife simply sighed, stepped over the driftwood and hoovered up the mud. She's never complained and she's only been to the foreshore with me once or twice. It's not her thing. She likes running marathons, which is an obsession in its own right so she understands. By this time I had begun to explore other parts of the foreshore too, travelling into central London to mudlark in the shadow of London Bridge and search the shoreline between Wapping and Limehouse. Then, in 2009, on the day before New Year's Eve, my difficult and complicated father died suddenly. For a year I haunted the quiet parts of the river, Rotherhithe, the Isle of Dogs, long stretches where I could rant and cry, where nobody could see my twisted face, trying to feel what I thought I should be feeling, to grieve and move on.

The river came to my rescue again in 2012 when Sarah and I had twins, a girl and a boy, who filled every second of every hour, sucked every ounce of energy from us and turned our lives upside down and inside out. It was exhausting, frustrating, endlessly fascinating, surprisingly liberating ... and I needed an outlet, just a few hours every now and then to re-find myself. On the foreshore I wasn't an exhausted new parent any more, nobody was demanding anything of me. I was a time traveller and a daydreamer. I searched for treasure and communed with the past. I lived in other people's lives through the objects I found.

One morning I arrived at the Greenwich foreshore to find a group of people gathered around the wooden posts that I'd been watching emerge from the mud over the years. They were members of the Thames Discovery Programme, a community archaeology group that monitors structures and deposits on the foreshore before they are washed away or covered over again. I said hello and got chatting to Nat, the lead archaeologist, who explained that the posts were thought to be part of a medieval jetty associated with the palace that had fronted the river between the fifteenth and seventeenth centuries. In recent years, even more posts and baseplates have appeared and disappeared on the tides. Some of the posts have large holes drilled into them – one even has a metal mooring loop attached to the top. Some still have wooden pegs holding them together. They are so well preserved by the mud that adze and saw marks can be seen on them. The wood is covered in a greenish-brown slime and the top half-inch or so is soft, but underneath it is hard, a testament to the properties of good English oak and elm.

It is the long-gone palace that was connected to the wooden posts and which lies in the bricks and masonry on the foreshore that draws me in here and keeps me coming back. Greenwich is unique. There is nowhere else I know of on the tidal Thames where the objects it reveals can be placed with such certainty. Most foreshore finds are a muddle of history that, unless they are marked in some way, are nearly impossible to attribute to a particular building or location. But at Greenwich, the objects have a provenance that's difficult to deny. Nearly every old object found here has an association with the palace and with the people who lived and worked in it.

I have a fascination with the Tudors that comes from growing up with them in a sixteenth-century farmhouse. Anyone who has lived in a very old house knows about the ghosts who inhabit its bricks and the lived-in feeling its previous occupants have given it. The house I grew up in had settled comfortably into its years and our ghosts were happy ones. The house itself was a traditional hall house, with red peg tiles that reached halfway down its walls and small windows to keep in the heat. My mother painted all the doors bright yellow to give it a welcoming look, and on cold nights we gathered by the large open inglenook fireplace, away from the draughts that you could almost see blowing across the hallway floor.

The low ceilings were criss-crossed by oak beams that had been ravaged over the centuries by beetles and worm, and wherever you went the floorboards creaked and moaned as if the house was complaining as you stepped on it. A colony of bats lived in the rafters and flitted out from a hole above my bedroom window at dusk every evening. The forgotten rooms at the back of the house smelled of mould and damp and terrified me at night when I was sent there to get more potatoes or dog food in the dark, but they fascinated me during the day when I could see past the junk and cobwebs to what they must once have been like. This was where the old kitchen and dairy had been. There were worn terracotta tiles on the floor of the kitchen and a Victorian iron range rusting away at one end. The dairy still had a pounded mud floor and a thick, wide wooden plank shelf under the small window. I went in there to feel the history of the house and to imagine the people who had cooked on the range and who had worn down the steps carrying the food they made through the now bricked-up door back into the main house.

I could only guess at who had lived in our house and what had happened there over the centuries, but the history of the medieval palace at Greenwich has been written down and recorded. History books tell me that Henry VIII was born there, as were his daughters Mary and Elizabeth, while his only son Edward died there at the age of fifteen, crying out in pain from the agony of his diseased body. Henry married two of his wives, Catherine of Aragon and Anne of Cleves at Greenwich, and on 29 May 1533, Anne Boleyn was escorted from there by a huge flotilla of sumptuously decorated barges four miles upriver to the Tower in advance of her coronation on 1 June. Her journey was quite the spectacle, she was dressed in gold cloth and accompanied by gun salutes and music, but less than three years later she made the same journey under very different circumstances. On 2 May 1536, she was taken under arrest from Greenwich upriver, past Rotherhithe and Wapping, to the entrance to Traitor's Gate. Seventeen days later, after a trial found her guilty of charges including incest, conspiracy and adultery, she was beheaded at the Tower.

There had been a large house on the river at Greenwich since at least early medieval times. The palace began life as a manor house called Bella Court, or Plesaunce, from the Latin meaning 'pleasant place to live'. When it came into the hands of Henry VII in the late fifteenth century he renamed it the Palace of Placentia, demolished much of it and set about rebuilding a fine riverside residence. The earliest depictions of the palace are two sketches by the Flemish artist Anthony van den Wyngaerde, who drew it from the front and the back in 1558. The riverfront view is drawn from the bank opposite and shows an imposing and rambling brick building around a series of courtyards with a chapel at the eastern end and a large gatehouse just off-centre, which opens onto the river. At the western end of the palace is a wooden jetty, which I'm sure corresponds with the posts and baseplates that are still emerging from the mud and washing away on the tides. Behind it is the hill where I made my decision to move to Greenwich on that hot summer day.

Henry VII was responsible for much of what we see in the sketches, but his son Henry VIII spent the most time and money on the palace, adding kennels, stables, a cockpit, armour workshops, tennis courts and a permanent tiltyard for jousting. Of all his sixty-three houses and palaces, Greenwich Palace, as it had become known, was one of his favourites and he made it his primary royal residence. It was close enough to the city to get to with ease by barge and far enough away to escape to when there was an outbreak of plague. The Royal Dockyards at Deptford and

Woolwich were close by and behind the palace was a deer park. Henry spent his time here hunting, jousting, courting, feasting and celebrating. He filled the palace with people and held extravagant entertainments.

The objects that are hidden in the mud at Greenwich fill in the details that are missing from the history books and bring the world of the Tudor palace to life. The foreshore here is like one large midden, a palatial version of the one in front of the house where I grew up, and in which are buried the ordinary lives behind the lavish parties. Here I can hold the tangible remains of everyday life in a Tudor palace: the soft remnants of reeds that may have covered its floors, the thick shards of pottery used in its kitchens, and even the food that was served and eaten.

Vast numbers of cooking pots and dishes were used in the preparation and presentation of food and many of those that broke ended up in the river. They are concentrated around the jetty, which must have been a convenient place for dumping rubbish and kitchen waste. I have quite a collection of feet and handles from pipkins, the pot-bellied earthenware cooking pots that were used in most houses from medieval times through to the eighteenth century. Pipkins came in a variety of styles and shapes, but most English-made pipkins had three stumpy legs and a single handle, which was usually hollow to disperse the heat. A stick could also be inserted in the handle, making it easier to move around when it was hot. Pipkins were sat close to or actually in the hot embers of the fire and the shards that lie on the foreshore are often blackened by soot from the last moments of their useful life; the handles are coloured more heavily on the side that was exposed to the fire.

Chafing dishes – ceramic braziers that held hot coals – were another common way of cooking food that required gentle heating. I have the flared bottom half of one of these and pieces of green and yellow glazed rims with little triangular projections for supporting a plate or bowl. Maybe they were used to prepare delicacies for the king and important guests or perhaps just to coddle an egg for the cook's late-night snack. Chafing dishes were also used to keep food warm, perhaps during the feasts at the palace, which could last for hours.

I have spent many absorbed and happy hours searching for the remains of feasts and everyday meals at court in the mud here. The bones that shift about the foreshore in long drifts and collect in corners against the wall are obvious to any visitor – apparently the police get a lot of calls from distressed people who think they have found evidence of a massacre. Among them I have found dogs' teeth, a cat's skull and the lower jaw of a rat – vermin from the halls and kitchens – but most of the bones are from the animals that were eaten at the palace. Wealthy Tudors and royalty enjoyed a rich diet that consisted mainly of meat. Drovers herded their animals from as far away as Wales to London, and flocks of geese, their feet dipped in tar and covered with sand to protect them, were driven in from the countryside. The large bones at Greenwich are mainly from domestic animals – cows, sheep, goats and pigs that would have been far smaller than the commercial beasts we breed today. Some of the bones have deep cut marks from sharp knives and cleavers and many of the larger ones have been smashed for the rich creamy marrow that was scooped out from inside them.

The bones of wild animals are here too – deer from the 200-acre royal park behind the palace, boar and maybe even seal and porpoise. I've found part of a large and once handsome deer antler, chopped off at one end, possibly by an axe. I have yet to find a seal or porpoise bone, but I know what a boar tusk looks like and I have found many of them on the Thames foreshore, especially at Greenwich. It is thought native wild boar had been hunted to extinction in Britain by the thirteenth century, and their reintroduced cousins had disappeared by the seventeenth century. Boar now thrive from released and escaped stock in certain parts of the country, but tusks from the foreshore are likely to date from a time when the nobility tested their skill and bravery against these wild pigs with long spears, daggers and heavyset dogs. Boar tusks don't last well once they're removed from the mud, though, and eventually shear apart and splinter into sharp fragments as they dry out.

It takes a keener eye to spot the smaller bones that are mixed in with the mud: the delicate skull of a rabbit, or possibly a hare, and countless fragile hollow bird bones. Most are about the right size for a chicken, but they could just as well be peacock, pheasant, heron, stork, goose, duck, gull, swan or even turkey bones, a new delicacy that arrived from America in the mid-sixteenth century. Beyond these bird bones are the frangible wishbones of pigeon, quail, teal, woodcock and the many songbirds that were consumed at court. The Tudors thought nothing of eating lark, robin, blackbird, thrush and linnet, beautiful delicate creatures that I'm sure were netted in their thousands on the marshes and scrublands close to Greenwich and across the water on the Isle of Dogs.

Fish replaced meat on Fridays and Saturdays, and also on the many religious holidays that occurred throughout the year. Sea fish were brought up the Thames from the Estuary and beyond, wrapped in seaweed to keep them fresh or salted in barrels. Freshwater fish were pulled from the river itself and kept alive in cisterns and ponds until they were needed. The tiny bones of the fish these people ate are perfectly preserved in the mud. All you have to do is look. I get down on my hands and knees, as close as I can to the foreshore, and pick a small patch of dark grey mud to analyse. Sometimes I find miniature hoards of fish bones, circular vertebrae with sharp spines that once supported the meaty flesh of cod, salmon, pike, haddock and perch. Other marine delicacies were also enjoyed at the palace. I have found the spiny armour from the skin of a thorn-back ray, the claws of large crabs and the shells of winkles, whelks, mussels, cockles and oysters.

The rough, grey, scab-like shells of oysters litter the foreshore in central London as well as at Greenwich. Harvested in the mouth of the Thames Estuary and along the coasts of Kent and Essex, packed into barrels, baskets and crates, and brought upriver to the city, they are the ancient remains of countless meals, common food for the masses throughout London's history. Native Britons regarded oysters as subsistence food, but the Romans considered them a delicacy and exported vast quantities of British oysters to Rome. They became protein for the poor, especially in Victorian times when they could be bought three for a penny. In the early 1900s, however, the filth that was being discharged into the Thames contaminated the oyster beds and the industry collapsed. The invasive Pacific oyster was introduced in 1926 to boost stocks, but most of the shells found on the foreshore are from native oysters, which have larger, more oval-shaped shells and a distinct hooked beak where the two shells meet. For mudlarks, oyster shells away from the Estuary are a good indicator of human population density – and where there are plenty of shells, there are likely to be good finds.

Close-up searching at Greenwich also reveals the remains of the fruit and nuts that were eaten between courses and at the end of meals. Ancient hazelnut and walnut shells survive miraculously well encased in oxygen-free mud. They are delicate, softened and waterlogged though, and dissolve quickly as soon as they are exposed to the tides. The apples, pears, blackberries and strawberries that were consumed have left no tangible evidence, but I have found plum and cherry pits and apricot stones, blackened by 500 years of darkness. I imagine a rakish courtier, lounging lazily against a window recess and looking out over the river as he rolls ripe cherries around in his mouth and spits the pits on to the flagstone floor. They mingle with the rest of the filth, and eventually, perhaps weeks or even months later, are swept up by a skivvy, dumped into a wheelbarrow and tipped off the wooden jetty into the river.

While more robust fruits such as oranges, lemons and pomegranates were brought to London on the ships that sailed past the palace on their way to the Pool, softer fruits like apricots and cherries were grown at specialist orchards in Kent on imported trees tended by the royal fruiterer. Henry VIII and Anne Boleyn were said to be particularly fond of fruit. Perhaps I have found the stones of apricots they shared together in the first bloom of their love.

Henry was also fond of sugar, which was a luxury at the time. There are references to it being kept under lock and key at Hampton Court, along with exotic spices, fruits and nuts. Sweet treats were prepared for the king by his confectioner, Mrs Cornwallis. She was the only woman listed as being a member of his kitchens and was described as 'the wife who makes the king's puddings'. I like to imagine her stirring her famous custards, jellies and quince marmalade in the vast, sweltering kitchens at Greenwich. Elizabeth inherited her father's love of sugar, which had become popular and fashionable, albeit still expensive by the time she lived at Greenwich Palace. It was eaten with vegetables and meat and used to preserve fruit. It was also used to produce all manner of sweetmeats, including marchpane, a type of almond and sugar 'dough', like marzipan, that was sculpted into elaborate centrepieces for banquets. It is said Elizabeth liked sugar so much that her teeth went black from it. Social climbers emulated this by rubbing soot into their own teeth to make them appear wealthy enough to afford sugar.

One morning a very friendly Swiss lady came up to me on the foreshore at Greenwich. Her English wasn't very good, but she made it clear she'd found something that interested her and motioned for me to hold out my hand, into which she dropped a human molar. The top surface was worn almost smooth, but apart from that it was a clean yellowy white and in very good condition, a distinct contrast to the three other human teeth I've found on the river, which were dirty grey with gingery-brown roots and eaten away by deep dark cavities that sent shivers down my spine.

I was reminded of something I had once been told by an archaeologist about the dating of teeth – that before the Elizabethans, since there wasn't much sugar and certainly no tobacco to discolour and rot them, teeth were often cleaner and less decayed. People kept their teeth for longer and through eating bread made with stone-ground, often gritty flour they wore the cusps of their teeth down. By this theory, the tooth I had just been given looked old.

It wasn't until the discovery of the New World, where sugar cane could be grown on vast plantations worked by armies of slaves, that sugar became cheaper and more widely available. By the eighteenth century, sugar refining was big business and there were hundreds of sugar houses in London making rock-hard sugar 'loaves' in moulds that varied in size. Thick syrupy refined raw sugar was poured into the mould and as it slowly dripped through the small hole in the bottom into a collecting pot, it left brown crystallised sugar behind. Poor-quality sugar crystallised less easily and was made in larger moulds, while white sugar fetched a better price and was made by slowly dripping a solution of white clay through it to draw out the remaining brown molasses. Once the mould was full, the sugar loaf was knocked out and dried in a stove room at sixty degrees Celsius.

Large shards of red earthenware moulds that were used to make sugar loaves are embedded in the foreshore just upstream from Greenwich Pier towards Deptford. There were two potteries at Deptford that made these moulds and it's possible that those that broke during the firing process were gathered up and used to fill and stabilise the foreshore here. The shards are thick and have white slip roughly painted on the inside, which helps to date them since sugar moulds were not slip-coated until the late seventeenth century. So they weren't destined for the palace.

Formal feasting at the Tudor court was not a greedy, gobbling free-for-all, but followed a strict code of etiquette. Manners were important. Plate after plate of food was brought out of the kitchens and presented to the king before being distributed to his guests, with sumptuary law restricting the number of dishes people were permitted to eat according to their social rank. A cardinal was allowed nine dishes, an earl seven, and knights of the garter six. They cut and stabbed their food with knives, used pewter spoons for soups, pottage and stews, but otherwise ate with their fingers which, in the palace at least, they wiped on a linen napkin draped over one shoulder.

I have quite a collection of bone, ivory and wooden knife handles that date back to early medieval times and several pieces of bone and pewter spoons: knops and broken handles, and an acorn finial from a sixteenth-century pewter spoon, which would have had a wide round bowl. Acorns were a remedy for cholera and the 'bloody flux' (dysentery), and acorn finials were popular at this time as a symbol of immortality and a talisman. People of all social classes carried their own knives and spoons for fear of infection and illness, which explains why so many are found on the foreshore.

Henry VIII also dined less formally in his private chambers, sometimes with close friends and occasionally with one of his wives. Large ceramic stoves covered with green-glazed earthenware tiles moulded with heraldic symbols probably heated some of these rooms. I know of one spot on the foreshore where fragments of similar stove tiles can be found, but they are rare and I have only three shards, one with the moulded top of a column that probably flanked the royal coat of arms or Tudor rose. Henry may have favoured glass goblets instead of gold or silver in his private rooms, perhaps a gift from the Venetian ambassador who was often seen at court. The goblet stems I have found at Greenwich match complete examples of sixteenth- and seventeenth-century Venetian goblets held at the Victoria and Albert Museum. They are shaped like large teardrops, hollow and rainbow-coloured with iridescence where the 400-year-old glass has begun to fracture into micro-fine layers that reflect light like a prism. What whispers of love and court gossip were they privy to?

For a time, there was a particularly fruitful spot at Greenwich that gave me Elizabethan fairy pipes and hammered coins, Tudor dress hooks, a wooden medieval knife handle, a fifteenth-century ear spoon with a thin twisted wire handle, a tiny bone die and hundreds and hundreds of pins of all styles and sizes. In fact, there were so many pins I had to be careful not to get pricked by them as I picked up other objects. This was also where I first noticed the little metal tubes that I later found out were lace aglets. I left scores of them to the mercy of the tide because I was convinced they were modern and for some reason something to do with electrical circuits.

Even to my relatively untrained eye I could tell this spot was special. I'd noticed water trickling through the lower part of the river wall nearby, so when I heard other river searchers talking about 'the sluice' it all fell into place.

Perhaps the objects I was finding had washed down with the effluent of the palace and out into the river where they had become trapped and embedded in the mud and muck on the foreshore? But whatever it was, it became my go-to spot and it yielded some lovely objects. Among them was a broken pottery whistle that came all the way from Belgium in the fourteenth century – a yellow-glazed cow-like creature, with long rabbit ears onto which a hooded rider is holding tight; the mouthpiece of the whistle emerges from the creature's rear end and it has a correspondingly confused look on its face – and a little flat clay cockerel, about as long as my little finger, which is thought by the Museum of London to be a seventeenth-century fairing, a child's toy bought for a penny or two from a fair or a pedlar. It was produced in a two-part mould with the same white clay that was used for tobacco pipes and he still has traces of salmon-pink paint on his wattle, which suggests he was once brightly painted. The end of his beak is chipped and most of his tail is missing, but I can see he has the long legs and rangy look of an old-fashioned breed of chicken, the type that was used in cockfights.

Henry VIII had a cockpit built at Greenwich Palace and cockfighting was a popular sport in England. It was banned in 1849, but continued illegally for much longer. Some taverns had their own pits where men gathered to watch the poor creatures, their wattles and combs removed to give them a more aggressive appearance and to help prevent them being damaged in the fights. Another barbaric game, which originally took place on Shrove Tuesday, involved throwing stones or cudgels at a live chicken buried up to its neck or tethered to the ground. The winner got to take the dead bird home for dinner and the bird's owner made his money by charging for each throw. An engraving of the Thames frost fair of 1683/4 shows a bird tethered to the ice and surrounded by excited men in hats and frock coats, which proves that by then it had moved beyond an Easter custom to become a popular London pastime. Crude little lead cockerels, looking very similar to my clay version, have been found on the foreshore by mudlarks. They are known as 'shies' and were specially produced for children to practise their skills in preparation for the adult sport. A clay shy may have been too delicate for a game of 'cockshy', but if the player aimed to destroy the cock completely it would have served its purpose well.

Giant nets of stones have now been placed two-deep against the river wall at Greenwich to try and shore it up against erosion. My special patch has been covered up, together with the top part of the foreshore, and half an hour on every tide has been taken away from me. But erosion, as ever, is a double-edged sword. It is stealing away the medieval jetty at Greenwich and compromising the river wall, but it is also washing out treasures for mudlarks and revealing the remains of the old palace itself.

In later life, Henry turned his attentions to Hampton Court, and although Elizabeth made Greenwich Palace her primary summer residence, she never had the same affection for it as her father did. By the end of the Civil War of 1642–51 it was in a dire state of disrepair. With no respect for its royal status, the Commonwealth ordered the state apartments to be turned into stables and later, it housed prisoners of war from the First Anglo-Dutch War of 1652–4. It was already a very old building and after years of neglect and wilful damage, Charles II decided to demolish it. Much of it, especially the valuable stone, was probably taken away and recycled, but some broken masonry, smashed floor and roof tiles and shallow irregular Tudor bricks still found their way onto the foreshore and lie scattered across its surface.

Tudor bricks are easy to identify among the rubble that covers the foreshore in central London. They are far thinner and lack a 'frog', the central depression that characterises bricks from around the late eighteenth century. Bricks became larger after 1784 to avoid a brick tax payable per thousand bricks, which was introduced to help pay for the wars in the American colonies. The government responded by passing a new law taxing larger bricks at double the rate and in 1839 they set a maximum volume of 150 cubic inches. This is still far larger than the average modern house brick, which is 87.41 cubic inches.

I came to bricks fairly late, having ignored them for many years, but they are surprisingly interesting and the Thames foreshore provides a seemingly unending supply of examples from every era. There are local red bricks, small yellow Flemish 'clinker' bricks, and hard-wearing nineteenth-century 'blue' bricks that were used to build the bridges and tunnels that came with the Industrial Revolution. Some have the maker's name stamped into them. If you are lucky you might find one stamped 'Diamond Jubilee' in celebration of Victoria's extended reign. Others have fragments of clay pipes embedded in them, perhaps dropped by accident into the clay as the brick-maker worked.

The bricks that built the palace and now lie in the mud at Greenwich were probably made of local clay, excavated in the autumn and overwintered to break it down and help remove the soluble salts before brick-making began in the spring. The clay was thrown into simple wooden frames that were open at the top and bottom, and excess clay was removed with a 'strike' before the frame was lifted off. The moulded bricks were laid out to dry until they were strong enough to be placed on edge. Then they were turned daily until they were fully dry and ready for firing. It took vast amounts of timber to fire the kilns and clamps. Even then the firing temperature was far lower than that of modern kilns and varied within the clamps, which meant that some bricks were underfired while others were overfired and vit-rified. As a result of this, and because of the speed at which bricks were made and the huge quantities that were needed for the project, their quality varied enormously.

Among the bricks and tiles, I have also found short strips of lead and tiny pieces of shattered window glass. Glass was expensive in Tudor times, and because it was diffi-cult to make large sheets of it, windows were constructed of smaller pieces held together by strips of lead, known as 'came', in a lattice pattern. The windows in the rooms the king used would have been glazed, but the best that ordinary people could expect was polished horn, paper or cloth. Many had nothing other than an old piece of sacking to pull across an open window to protect them from the worst of the elements.

The glass is particularly poignant. Had it been in a window in the monarch's private apartments? Had Henry looked through it as he deliberated over his decision to have

Anne Boleyn executed? Or had his daughter Elizabeth, as she wrestled with her conscience before signing the death warrant of her cousin, Mary Queen of Scots? Henry may have watched his warships as they sailed past from the royal dockyard, just to the west of Greenwich, from behind this piece of glass, and Elizabeth might have seen her ships set sail and return from newly discovered worlds through it. Did they look out at low tide? Could they see the foreshore I search today?

The palace was replaced with the classical buildings and twin domes of the Old Royal Naval College that still stands today. The college was originally designed by Christopher Wren as a Royal Hospital for Seamen and opened its doors to the first pensioners in 1705, admitting elderly or injured seamen who could no longer serve in the navy and who had no other means of support. They were like the army's Chelsea Pensioners, only they were known as Greenwich Pensioners, and their frock coats were blue instead of red. At its peak, in 1814 during the Napoleonic Wars, it provided accommodation for over 2,700 men, but by 1869 numbers were dwindling and the hospital closed.

I imagine them walking along the river in front of the hospital buildings, wearing tricorn hats and the traditional blue frock coats, smoking clay pipes with long curved stems and the royal coat of arms or the Prince of Wales plume of feathers moulded into the bowl. I've found more of these decorated eighteenth-century pipes at Greenwich than any-where else, along with the bottoms of several dark green, early nineteenth-century square gin bottles.

Complete square gin bottles are rare. Most have been shattered and battered by the resting hulls of ships and barges and the shifting tides and I am still searching for a whole one. But they were once common and the standard method of transporting gin. Their tapered shape allowed them to be packed in sets of six to twenty-four in wooden crates for safer, easier and more space-efficient transport and storage. Gin originally came to England from Holland in the seventeenth century, with soldiers returning from the Thirty Years War. They drank it to keep warm on the battlefield and to steel their nerves – it was the original 'Dutch courage' – but it quickly became popular on the streets of London too. By the mid-eighteenth century, it was the scourge of the city and being cheap it was consumed in vast quantities by men, women and children alike. But navy gin was even stronger and it was said that ship's captains tested its strength by mixing it with gunpowder. If it failed to light, chances were it had been watered down by the distiller or by someone on the ship hoping to get away with an extra ration.

I've found naval buttons at Greenwich, lost and pulled from the uniforms of sailors as they embarked and disembarked from their ships. They are gratifyingly easy to date, thanks to their design. The earliest British naval buttons have the stylised round-petalled rose on them and date from 1748, when uniform regulations for officers were first introduced. The rose was changed to an anchor in 1774. In 1812, after the design on Merchant Navy buttons changed from a plain anchor to a fouled anchor, a crown was added to most Royal Navy buttons to distinguish them and the design has remained much the same ever since. It was the officers who 'wished to be recognised as being in the service of the Crown' who lobbied for regulation uniforms. It is said that George II chose blue after seeing the Duchess of Bedford in a riding habit of blue faced with white. Some captains established general standards of appearance for the seamen on their vessels, but there was little or no uniformity between ships, and ordinary seamen continued to dress in 'slops', jackets, waistcoats and trousers that were made to specifications set out by the Admiralty, until the mid-nineteenth century when uniforms were introduced for all ranks.

The pretty porcelain head of a Victorian sailor figurine that I found rolling around at the edge of the water at Greenwich is wearing a straw hat, which was standard issue in the navy at that time. I found him at the bottom of the sweeping steps up which Nelson's coffin was carried following his death at the Battle of Trafalgar. His body had been preserved on board ship in a cask of brandy mixed with camphor and myrrh and he lay in state for three days in the Painted Hall at the Royal Hospital where more than 15,000 people came to pay their respects. On 8 January 1806 he was carried back to the river stairs to a waiting black-canopied funeral barge that took him upstream to Whitehall, where he spent the night at the Admiralty before his funeral at St Paul's Cathedral the next day.

I moved away from my precious Greenwich in 2015, when the twins got bigger and our little house began to strain at the seams. We left the river and made a home by the sea, not far from the Estuary. But Greenwich still pulls me back – it's an old friend now and I'd miss it too much if I didn't visit. I come for an early tide, arriving when the sun is rising and the water is still lapping the green-fuzzed stone wall, and stay searching until the river creeps back in and gently shoos me away.

TILBURY

The sewer-hunters occasionally find plate, such as spoons, ladles, silver-handled knives and forks, mugs and drinking cups, and now and then articles of jewellery; but even while thus in 'luck' as they call it, they do not omit to fill the bags on their backs with the more cumbrous articles they meet with – such as metals of every description, rope and bones. There is always a great quantity of these things to be met with in the sewers, they being continually washed down from the cesspools and drains of the houses.

Henry Mayhew, *London Labour and the London Poor* (1851)

The foreshore after heavy rain can be quite repulsive. Even after relatively light rainfall, London's Victorian sewers, which were built to deal with a population half the size it is now, simply can't cope and they overflow into the storm drains that lead directly into the river. Each year around 7,200 Olympic-sized swimming pools of untreated waste water is discharged into the Thames. There is no mistaking a sewage-spill day. One of the first things you notice is the smell that overrides the usual clean alkaline odour of the river and replaces it with a repellent human essence that hits your nose in wafts and thickens at the back of your throat. The smell is worse close to the storm drains, where it's concentrated and soaked into the mud and sand.

The drains themselves are often skirted with unmentionable filth. Many have heavy iron covers that swing open as the water flows out. Some of these openings are quite small, but others are large enough to crawl into, which is what the specialist tribe of sewer hunters called toshers did to earn their living in the nineteenth century. Toshers were the mudlarks' subterranean counterparts. Mayhew described them as 'strong, robust, and healthy men, generally florid in their complexion', whose escapades underground earned them an elite wage among the working classes of the time. 'Sometimes they dive their arm down to the elbow in the mud and filth and bring up shillings, sixpences, half-crowns, and occasionally half-sovereigns and sovereigns. They always find the coins standing edge uppermost between the bricks in the bottom, where the mortar has been worn away.'

Toshers dressed distinctively in long greasy velveteen coats with large pockets, canvas trousers and a canvas apron to which a lantern was strapped. They carried a long pole with a large iron hoe at one end to rake through the muck and to help steady themselves in the sludge; it was also to defend themselves from the packs of huge rats that lived in the sewers. The men had nicknames like Lanky Bill, Long Tom, One-eyed George and Short-armed Jack, and worked in gangs of three or four, accessing the sewers from the outlets on the river and searching for anything of value that had passed down the drains – coins, nails and scrap metal, jewellery, plates, knives and forks. It was a dangerous occupation, and in 1840 unauthorised entry into the sewers was made illegal, which is one reason it was done mostly at night. Toshers risked drowning on incoming tides, getting lost in the miles of crumbling sewers and being overcome by the poisonous gases that rose from the filth. A bite from a rat could turn septic and often proved fatal.

Fantastic stories circulated among them, like the legend of the wild hogs who lived in the sewers beneath Hampstead, and the myth of the Queen Rat, a supernatural creature who was said to invisibly follow the toshers around as they worked. If she liked the look of one of them, she would turn herself into a beautiful young woman, albeit with claws on her toes and rat-like eyes that reflected the light, seduce him and then would reward him with good finds. If he offended her, however, his luck would soon change. One tosher, named Jerry Sweetly, is said to have lashed out at the Queen Rat after she bit him on the neck while they were making love – she did this to protect her lovers from other rats. She gave Jerry Sweetly his luck in the sewers, but she cursed his wives, the first of whom died in childbirth and the second after falling into the river. His children were all blessed with luck, but in every generation of the Sweetly family since there is said to be a child born with one blue eye and the other the colour of the river, a reminder of their ancestor's brush with the Queen of the Sewers.

The river has been used as a convenient dump ever since the Romans. Refuse and human waste was thrown directly from the houses on London Bridge and the buildings along the river's banks; the city's privies and cesspools were carted to the river and dumped in it; the middens and piles of rubbish that grew up around the city were periodically shovelled up and taken to the river; and it was a useful repository for the butchers, tanners and fishmongers who worked along the riverfront. By the nineteenth century, it was little more than a tidal sewer with a floating scum of street muck, domestic waste, animal dung and ashes from the city's hearths. The increasing popularity of flushing toilets, which emptied into sewers that led directly to the river, and London's growing population eventually tipped the balance. By the 1840s, 200 tons of human waste was gushing into the Thames every day. In 1858, after a long hot summer, the smell rising off the river was so overwhelming that Parliament was almost abandoned. It became known as the Great Stink and an Act of Parliament was passed to find a solution.

The engineer Joseph Bazalgette was commissioned to design a system of large sewers to run along the edge of the river in newly constructed embankments built on land reclaimed from the foreshore. The new system intercepted the existing sewers and took the waste to the eastern edge of the city. Bazalgette's sewers improved the quality of the water in central London, but the problem didn't just go away. It simply moved downstream to the river just east of Woolwich. Huge 'mud' banks built up around the sewage outlets at Crossness and Beckton, and two continuous streams of fermenting sewage, ripe with noxious gases, turned the river here into a thick, slimy, stinking cesspool that moved slowly on each tide towards the sea. Its true horror became apparent in 1878 when the paddle steamer the *Princess Alice* collided with a collier and sank in this most polluted part of the river. Of the 900 passengers on board, only around 130 survived and it remains Britain's worst peacetime disaster. The chemicals in the water bleached the clothes of the corpses and discoloured their skin. The effects of the sewage caused them to bloat to such an extent that extra-large coffins had to be made, and of those fortunate enough to be plucked from the river, many died later from the effects of ingesting the water.

Sewage and industrial waste continued to pour into the river and bomb damage to London's sewage system during the Second World War made matters even worse. Eventually, in 1957, the Natural History Museum declared the Thames 'biologically dead' and surveys concluded that there were no fish between Kew and Gravesend. A campaign to clean up the Thames began in the 1960s and by the end of the 1970s the river was considered to be 'rehabilitated'. It is now cleaner than it has been in living memory and supports over 125 species of fish. The Estuary is the largest spawning ground for sole in England, oysters have returned and even lobsters live in its muddied waters. Further inland the river is home to long black leeches and freshwater mussels. At the tidal head, spiny sticklebacks, red-throated in the breeding season, flit about in the shallows and perch spawn in the shade of the willows that clutch the banks. At Hammersmith I once watched a little miller's thumb fish, his oversized head pointing into the gentle current, guarding a batch of eggs in the gravel beneath him. If I'm lucky, on a bright sunny day when the water in the shallows is clear, a baby flatfish might flip and float over my boots.

Some today hail the Thames as the cleanest urban river in the world, but it still carries dangerous microbes. Most of those who row on the river have at some point suffered from a bout of 'Thames tummy'. I have myself, and I know of several other mudlarks who have been brought down, even hospitalised, by mysterious illnesses. Sewage spills bring with them all sorts of other nasty foreshore finds too. The retreating tide leaves behind a fine mesh of wet wipes, sanitary towels and condoms, and multicoloured strandlines filled with thousands of plastic cotton-bud sticks, tampon applicators, disposable plastic contact lens cases and plastic teeth-cleaning sticks. Pretty much anything that fits down a toilet will find its way onto the foreshore after a sewage spill: plastic bath toys, combs, disposable razors, toothbrushes and tubes of toothpaste. And the same goes for medical waste – colostomy bags, cannulas, plastic saline containers, drip bags, syringes, drug packaging and once even a hospital wristband with a name, date of birth and hospital number written on it in blue ink.

I sometimes wonder if the sewers spill out some of the most personal possessions I find too: glasses, hearing aids and, rather shockingly, a prosthetic eye that I spotted winking back at me from the mud. It is a work of art. The small cup-shaped piece of glass was tailor-made for its owner, and the hazel iris and tiny blood vessels that spider across the white are hauntingly realistic. I didn't hesitate in taking the eye home with me, but I can't touch the false teeth and dental plates I find. There's something creepily intimate and a bit dirty about them, even those from the 1950s or earlier, with salmon-pink gums made of vulcanite rubber and bright white porcelain teeth.

Worst of all, though, are the congealed yellow-grey blobs that I sometimes find lurking inconspicuously among the gravel after a sewage spill. They are putrid pieces of a 'fatberg'. The fatbergs that grow in London's sewers can become immense. The largest to date, discovered beneath the streets of Whitechapel, was longer than Tower Bridge and thought to weigh as much as eleven double-decker buses. They are made up of fat, dumped down kitchen and restaurant drains, which congeals into lumps and clings to the sewer walls. As it gets larger it attracts more fat, which acts as a binding agent for the organic material in sewage. Wet wipes, toilet paper, hypodermic needles and sanitary products become embedded in the stinking mass as it grows and grows, gradually turning as hard as concrete until it blocks the sewer or breaks up and washes away in foul-smelling greasy lumps.

Sewage-spilled rubbish is usually worse on early-morning tides in central London, before the river busies up and the wake of passing boats starts to wash it away. The rubbish that flows out with the Thames also varies with the seasons. Christmas trees, stripped of their festive finery, float down the river in January; champagne bottles litter the foreshore after New Year, especially near the bridges; and tennis balls bob out to the Estuary by the score during Wimbledon. More coffee cups litter the foreshore in the winter and plastic bottles and food packaging increase in the summer. This is now the most common type of rubbish washing up on the foreshore.

Rubbish tends to be larger to the east of the city, where the river flows through more remote and run-down areas: bicycles, motorcycles, car tyres and shopping trolleys. Most of this sinks slowly where it's dumped, but I've also seen fridges and car bumpers floating away into the distance. Some things look as though they have been there for years; others look new, freshly jettisoned and abandoned.

Perhaps it's easier to get heavy objects to the river's edge without being seen in this part of London.

The river sorts rubbish like an obsessional old man. It gathers plastic bottles, food packaging and polystyrene in inlets and in the corners of its walls, and strews cotton-bud sticks, straws and plastic bottle tops in long thin strandlines. Towards the Estuary, it collects all manner of floating debris in huge multicoloured banks, storing it high up on the fore-shore, often on the outside of its bends, out of reach of all but the highest spring tides. There are sink spots on the bends too, on the inside where the river slows and drops its invisible load: the wet wipes and plastic bags that tumble unseen below its surface. It fills the bags with silt so that they sink and turns the wet wipes into a thick spongy blanket. In Hammersmith there are now so many wet wipes in the river that they have formed a small island. I first noticed it several years ago when I stepped on what looked like a hump of brown rags and realised to my horror that it was a mass of filthy wipes. The last time I visited, the island was much larger. It had trapped tree branches that were snaring even more passing trash. A duck was sitting happily on this filthy reef and it occurred to me that our rubbish is actually changing the geography of the river.

Work is under way on a giant twenty-four-foot-wide, sixteen-mile-long 'Super Sewer', most of which will run deep beneath the Thames between Hammersmith and Limehouse. It will eventually store London's sewage and transfer it to updated treatment plants east of the city, making sewage spills a thing of the past. Large floating objects are dealt with by the PLA's driftwood craft and there are sixteen passive driftwood collectors. These are giant floating cages that are moored at strategically chosen points where the currents carry the most debris. They swing on a single mooring on each tide to gape into the flow of water, trapping rubbish from the top four feet of the river in the back of the cage. Each cage can collect up to forty tons of rubbish a year and much of their harvest is taken downstream for disposal. The city's domestic refuse also travels east in huge rubbish barges, filling up at four central riverside collection points, including one at Cannon Street, where they sit, tawny with rust, creaking and booming as they slowly rise and fall on the tide. They travel downstream on the ebb tide, pulled by tug to an incinerator at Belvedere, just east of the Thames Barrier at Woolwich. The city's rubbish is burned at a temperature of at least 850 degrees Celsius and the heat is used to generate electricity. The by-product, ash, is loaded back into barges and taken by river further east to Tilbury where it is converted into building aggregate to build and repair the roads in the city that consumes the electricity.

But this approach to London's waste is relatively new. When I first started visiting the river, the rubbish barges that slid east on the high tide were destined for the aptly named Mucking Marshes landfill site on the Essex (north) side of the river, thirty-two miles downstream from Cannon Street, on the edge of the Thames Estuary. This is where London has been hauling its rubbish since the late nineteenth century. Before then, there was less rubbish and less need to dispose of it in such a way. It was pretty much the same type of waste it had been for centuries – ash from fires, pottery, bones and shells. Private contractors paid for the privilege of sorting through it for anything they could resell and most of what was left was burned. But by 1890 all that had changed. Mass production meant cheaper goods and ordinary people had more money in their pockets to buy them. Firms responded to this by producing more and cheaper products in what was essentially worthless, throwaway packaging. As London grew in size and consumed more and more, rubbish lost its value and instead of being paid for their rubbish, parish authorities began to pay to have it taken away. They bought up cheap, remote marshland beside the river in Kent and Essex and the tons of rubbish London produced was towed east by barge and dumped there.

Acres of riverside marshes in Essex are filled with London's waste. Mucking received London's rubbish for fifty years before it closed in 2011, when it was capped off with a 100-foot 'pie crust' of soil. It has now been transformed into a nature reserve. But at Tilbury, opposite Gravesend, a little further west, the rubbish from an old landfill site is spilling out of the bank, onto the foreshore and into the river.

It was curiosity that first drew me to Tilbury. I'd heard from other mudlarks about the bottle diggers who worked the riverbank and the bottles and glass that stretched into the distance on Bottle Beach, and I wanted to see it for myself. On the handful of times I've been, my adventure has always begun at Gravesend, with the little ferry that leaves around every half an hour from the pier, although the timetable is confusing and it can be a bit random. A ferry has been plying its trade between Gravesend and Tilbury for at least 500 years and its latest incarnation – at least when I was last there about a year ago – is the *Duchess*, a rusting relic with a smashed wheelhouse window covered over by torn cardboard boxes to keep out the wind. I join a group of other passengers – locals returning from the shops in Gravesend, a couple of men with mountain bikes and some walkers – and we file silently on board.

Inside, the *Duchess* is basic and I have the distinct feeling that nothing about it has changed in years. There are wooden benches around the edge and a few old kitchen chairs lashed to the side with rope in case the river gets choppy. It is much too warm and fuggy, and condensation slides down the dirty windows and drips onto the lino-covered floor. Each time the door swings open it lets in a tempting breath of cold river air and I soon decide to stand outside on the small deck for the duration of the journey. A man unties the ropes, the captain folds up his newspaper and we push off. The *Duchess* revs loudly, engulfing us in a cloud of black smelly diesel smoke, and is briefly taken by the retreating tide. The water looks slow, but it is slick and fast-moving and the ferry struggles a little to regain its direction before it pushes steadily towards the north shore. It is a short journey. We reach Tilbury within five minutes.

We dock at the end of the old cruise ship terminal, a low, solid, brick-built building, and walk up a long wooden gangplank alongside the deserted station. The passenger landing stage opened in 1930 and the station brought people to and from the boats until the terminal closed in the 1960s. This dock is where £10 Poms left on assisted passages to start a new life in Australia, and where the *Windrush* arrived in 1948, bringing the first people in a wave of migration from the Caribbean to the UK. It is abandoned and dilapidated now. The old light green and cream paint is peeling, many of the windows are smashed and the metal girders that once supported parts of the roof are streaked with rust. I squint through a gap between the heavy wooden padlocked doors into the large open hall, which has a semi-glass roof. There's a dusty free-standing ticket office in there, untouched since the day it sold its last ticket, frozen in time.

The railway station closed in 1992, but the ship terminal reopened in 1995 and today is disembarkation day. A cruise ship is docked in front of the building and the area is buzzing with cars and taxis. Behind the terminal, thousands of newly imported cars sit in neat rows and stacked containers wait to be loaded onto the large container ships that moor at Tilbury Docks. Tilbury Docks was opened by the East and West Indian Dock Company in 1886, but it wasn't until the central London docks and warehouses closed in the late 1960s that it came into its own. Its proximity to the sea and ability to accommodate large container ships finally made it a success and it is now one of Britain's three major container ports. But I turn away from all this and start walking east at a pace. I have a way to go and the tide is already falling.

This Essex stretch of the Thames is a strange, ugly-beautiful place of industrial sprawl and tangled electricity pylons against wide skies that can quickly lower and turn angry. I find the river path in front of the aptly named World's End pub. There's a concrete wall, but it is low enough to see over and I look out at the falling water as I walk. The river is much wider here than I am used to further west and below me the foreshore is a smooth expanse of deep gloopy mud. I won't be venturing onto that. It is scored into a series of tiny valleys by rivulets of water and a solitary wading bird is picking its way between washed-up strands of seaweed. I can sense the sea. The light has changed; it is brighter and cleaner and I can see for miles.

Tilbury is London's handmaid, its engine room, spoil heap and protector. Just before the sewage works and a soon-to-be-demolished power station, on the outer edge of the port complex and surrounded by scrubby marshland grazed by hairy black-and-white horses, is Tilbury Fort. The fort was first built by Henry VIII to protect London from invasion along the Thames and was enlarged with distinctive star-shaped defences in the late seventeenth century that give it a futuristic look when seen from the air. Close by, in 1588, Elizabeth I gave one of the most famous speeches in English history. Dressed in white, her torso armoured by a shiny silver cuirass and mounted on a white charger, she rallied her troops in advance of the Armada, defending her strength as a queen and promising to live and die among them in battle. As I near the plant I can smell the sewage, but I notice yellow lichen growing on the wall. I'm pretty sure it doesn't grow where there's pollution, so I reason the air must be quite clean despite the smell. There were small patches of it as I passed the fort and now round, flat crusty blooms, the size of saucers, are fighting for space with each other and covering the concrete.

I am heading for a small 'cove' just beyond the power station and reach a short flight of metal stairs that take me down a level to pass in front of it. The other side of the stairs is a tall concrete security wall, topped in places with rusty barbed wire and covered in old-style graffiti, scribbles, rude words and people's names. The wide tarmac path has gone; it's a thin dusty trail now, which winds along the wall, through the reeds and grass that grow down to the foreshore. There is evidence of the high spring tides in the dust and caught among the reeds, a tangle of multicoloured cotton-bud sticks, straws, bottle caps and other miscellaneous bits of plastic. I pass a red football, dried out and crazed with cracks. Large pieces of driftwood lie stranded – tree trunks, pieces of broken jetties and telephone poles, bleached and rotting, carved by the water.

I carry on under a concrete walkway that leads to a large jetty. It was built when the power station was still active and at one time took huge ships carrying up to 66,000 tons of coal. It's a depressing sight now, strung with coils of razor wire and covered with more crap graffiti, but I am almost at the cove. Suddenly, the concrete wall ends and the land opens up. I can see electricity pylons marching away across the marsh, white aeroplane scratches high up in the sky, and a tiny fluttering speck – a skylark that is filling the silence with its frantic song.

I search two spots at Tilbury and the cove is the first I come to. It's more intimate than the second, which is a long straight empty beach, and I feel more comfortable here. The river has eaten a small deep semicircle into the bank next to a jetty to which a couple of barges are moored, so I'm enclosed on all sides. From the path above I can already see bottles and shards of china scattered across the foreshore and I know that beneath my feet, just below the surface, there are thousands more. This is the site of one of the Essex marsh dumps and it is slowly eroding into the river. Since the rubbish was dumped here, sea levels have risen by around four inches, and with no river wall to protect it, very high tides are slowly mining the riverbank for its treasures, revealing layer upon layer of ancient landfill.

I wade through the tall grass, then scramble and jump over the deep holes left by bottle diggers and slither down the steep side of the riverbank, bringing a landslide of broken crockery and thin dusty soil filled with ashes and cinders with me. The tide is quite low and I look around to see what it has left behind. I am surrounded by rubbish up to a century old, household waste and the ordinary detritus of everyday life. Almost everything I can see is glass, ceramic or rusting metal, and everything is broken, chipped, worn out and empty.

My visits to Tilbury have yielded smashed china dolls' heads and twisted lead toys; single glass lenses from old-fashioned round spectacles; worn-out shoes; and a large brown earthenware hot-water bottle, shaped like a loaf of bread, chipped and missing its stopper. I've found a flattened doll's pram; a crushed cigarette case; the metal frame of a purse; broken glass lampshades, still blackened by lamp soot on the inside; thick white utility crockery with the names of long-closed-down hotels, restaurants and cafes; smashed ornaments – heads, legs, bodies and empty plinths; a headless glass pig; a small porcelain Christmas cake decoration, a 'snowbaby' in a white fuzzy suit that once sat proudly on top of someone's cake; and a compressed lump of eighty-year-old newspaper, sodden and yellowed, but still readable, a simple snapshot of everyday life before the Second World War turned it upside down. On one piece there were advertisements for second-hand cars – £175 for a 1933 Daimler – and for indigestion relief. On a second piece there were situations vacant, although just the 'F' and the 'P' sections: a Fish Fryer and wife with experience; a Fishmonger in Marble Arch; Fitters for the RAF; a Floor Inspector in a press shop; Piano Polishers; Piano Stainers; Piano Fly-Finishers and Plasterers. It was too fragile to take home and I left it to float away on the next tide.

Rayon, silk or even early nylon stockings hang out of the low stratified waste-filled cliffs, waving like windsocks in the breeze, and all around me are the broken and cracked bellies of teapots, their spouts and lids. It's all very British and I imagine the millions of cups of tea that have been poured and drunk from the remnants lying here. Most of the teapots are stained brown inside with tannin. Some are delicately patterned and painted with pastel flowers, while others are plain glazed in rich green and blue. The most common are the 'Brown Bettys', traditional dark brown glazed pots that reached the peak of their popularity at the turn of the last century. The Victorians considered tea brewed in a Brown Betty to be the best, since its rounded shape allowed the leaves to circulate more freely, releasing more flavour.

Much of the pottery is blue-and-white domestic china, most of it is transfer-printed, a technique developed in the mid-eighteenth century to enable the potteries to keep up with the demands of the emerging middle classes for affordable, decorated tableware. By far the most common design is the Willow pattern, a scene adapted by English potters from imported Chinese wares. By the time it has reached the river the Willow pattern is usually shattered and fragmented – two doves swooping amorously over a waterside landscape, a willow tree, three figures on a bridge, a boat and a pagoda-style house – but brought together they tell a story of love and devotion, albeit invented by the potteries to improve sales. One version, which has no links to China at all, goes something like this. The beautiful daughter of a wealthy Mandarin fell in love with a humble accounting assistant, angering her father. He dismissed the man and built a high fence around his house to keep the lovers apart. He had planned for his daughter to marry a rich and powerful duke, who arrived by boat bringing jewels for his new bride. The wedding was to take place the day the blossom fell from the willow tree, but on the eve of the wedding the accounting assistant sneaked into the house disguised as a servant. The lovers escaped over the bridge with the jewels, pursued by the girl's father, whip in hand, and sailed away on the duke's boat to an island where they lived happily for many years. When the duke discovered their hideaway, he sent his soldiers to kill them, but moved by their plight, the gods transformed the lovers into doves. It is the doves that are the most sought-after shard among foreshore collectors.

For all its multifarious bounty, Tilbury is best known for its bottles. You can see where the bottle diggers have been at work, digging warren-like holes in the bank in search of their glass treasure. They dump their rejects, and throw them down onto the foreshore below. There are so many that I don't take them home unless they are unusual, pretty or small. I have to draw the line somewhere. At the cove, there are small fish paste pots by the dozen and squat brown glass Bovril jars in every size. Knocking around among them are ink bottles, long thin phials that once contained olive and clove oil, and glass bottles with the names of chemists, cleaning products and cure-alls pressed into them. Heavy dark brown beer bottles with thick molten glass blobbed lips are common at Tilbury and usually discarded by the bottle diggers, but I've been lucky and claimed a much rarer Codd bottle, complete with marble, a small late nineteenth-century Schweppes torpedo bottle and three Victorian poison bottles. By the late nineteenth century there was an array of poisonous substances available to pretty much anyone who wanted to buy them. To help people avoid confusing arsenic with indigestion relief, they were sold in coloured glass bottles with raised patterns and designs that could be felt in the dark or by the dim light of a candle. One of mine is a beautiful dark blue and the other two are emerald green. They remind me of the magic potion bottle in *Alice in Wonderland*. But instead of 'Drink Me' my bottles come with a more sinister warning: 'Poison, Not to be Taken'.

Milk glass, opaque and white, is easy to spot against the dark cinder-rich mud. The pressed-glass jars that once held cold cream and cosmetics lie everywhere, but again I am choosy about what I take and only collect the geometric, linear, art deco designs of the 1920s that shout the Age of Jazz, flappers and carefree times. Perhaps they once shared a dressing table with the perfume bottles that occasionally tumble from the banks. I have one very special small bottle, dating from around 1905, that was a collaboration between the perfume manufacturer Coty and two of the world's finest glass manufacturers. The bottle was designed by Baccarat, famed for its crystal glass, and the delicate frosted stopper wreathed with tiny flowers was created by René Lalique. I have tried to pull the stopper out, to sniff the dribble of yellowing perfume that is left in the bottom, but it is wedged in too tightly and the scent that would once have freshened the wrists of an Edwardian lady remains a mystery.

The number of bottles and pieces of broken glass at my second search site, 150 yards east of the cove, has earned it the moniker 'Bottle Beach'. Bottles spill out of the banks and onto the foreshore and glass of one kind or another covers the whole half-mile stretch. The river is gradually transforming it into river-glass, spreading it over the foreshore and washing it into great piles of smooth, colourful glass pebbles. This is a different kind of treasure and attracts the sea-glass collectors, but I was the only person on the beach that day. In the four hours I was there I didn't see another soul – and that might have been just as well, since I've recently learned about the hidden horrors of Bottle Beach.

Lying among the bottles are hundreds of little black degrading batteries. Plastic bags and synthetic clothes are emerging from the riverbank too. This part of the dump isn't as old as the cove. The bottles help to date it, and I even recognise one of them, a quarter-pint milk bottle like the ones we had at school in the 1970s. At a guess, I'd say the rubbish here dates back to around the 1950s. It's a mixture of household, commercial and industrial waste and the truth is nobody really knows what's here – it was dumped before records were kept – but a recent survey of the soil at Bottle Beach discovered asbestos, lead, arsenic and cadmium. It is filled with poisons and carcinogens, not to mention the micro-plastics, which are washing into the river and out to sea.

I was glad I'd worn my latex gloves when I heard about this and I haven't been back to Tilbury since. It is not my kind of mudlarking anyway. There is no real hunt or discovery here – it's just picking through trash, a mound of mass-produced objects, many of which were made to be thrown away. It's all too recent and there's way too much of it. The stories are jumbled and massed together and the voices of the past are loud and angry: countless sobbing children and cursing housewives. Each smashed ornament is a sigh and every broken toy a tantrum.

Tilbury paints a picture of emerging consumerism and of a society on the brink of overindulgence. It provides a depressing glimpse of our recent legacy. The wood, straw, reeds, leather and bone our ancestors left behind have mostly rotted away, and the bricks, tiles, pottery, clay pipes and glass they made and used are slowly eroding, chipping and wearing down, returning to the sand and mud from whence they came. But Tilbury is a reminder of the permanence of the things we throw away today. It tells a story of overconsumption and wanton waste, and sends us a message for the future. We may ship our rubbish east and hide it in landfill sites. We might even build nature reserves on top of it. But much of it is never going away.

ESTUARY

Did I ever find a dead body on the shore? Yes, a goodish few – eight
or nine, I dessay. Five shillings reward it is to find 'em; but I'd a
jolly sight sooner find a good boat's grating, or a few fathom of
cable. There's a lot of trouble about finding a body, and what with
the inquest and one thing and another it don't pay. Still, it isn't in
human nature to see a fellow-creeter, man or woman, layin' there,
lookin' like they do look, and know if you don't look after 'em they'll
be took off again by the next tide.

James Greenwood, 'Gleaners of the Thames Bank',
Toilers in London, by One of the Crowd (1883)

As the river slides eastwards from Tilbury towards the sea
it rounds Lower Hope Point, a bleak, flat marshland,
criss-crossed by wriggling creeks and drainage channels and
dotted with low ruined buildings, which are the remains of
a gunpowder and explosives works that closed in 1921. The
name 'Lower Hope Point' is an optimistic suggestion of the
river's final destination, where new journeys start and old
ones end, but in many ways the river's own journey never
really ends. Instead, it merges imperceptibly with the North
Sea, somewhere in the Estuary, at a point that changes with
the wind, weather and tides, when the balance tips and the
water becomes more sea than river.

Lower Hope Point is on the south, or Kent, side of the river on the Hoo Peninsula, a spur of marshland that lay in one of the Saxon divisions of England called 'hundreds'. Once known as the Hundred of Hoo, it was a thriving area until the sixteenth century, when malaria, carried by mosquitoes that bred in the brackish marsh water, began to decimate its ancient communities and it grew desolate and lawless. The north, or Essex, side, has been at least partially tamed by London's deep-sea cargo port, the London Gateway, and Southend-on-Sea, a grey mass on the horizon, but the south side is still wild, remote and empty, a bleak but beautiful land of pewter skies and wind-blown, treeless marshes, little changed since Abel Magwitch crawled away from his prison hulk and chanced upon young Pip, whose family lay in a pitiful row in the graveyard of one of the Hoo's ancient churches.

There is no simple way to get to the river here. There is no train or bus that will conveniently drop you off at the riverside, no set of stairs leading to the water. For the most part, the foreshore is inaccessible, and with its fast tides and deep mud, mudlarking here can be treacherous. I never attempt it alone, but always go with my friend James who calls ahead to let the coastguard know we'll be on the mudflats. James knows the mud as well as it can be known and is an extra pair of eyes on the turning tide.

We usually choose an early-morning tide for our visits and it's still dark when we meet in a car park far from the river. I jump into James's car and we drive down winding empty roads for fifteen minutes or so, past sleeping houses and shadowy churches until we get to the first of a series of metal farm gates that leads onto rough tracks and eventually out to the tufted marsh meadows. After another ten minutes of bumpy driving, scaring frogs that jump in our headlights, we reach the bottom of a tall bank where the marsh ends and the river starts, though it's still a good walk from here to where it is safest to step off the riverside onto the mud to begin our search.

Our main quarry is early wine bottles. These dark green, almost black, seventeenth- and eighteenth-century beauties are classified, according to their shape, as 'onions', 'shaft and globes' and 'mallets', while those that have morphed between them over time are called 'transitionals'. Since they are all free-blown they are delightfully individual, all a bit wonky with trapped bubbles of air and twists in the glass from being turned on the glassblower's blowpipe. They survive cushioned and preserved in the thick soft mud, though the river is fickle and can be reluctant to release them. Early bottles are elusive, lucky finds and we often don't find any, although once, typically when I wasn't with him, James found so many he couldn't carry them all back. He made do with four and photographic evidence of those he had left and that had vanished back into the mud by the next time we went.

Leaving the cosiness of the car, I notice the sky is beginning to lighten, and I can smell salt in the air. We pull on our hi-vis vests and waterproofs, check the batteries on our phones, then set off on foot along the bottom of the bank. The sun rises behind us as we walk, casting a warm orange glow across the empty marshes, but it doesn't last long and the light soon grows hard and bright. It is March and we have come for one of the very low spring equinox tides in the hope that the water will pull back far enough to reveal our hunting grounds and give us time to search them.

As dawn breaks, birds come to life all around us. I can't see them, but I can hear hundreds of geese and ducks and, somewhere in the distance, the mournful cry of a lone curlew. We walk for perhaps three-quarters of an hour until we finally reach the point we want and climb the bank, grabbing handfuls of dry tufted grass to pull ourselves up. The river has been hidden from us until now and when I reach the top I'm hit by the wind and a wonderful sight. For as far as the eye can see, there is mile upon mile of smooth sludge, its watery surface reflecting the thin early-morning light. The Estuary is where boundaries blur, where the river meets the sea, and the earth, water and sky blend together. I can barely distinguish the river in the distance; the north shore is only a dark pencil line that separates the concrete-coloured water from the light grey sky above it.

The specks on the horizon, to the east, are Maunsell forts, metal towers that look like alien sentries, built to defend the nation from German attack in the Second World War. To the west, just out of sight, behind the wall at Lower Hope Point, is the Waterman's Stone, the obelisk which marks the most easterly extent of the old Thames waterman's licence. Just east from where I am now are two more obelisks: the London Stone on the Kent side and the Crow Stone on the Essex side. The London Stone was erected in 1856 and stands at the mouth of Yantlet Creek on the Isle of Grain at the furthest end of the Hoo Peninsula. It is almost impossible to get to. The other obelisk, the Crow Stone, stands in the mud at Southend-on-Sea and is only accessible at low tide. The invisible line drawn across the river between the two is known the Yantlet Line. It is around thirty-four miles from London Bridge and once marked the limits of the City of London's control over fishing rights and tolls on the river.

I zip my coat high around my ears and climb over the wall, sliding down the concrete slope on the other side to a pile of rocks that's covered with slippery brown bladder-wrack, evidence of how far the tide comes up when it's in. There is no other option here than to cross this slippery mass, so I crawl low to the ground, hands outstretched. I don't want to fall and risk a broken bone. Where the rocks and seaweed ends, before the mud begins, there's a thin strip of coarse yellow sand and I pause for a moment to prepare myself for what is to come.

I look briefly towards the invisible Yantlet Line and out over the mudflats that I'm about to try and conquer, then I step off the reassuringly sound strip of sand into the thick, custardy mud. Instantly, I sink six inches in and I have to keep treading to stop myself from sinking any further. If I stop, I will get stuck, so I keep walking, leaning forwards, half stooping, knees bent, walking on tiptoe to avoid cre-ating a vacuum. And it hurts. I try to ski my foot across the surface, pressing down as gently and evenly as I can. I feel like a kung fu master. I am walking across rice paper without breaking it. Except I'm not. I'm a five foot ten inch middle-aged woman, dressed in an electric-blue waterproof and hi-vis vest with wellies that are a bit too big and keep slipping off.

I manage to walk about a quarter of a mile before I stumble and fall with a splat onto my knees, leaving a wel-lington boot behind, my socked foot squishing into the cold wet mud. I struggle to my feet and stand on one leg, twisting around and trying to pull my lost boot out with my hands, but the mud stops my fingers from getting a purchase on it. Now that I am standing still, my other foot is sinking. I am in a bit of a pickle, so James comes to my rescue. He pulls my boot out of the mud with a delicious slurp, helps me back into it and hauls me out of my predicament. Then he takes my arm to help me along and we're off again, heading towards a small hump that's darker and dotted with bricks where the mud is firmer and we can rest.

James is really, really good at mud walking and I'm jealous because I'm rubbish. He once bought me a pair of inflatable snowshoes to stop me from sinking so deep, but I kept falling over them and eventually they popped. I've watched him and tried to copy what he does, but I still sink. He's tall and his feet are bigger than mine, so I like to think that's his secret but really I know it's more a matter of technique. He's got a knack I haven't, a kind of quick slide, twist and hop.

I'm exhausted by the time we reach the hump. I must make a decision. If I go on, I'll need enough strength to get back. Should I shelve my eagerness to go further, to where the bottles are, in favour of good sense? If I give up, I'll probably make my way slowly back to the edge of the mud to look for the Roman pottery shards and Victorian bottles that sometimes wash up where the rocks meet the sand, or I'll crawl back over the seaweed and find a strandline of plastic to search for bottles with messages in them. I've found quite a few of these in the past – children's drawings and fantasies of pirates and deserted islands corked into bottles, stories of captured princesses, invading aliens and superheroes. I have also found deeply personal notes, demons trapped and thrown away: heartfelt wishes, regrets and disappointments, and once an intimate goodbye to a loved one.

Some bottles ride the currents for years, like the one containing a message written in 1914 that was found in the Thames Estuary in 1999. It was written by a soldier to his wife as he crossed the English Channel on his way to France, and had been pushed into a ginger-beer bottle. The note read: 'Sir or madam, youth or maid, Would you kindly forward the enclosed letter and earn the blessing of a poor British soldier on his way to the front this ninth day of September, 1914. Signed Private T. Hughes, Second Durham Light Infantry, Third Army Corp Expeditionary Force.' Hughes was killed twelve days later and the bottle remained at sea for another eighty-four years before it was snagged in a fisherman's net. Hughes's daughter Emily, who was only two years old when she lost her father, was an eighty-six-year-old grandmother living in New Zealand when she was tracked down and given the letter.

Sometimes I stay on the hump and enjoy just being there. I've done it quite a few times and it's magical. If the wind isn't roaring in my ears, it's quiet enough to hear barnacles turning in their cones and wormholes opening up all around me. Huge container ships slide by at eye level and flocks of wading birds pass in tight formation. I sit there mesmerised by the dark sheets of rain rolling across the horizon while James becomes a bright yellow speck in the distance. To sit on a hump of mud in the middle of the Thames Estuary is the most exhilarating feeling of absolute remoteness. But this time I decide to slap on through the mud.

It is a very different style of mudlarking out here. There is no point in looking down, because mostly there is nothing to see but plain, empty mud. You have to look ahead into the distance for objects, black dots that almost seem to be hovering just above the surface. James knows where the early bottles are most likely to wash up in this vast expanse, but even so often all we return with are muddy clothes, aching legs and flushed cheeks. Victorian bottles are easier to find out here, but they are heavy and slow me down, so I don't usually collect them. I stand them up in the mud, however, so that I can see them more easily on my way back, in case my rucksack is empty. James sometimes leaves finds out on the mudflats too, including two human skulls that I wish he'd brought back, but which were too much for him to carry. It's impossible to say where they had come from. Perhaps they had tumbled down the river from further upstream or maybe they are the remains of dead sailors, thrown overboard before their ship began its final journey upriver to port. It would have been a cheap and convenient way to cover up disease among the crew, which may have prevented the ship from docking and everyone on board from being paid.

It's not unusual to come across human remains on the river. Mudlarks have found finger bones, jaws with teeth still firmly inserted into their sockets, ribs and long smooth arm and leg bones muddled in with the cow, pig, sheep and horse bones that litter the foreshore, but it takes some knowledge of anatomy to pick them out and I'm sure I've passed a lot by without noticing them. The section of human skull I did find was unmistakable though. I could tell it was human by the size and shape of it, a shallow, dirty, creamy-yellow cup that fitted neatly in the palm of my hand. On the inside were faint grooves and ridges where someone's brain had once pressed against it and the edges were ragged where it had broken along its natural sutures. It looked very old, just like most of the human bones found by mudlarks on the foreshore, but they all have to be reported to the police just in case foul play is at hand.

I'm not squeamish about human remains. In fact, they've always intrigued me. I was ten years old when I found my first human bone. My birthday treat that year was a trip to the London Dungeons, a chamber of horrors, which was then beneath London Bridge station. It appealed to my fascination with the macabre and was gloriously terrifying. Afterwards, still buzzing on self-inflicted terror, Mum and I went to the churchyard at Southwark Cathedral to eat our packed lunches. Sated on honey sandwiches and a can of Pepsi, I decided to explore the small green space we were sitting in. The closely pruned roses had just been dug over, and to my joy, on top of the freshly turned yellow clay was half a lower human jawbone complete with teeth. As far as I was concerned, this was the perfect end to a perfect day.

I quickly finished the crisps I was eating and dropped my treasure into the empty bag, stuffing it deep into the pocket of my jeans before I was seen. It took all the limited self-control of a newly turned ten-year-old not to sneak a peek on the train home, but as soon as I was alone, I took it out and gazed at it. It was old and brittle and had been broken many years ago, perhaps by a gardener's fork. Two of the teeth were in excellent condition and to my delight one had a gaping black cavity that had eaten away a quarter of the tooth. Either side were several empty sockets where teeth had been lost, either in life or more recently to the rose bed.

The jawbone became the star of my chest-of-drawers museum and rested in its own box, lined with scrunched-up pink tissues. I daydreamed about the person it might have belonged to – a wicked pirate, an old lady in a frilly bonnet, a brave man killed in a duel – and for weeks I went to look at it every day after school, until one day it disappeared. I searched high and low. I blamed the dog and I even debated its magical ability to move on its own, but I never found it. Years later my mother confessed. Alerted by my increased visits to the barn she'd looked in the museum and was horrified by what she found. The jawbone hadn't disappeared of its own accord; Mum had taken it to the local vicar, who had buried it in consecrated ground.

Sometimes a complete human skull, or even an entire skeleton, pushes its way out of the foreshore. In 2009, a mudlark found a partially submerged skull at low tide on the Isle of Dogs. It was removed by the police and once they had concluded that it wasn't a recent death, they passed it to the Museum of London. It was radiocarbon dated to 1735–1805, a time when the area was largely empty save for a line of windmills that stood beside the river along its western side. Archaeologists returned to the site eight months later and found the mostly complete skeleton of what turned out to be a twelve-year-old girl, who had been buried in a hole deliberately dug into the foreshore close to the low-tide level. This made excavation difficult. It meant they had about an hour when the tide was at its lowest to lift the remains. Every time a boat passed, the site was swamped by the wake and the bones risked floating away, so they worked quickly, lifting and photographing each bone one at a time until the girl was finally free of her cold and lonely grave. Her life and death remain a mystery. Whether she was killed by accident or murdered, whoever disposed of her body had gone to great lengths to ensure she was not found.

Bodies found their way into the river in all kinds of ways. Georgian and Victorian London was notoriously dangerous and people disappeared easily. Corpses could be disposed of with no trouble at all in the stinking body of water that flowed through the capital and the Thames was a useful conspirator. It swallowed the bodies of elderly relatives to save their families the shame of a pauper's funeral, and centuries earlier it hid those of plague victims from terrified neighbours. Even taking a wherry from one side of the river to the other was fraught with danger. Slippery stairs and jetties, poor lighting and often an excess of ale or gin, meant that many simply fell in and were washed away with the city's refuse. People fell from the ships and barges that moored along the Thames; ropes tripped the unwary and wooden decks became slippery in the rain. Sailors with a belly full of grog from riverside taverns often fell in. It was considered bad luck for a sailor to know how to swim and many found themselves welcomed into Davy Jones's riverine locker sooner than they had expected.

The battles that have taken place along the Thames also added to the river's burden. The Romans fought the Britons on its banks; Viking raiders sailed upriver to attack the Saxons from their longboats; and the great Iceni queen Boudicca laid siege to Roman London in AD 60, slaughtering every man, woman and child in her path. There are the bones of Napoleonic prisoners who died on board the prison hulks in the eighteenth century and Second World

War pilots whose planes crashed in the wide expanse of the Estuary. Every century has added more victims of warfare to the river.

Their bodies sank down into the brown water and tumbled away with the tide. Swollen flesh separated from bones, rings slipped from fingers, shoes were pulled off feet, knives fell from belts and swords slid from hands. Clothes worked free from corpses and became embedded in the thick mud. As the fabric rotted, clusters of buttons, buckles, cufflinks and brooches were left behind for the mudlarks to find. Often the tides and currents swept the bodies many miles away from where they first entered the water. Some were never found, sucked down into the mud or washed far out to sea. I've been told stories of corpses found on the Estuary filled with river shrimp and crabs, and others so bloated they were mistaken for armchairs.

If you spend enough time around the Thames you will eventually come across a dead body, or a part of one. A few years ago, a mudlark found a severed human foot at Bermondsey, which came from a particularly grisly murder nearby. The Marine Policing Unit recovers around thirty-five bodies every year – about 90 per cent are attributed to suicide, some are tragic accidents, but either way the Thames is a master at claiming its victims. Survival depends on a set of circumstances: tide, water temperature and the height from which someone falls. The Thames is at its coldest in April, after the winter months have sucked out any warmth it might have had, and at its warmest in September, after it has spent all summer absorbing the sun's rays. But it is never actually 'warm' and the simple shock of entering the water suddenly can be enough to stop a heart beating.

I have seen two bodies in the Thames. I saw my first as I was walking along the river path from the Isle of Dogs towards Limehouse. It was a particularly high spring tide, and the water was lapping closer than usual to the top of the river wall. It was overcast, cold and grey, and the water matched the sullen clouds. The wind was in my face and I paused for a moment on a bend in the path to look back over the river and that's when I saw her, caught where the wall stepped in and the currents couldn't reach her. She was in a dark coat, floating face down, arms outstretched, her long hair spread out like a soft halo. Small choppy waves broke gently over her head and she looked peaceful, angelic. In that moment I surprised myself. Instead of panic and shock, I felt a deep connection with the woman held in front of me by the turning tide. She was a stranger, but I was the first to be with her after her final and most private moment.

The second person I saw was in central London very early one morning. Two police officers had arrived before me and were standing beside him, discussing what to do next. I caught a glimpse of the body between them as I walked past. It was a young man with short dark hair and a white shirt and jeans, lying face down in the jagged dip of an eroding barge bed. He didn't look as if he had been tumbled around in the river. His shirt was still tucked in and his hair was already dry. He could have been sleeping, but he lay awkwardly with both arms beneath him and his bottom slightly raised in the air. One of the police officers caught my eye and I looked away slightly ashamed. By the time I walked back, he had been taken away. Even now, I don't like to linger or search the spot where I saw him, but I think about the young man often and wonder who he was.

For all its bleak beauty, the Estuary is merciless and its tides and currents have claimed its fair share of lives. There are estimated to be around a thousand shipwrecks lying on its bed along with several planes, one of which I learned about through a chance find on the foreshore. Several years ago, I found a small die-cast brass brooch in the shape of an old-fashioned plane. It wasn't in good condition – all of the green enamel had gone and the pin was missing – but I could just make out the name 'Amy' written across its wings and a tiny map of Britain on one wing tip and of Australia on the other. These were the clues that led me to its story. 'Amy' was Amy Johnson, who flew solo in May 1930 from England to Australia in nineteen and a half days. The event began as a small and private affair, but as her journey progressed she became an international media sensation. Songs were written about her and badges were cast in commemoration, and it was one of these that I had found.

As I read about this woman I had never heard of before, I discovered the life and death of a remarkable individual. Amy Johnson was the first person to fly from London to Moscow in one day; she set a solo record for her flight from London to Cape Town, and time records for flying from Britain to Japan and from Britain to India. She continued her flying career into the Second World War, joining the newly formed Air Transport Auxiliary and moving Royal Air Force aircraft around the country. On 5 January 1941, while flying from Blackpool to RAF Kidlington near Oxford, she went off course in adverse weather and bailed out as her plane crashed into the Thames Estuary. The crew of HMS *Haslemere* spotted a parachute floating down through the snow and then saw a figure wearing a pilot's helmet calling for help from the water. They watched as she was pulled closer to the ship's propellers by the current, and although there was no hope of saving her, Lieutenant Commander Walter Fletcher dived into the freezing water to rescue what he took to be a passenger. He failed and died from exposure in hospital days later. It is likely Johnson was sucked down into the blades of the ship's propeller and although parts of her plane, her logbook, chequebook and travelling bag were washed up nearby, her body and that of the 'passenger' were never recovered.

Ahead of me, James turns. I can see his lips moving, but his words are snatched away by the wind and I shake my head. He points to his watch. We have been out here almost two hours and it's time to go. The river is sliding past, still heading seawards, which is good, but it will turn in thirty minutes. I look at our footsteps, snaking back around patches of deep mud and rest spots of rubble vanishing in the distance towards the shoreline. We are far from where we need to be and it's not a direct route back either. We must retrace our footsteps east before we can start to head south to the safety of the shore, and that will take time.

Several Victorian bottles and plain stoneware pots are standing in the mud along our path back. If I have the energy, I'll collect them as we pass, though they're not particularly special and I'm thinking I will probably leave them today. I'm happy with the three barnacle-encrusted early free-blown wine bottles we found, a beautiful clay pipe with roses and thistles entwined around the bowl, and the lid of a Gosnell Brothers Cherry Tooth Paste pot. I have seen these before. They are often embellished with a portrait of the young Queen Victoria to support the manufacturer's claim that the paste was used by 'all the courts in Europe', but I hadn't realised how brightly coloured the pots once were until now. Freshly plucked from the Estuary mud, the pot I picked up had a few vivid moments of almost-newness before the air dulled it, ageing it 150 years before my eyes.

We begin our laborious trudge back, James half pulling, half supporting me. He has one of the precious free-blown bottles tucked under his other arm and I have two in my backpack. They are leaking liquid mud and it is dribbling out of the bottom of my bag, but I am up to my elbows in it anyway. It is splattered across my face and squelching in the welly that came off earlier, warm and soft. This is MUDlarking. I am starting to flag when we see a small hump of rubble that's just large enough for both of us to stand on. We catch our breath and rest our legs, and I look to the land, which is getting closer, but still seems desperately far away. Then I look back over my shoulder, past James, along the winding path we've made in the mud to the river. The tide has turned behind our backs and the water is chasing us.

The speed at which the water moves varies in different parts of the river and according to weather conditions. It is mostly influenced by the tides, but above Putney the amount of water flowing over Teddington Weir also plays a part. The speed of the water above London Bridge is usually between 1 and 3 knots. Below London Bridge and as far as Woolwich, the average speed is around 2.3 knots on the falling tide and 2 knots on the rising tide. Further downstream, the speed of the tide is affected by pressure and wind that can act with or against the tide to create positive or negative storm surges. In the Estuary, the tides move at an average of 2.6 knots, or 3 mph. The average walking speed of a human being on flat, sound land is about 3.1 mph. I estimate that we are barely touching 2 mph.

With the river fast on our heels I think of the wall of water that inundated the Estuary one cold night in January 1953, gushing through homes and sweeping people away. The Estuary is the first part of the river to feel the effects of the sea, and when exceptionally high tides combine with storm surges in the North Sea, the Thames can flood. Floods have been recorded in London since AD 9. In AD 38 a great flood is thought to have killed as many as 10,000 people, and in December 1663 Pepys recorded in his diary the 'greatest tide that ever was remembered in England', which inundated Whitehall. The last major flood in central London was in 1928, when the Thames overwhelmed the river wall at Hammersmith and Millbank in the dead of night, drowning fourteen people, filling the streets with up to four feet of water – and taking T. J. Cobden-Sanderson's ashes from their nook in his garden wall. In virtually every recorded century, heavy rainfall upriver combined with tidal surges from the North Sea has caused severe flooding. By the law of averages, it won't be long until London floods again.

Out on the Estuary, the only protection from the river is sea walls and flood defences, which were improved and updated after the flood of 1953. The most crucial structure protecting central London is the Thames Barrier at Woolwich, which is one of the largest movable tide barriers in the world. Since becoming operational in 1982 it has closed 183 times: 96 against tidal flooding and 87 against the type of combined tidal and fluvial conditions that caused the flood of 1928. But although it was designed to last 200 years, people are doubting its longevity: the plaque on the Barrier reads 'Here the tide is ruled, by the wind, the moon and us', but there is no mention of rising sea levels and global warming.

Once a month the Thames Barrier is tested and partially closed to allow maintenance work to take place. On these days strange things can happen to the river upstream. Sometimes it takes for ever to drop, never fully reaching the low tide that was promised; other times it stays low far longer than it should and rushes back in faster than normal. When I'm planning a trip to the river, I try to remember to check what the Barrier is doing. On the one day a year that the Thames Barrier closes fully against a high spring tide, usually in September or October, the river stays low for hours and a mudlarking session can extend all day.

Standing in the middle of the Estuary, where the river is at its widest and most powerful, I suddenly remember the little river on the farm and how some days I would wake to find it spread across the garden, unrecognisable, no longer a gentle clear stream but an angry muddy stranger creeping slowly up the lawn. My parents told me stories of how the river used to flood the house when they first moved there, running through the pigsties before it seeped up through the cellar and into the kitchen, leaving behind a thick layer of sludge and the stink of pigs. Dad once had to rescue my brothers, driving a tractor through the flood water to where they stood waiting in their wellies by the back door. The course of the river was straightened before I was born and forced further north, but I still feared the rain as I lay in bed listening to it fall on the old tiles above me, and dreaded the river's transformation, terrified of it invading the house again.

Now, panic flutters in my gut as I watch the water inch closer. In central London the tides cover the riverbed gradually, licking my heels and nudging me off the foreshore bit by bit, back to the river wall where a set of stairs or a ladder will take me to safety. But so close to the source of the tide itself, the water moves quickly, spreading across the mud and filling the channel before you know it. A fast-moving tide will overtake sluggish legs mired in mud and swiftly surround sandbanks, cutting off the way back to the shore. The water has already covered our footprints behind us and it won't be long before it has erased the ones we're making now. If I were to stay standing where I am, I'd be at least twelve foot under water by the time it reached the top of the seaweed-covered rocks under the concrete wall where James and I scrambled down just a few hours ago.

I cast my eye to land and calculate the distance still to go, picturing the water on its journey upstream. The river is like a great khaki snake-dragon, smoothing and stroking its treasures, hiding them in its coils. It has already rounded the bend at Lower Hope Point and will be passing the dump at Tilbury, drawing over broken bottles and teapots, silencing the cursing housewives and crying children. At Blackwall it will flow over the possessions dropped by pilgrims and adventurers before it loops its way around the Isle of Dogs to Greenwich to sort the remains of Tudor feasts for the next low tide. I watch it in my mind's eye, as it travels on past Cuckold's Point and into the Pool, where it will play on the bones of abandoned warships and pluck nails from the mud as it journeys to Tower Bridge. Now it makes its way through the city, past Trig Lane, where last week it handed me half the grizzled face of a beardy Bellarmine, and Queenhithe, where I collected a handful of Georgian clay pipes, then it pushes west to swirl around the prehistoric remains at Vauxhall. At Hammersmith it will check its cache for a special secret, ensuring the pieces of metal type that were passed into its care are still squirrelled away, out of the reach of mudlarks, before it crawls on westwards to the tidal head. Around four and a half hours from now, the river will have reached the locks and weir at Teddington. Here it will take a deep, earthy, leaf-scented breath, before beginning its journey seawards once more.

My legs are starting to get stiff and I know I need to keep moving. I turn my back on the river and step off the rubble back into the mud. I lurch a few feet landwards, but my river ancestors are holding tight to my boots. They don't want me to leave. I fix my eyes on the thin yellow strip of sand in the distance and force myself forwards through the sludge, conjuring the week's tide tables in my mind as a distraction. I'm exhausted, but I'm planning my next trip. The tides are good for the next seven days and with a bit of shuffling, pleading and creative planning I am sure I can rearrange my schedule around them. I've got to pick the kids up from school tomorrow, but I have a meeting near London Bridge on Friday and I should be able to fit in a quick lark afterwards. In my head I tell my river forebears: I'll be back with you on the river soon.

PEGGY JONES,

The well known Mud Lark,

at Black Friars.

Pub.d June 26.th 1805 by R.S.Kirby 11 London House Yard S.t Pauls.

ACKNOWLEDGEMENTS

My knowledge barely grazes that of the specialists and professionals I've met and consulted in my years as a mudlark. They have helped me to turn anonymous objects into living history and to understand the river itself. There's a long list of people I am indebted to for helping me with my research for this book and for reading and checking my facts. The mudlarks that shared their stories with me are another special group, they are the ones that know the true value of the river and the treasures it holds. For everyone's kindness, help and support, thank you:

Anton Vamplew (astronomer), Chiz Harward (archaeologist), Chris Coode (Thames21), Chris Knight (St Austell Brewery), Claire Newton (photographer and artist), the Company of Watermen and Lightermen, Dave (mudlark), Dr David Higgins (clay pipe specialist and chair of the National Pipe Archive and the Society for Clay Pipe Research), David Pearson (conservation manager at the Mary Rose Trust, Portsmouth), David Powell (lead token specialist and editor of the *Leaden Tokens Telegraph*, who helped me to resurrect Robert Kingsland), Eliott Wragg (archaeologist), Dr Fiona Fearnhead (palaeontologist at the Natural History Museum), Dr Fiona Haughey (foreshore archaeologist), Gerald A. Livings (jeweller and reproduction aglet maker, Wisconsin), Graham (mudlark), Heather Coleman (clay pipe maker), Ian Richardson (Treasure Registrar, British Museum), James (mudlark), Jane

Henderson (Department of Archaeology and Conservation at Cardiff University), Jane Sidell (Inspector of Ancient Monuments, thank you for patiently explaining the mysteries of prehistory to me – over and over again), Johnny (mudlark and artist), Julia Smith (mudlark), Kimberley Roche (archaeological conservator), Kristian Schug (for his research on Private French), Livetts Marine Logistics (Chris Livett, Edward Livett, William Waylet, Alex Miles, Adam Davis), Lynn Burchell, Metropolitan Police Marine Policing Unit (Sergeant Ian Spooner, PC Martin Davis, PC Peter Sandell, Adam O'Grady), Michael Lewis (Portable Antiquities Scheme and Treasure Finds, British Museum), Mike Webber (archaeologist), Nathalie Cohen (archaeologist), Ninya Mikhaila (Tudor tailor), Port of London Authority (Martin Garside and Alex Mortley), Richard Carey (mudlark and clay pipe collector and specialist), Richard Hemery (mudlark and pottery specialist), Robert Green (type designer), Robert Jeffries (Hon Curator at the Thames River Police Museum), Stuart Wyatt (Finds Liaison Officer at the Museum of London), Tim Ash (RNLI), Yogesh Patel (BAPS Shri Swaminarayan Mandir, Neasden, London), Yvonne Saunderson (Marine Police Suicide Prevention Team).

I can't thank the team at Bloomsbury enough for their insight, creativity, hard work and professionalism, especially Alexis Kirschbaum for her unwavering faith and support throughout – it was a long road, but we got there in the end! Huge thanks to my very brilliant editor Anna Vaux, who just 'got' me, and to Marigold Atkey and Jasmine Horsey for being such a delight to work with. The publicity and marketing team at Bloomsbury is second to none, so big thanks to Emma Bal, Genista Tate-Alexander and Ella Harold for all their hard work. Thank you to Johnny Mudlark for letting me loose on his precious sketchbooks and to David Mann for creating such a beautiful jacket with the amazing illustrations they contain. I wouldn't be sitting here writing any of this without my agent Sarah Ballard and her assistant Eli Keren at United Agents: your excellent instinct was right, Sarah. Thank you for persuading me to do it.

Special thanks to James for sharing so much, to Geoff for my floating hotel room in the Docklands and Bob and Philly for their open house. To all my friends and family, who have been so patient and supportive, I'm sorry for being 'absent' for two years, but I'm back now. To my mother, above all others, thank you for teaching me to look, for opening my eyes to the wonders around me and for nurturing my inquisitive soul. Of all your gifts this is the most valuable and enduring. For the twins, my little life-changers, who tiptoed past my room for what must have felt like an eternity, this book is my gift to you.

Finally Sarah, my ever-patient wife, for keeping the world at bay, listening unendingly to me bleat on about 'the book' and celebrating with me every time I 'finished'. You made all this possible by giving me the most precious gifts of all: time and freedom. For that, from the very bottom of my heart, I thank you.

SELECT BIBLIOGRAPHY

Books and publications listed once, under the chapter where they are first used.

MAIN EPIGRAPH

Richard Rowe, 'A Pair of Mudlarks', *Life in the London Streets* (1881)

MUDLARK

Lesley Brown (Ed), *The New Shorter Oxford English Dictionary on Historical Principles*, (Oxford, 1993) [epigraph]

Jerzy Gawronski and Peter Kranendonk, *Stuff: Catalogue Archaeological Finds, Amsterdam's North/South Metro Line* (Amsterdam, 2018)

TIDAL HEAD

St. James's Gazette, June 1884 [epigraph]

Globe, 25 June 1884

Peter Ackroyd, *Thames: Sacred River* (London, 2008)

A. A. C. Hedges, *Bottles and Bottle Collecting* (Buckinghamshire, 1996)

'All About Richmond Lock and Weir on the Thames', Port of London Authority (2014) [film]

HAMMERSMITH

Letter to a Customer from T. J. Cobden-Sanderson, 14 February 1918 [epigraph]

T. J. Cobden-Sanderson, *The Journals of Thomas James Cobden-Sanderson 1879–1922* (New York, 1969)

Colin Franklin, *The Private Presses* (London, 1990)

Ruari McLean (ed.), *Typographers on Type: An Illustrated Anthology from William Morris to the Present Day* (London, 1995)

Marianne Tidcombe, *The Doves Bindery* (London, 1991)

VAUXHALL

John Burns (Liberal MP 1892–1918), quoted in a *Daily Mail* report of his death, 25 January 1943. The remark was reputedly made to an American who had spoken disparagingly about the River Thames [epigraph]

Nathalie Cohen and Eliott Wragg, *The River's Tale: Archaeology on the Thames Foreshore in Greater London* (Museum of London Archaeology, 2017)

Ivor Noël Hume, *Treasure in the Thames* (London, 1956)

Ivor Noël Hume, *All the Best Rubbish* (New York, 1974)

Samuel Pepys, *The Diary of Samuel Pepys Esquire* (London, first published 1825)

Simon Webb, *Life in Roman London* (Stroud, 2011)

The Archaeology of Greater London: An Assessment of Archaeological Evidence for Human Presence in the Area Now Covered by Greater London, Museum of London Archaeology Service (London, 2000)

TRIG LANE

Ivor Noël Hume, *Treasure in the Thames* (London, 1956) [epigraph]

Janet Arnold, *Queen Elizabeth's Wardrobe Unlock'd* (London, 1988)

Peter Barber, *London, A History in Maps* (London, 2012)

Geoff Egan and Frances Pritchard, *Dress Accessories 1150–1450* (London, 1991)

Lois Sherr Dubin, *The History of Beads* (New York, 1987)

Kevin Leahy and Michael Lewis, *Finds Identified: The British Museum's Portable Antiquities Scheme* (London, 2018)

Bridget McConnel, *The Collector's Guide to Thimbles* (London, 1995)

Gustav and Chrissie Milne, *Medieval Waterfront Development at Trig Lane, London* (London, 1982)

Hans Van Lemmen, *Medieval Tiles* (Princes Risborough, 2000)

BANKSIDE

Ivor Noël Hume, *Treasure in the Thames* (London, 1956) [epigraph]

Kirby's Wonderful and Eccentric Museum; or Magazine of Remarkable Characters, Vol. III (London, 1820)

Matthew Green, *London: A Travel Guide Through Time* (London, 2015)

Ivor Noël Hume, *If These Pots Could Talk: Collecting 2,000 Years of British Household Pottery* (Milwaukee, 2001)

Lloyd Laing, *Pottery in Britain 4000 BC to AD 1900: A Guide to Identifying Pot Sherds* (Essex, 2014)

Ian Mortimer, *The Time Traveller's Guide to Elizabethan England* (London, 2012)

Stephen Porter, *Shakespeare's London* (Stroud, 2011)

Brian Read, *Hooked-Clasps and Eyes* (Somerset, 2008)

Gillian Tindall, *The House by the Thames and the People who Lived There* (London, 2006)

QUEENHITHE

Charles Manby Smith, 'The Tide Waitress', *Curiosities of London Life or Phases, Physiological and Social of the Great Metropolis* (1853) [epigraph]

Francis Grew and Margrethe de Neergaard, *Shoes and Pattens: Medieval Finds from Excavations in London* (London, 1988)

John Matusiak, *The Tudors in 100 Objects* (Stroud, 2016)

LONDON BRIDGE

James Greenwood, 'Gleaners of Thames Bank', *Toilers in London, by One of the Crowd* (1883) [epigraph]

TOWER BEACH

Charles Manby Smith, 'The Tide Waitress', *Curiosities of London Life or Phases, Physiological and Social of the Great Metropolis* (1853) [epigraph]

Caitlin Davies, *Downstream: A History and Celebration of Swimming the River Thames* (London, 2015)

Kenneth Porter and Stephen Wynn, *Castle Point in the Great War* (Barnsley, 2015)

Harriet White, *Legge's Mount, The Tower of London, London: Scientific Examination of the Crucibles*, Research Department Report Series, English Heritage (2010)

ROTHERHITHE

Henry Mayhew, *Letters to the Morning Chronicle* (1849–50) [epigraph]

Daniel Defoe, *A Tour Through the Whole Island of Great Britain* (1724–7)

John Evelyn, *The Diary of John Evelyn* (first published 1818)

WAPPING

Frederick Marryat, *Poor Jack* (1840) [epigraph]

Patrick Colquhoun, *A Treatise on the Police of the Metropolis; Containing a Detail of the Various Crimes and Misdemeanors By Which Public and Private Property and Security are, at Present, injured and Endangered: and Suggesting Remedies for their Prevention* (London, 1796)

Geoff Egan and Hazel Forsyth, *Toys, Trifles and Trinkets* (London, 2005)

Michele Field and Timothy Millett, *Convict Love Tokens: The Leaden Hearts the Convicts Left Behind* (Adelaide, 1998)

Henry Mayhew, *London Labour and the London Poor* (1851)

James Hardy Vaux, *Memoirs of James Hardy Vaux* (1819)

GREENWICH

Richard Rowe, 'A Brood of Mudlarks', *Episodes in an Obscure Life* (1871) [epigraph]

Clive Aslet, *The Story of Greenwich* (London, 1999)

Tracy Borman, *The Private Lives of the Tudors* (London, 2016)

Geoff Egan, *The Medieval Household: Medieval Finds From Excavations in London* (London, 1998)

Martin Hammond, *Bricks and Brickmaking* (London, 1981)

Drew Smith, *Oyster: A Gastronomic History* (London, 2015)

Olivia Williams, *Gin Glorious Gin: How Mother's Ruin Became the Spirit of London* (London, 2014)

TILBURY

Henry Mayhew, 'Of the Sewer Hunters', *London Labour and the London Poor* (1851) [epigraph]

Helen East, *London Folk Tales* (Stroud, 2012)

Alexander Moring (ed.), *The Story of the Willow Pattern Plate* (London, 1952)

Phil Stride, *The Thames Thideway: Preventing Another Stink* (Stroud, 2019)

Nigel Watson, *The Port of London Authority: A Century of Service 1909–2009* (London, 2009)

The Secret Life of Landfill, BBC4 (first aired October 2018)

ESTUARY

James Greenwood, 'Gleaners of Thames Bank', *Toilers in London, by One of the Crowd* (1883) [epigraph]

Edward Carpenter, Peter Kendall and Sarah Newsome, *The Hoo Peninsula Landscape* (Historic England, 2015)

WEBSITES

Agas Map: https://mapoflondon.uvic.ca/map.htm

Amy Johnson Trust: www.amyjohnsonartstrust.co.uk

British Museum: www.britishmuseum.org

Convict records: https://convictrecords.com.au

Cory Riverside Energy: www.coryenergy.com

Currency converter: www.nationalarchives.gov.uk/currency-converter

Diary of Samuel Pepys: www.pepysdiary.com

Doves type: https://typespec.co.uk/doves-type/

English Heritage: www.english-heritage.org.uk

Friends of Ham Lands: www.hamunitedgroup.org.uk

Geological Society: www.geolsoc.org.uk

Historic England: https://historicengland.org.uk/

Historic Jamestown: https://historicjamestowne.org

Leaden Tokens Telegraph: www.leadtokens.org.uk

Libraries Tasmania convict records: https://www.libraries.tas.gov.au

Marine Biological Association Recording Scheme: www.mittencrabs.org.uk

Mary Rose: www.maryrose.org

Mayflower: www.mayflower400uk.org

National Archives: www.nationalarchives.gov.uk

National Museum of the Royal Navy: www.nmrn.org.uk

Old Royal Naval College Greenwich: www.ornc.org

Portable Antiquities Scheme database: www.finds.org.uk

Port of London Authority: www.pla.co.uk

Pub History and Historical Street Directories: www.pubshistory.com

Richmond Council: www.richmond.gov.uk

Rocque map: www.locatinglondon.org

Rose farthings: www.britnumsoc.org
Royal Armouries: www.royalarmouries.org
Royal Mint: www.royalmint.com
Royal Museums Greenwich: www.rmg.org
Royal Palaces: www.hrp.org.uk
St Margaret's Community: www.stmargarets.london
St Mary's, Willesden (the Shrine of Our Lady of Willesden):
    www.shrineofmary.org
Sugar refining: www.mawer.clara.net
Thames Barrier: https://www.gov.uk/guidance/the-thames-barrier
Thames Discovery Programme: www.thamesdiscovery.org
Thames21: www.thames21.org.uk
UK Detector Finds database: www.ukdfd.co.uk
Victoria and Albert Museum Collections (Penn Tile):
    https://www.vam.ac.uk/collections
Visscher map: www.panoramaofthethames.com
Wilson Art Gallery and Museum: www.cheltenhammuseum.org.uk
Zoological Society of London: www.zsl.org

MUSEUMS

Brandon Heritage Centre, Suffolk
British Museum, London
Fitzwilliam Museum, Cambridge
Globe Exhibition, London
Little Woodham Living History Village, Hampshire
Mary Rose, Portsmouth
Museum of London
National Maritime Museum, London
Natural History Museum, London
Royal Armouries, Leeds
Thames River Police Museum, London
Tower of London
Victoria and Albert Museum, London

INDEX

abalone 78
acorns 245
advertisements 269–70
Aesop's Fables 112
Aethelred's Hythe 118
Agas Map 66, 75, 96, 176
aglets 128, 246
Albert Embankment 44
Alfred the Great 119
Alice in Wonderland 272
Amstel, river 5
animal bones 239–40
Anne of Cleves 236
Apollo 148
arsenic 272
Arts and Crafts movement 31
ashes, human 30, 35, 291
Attis 148

Baccarat 272
Ballu, Baccgalupo 103
barge beds 46, 99, 105
Barklie, Lieutenant 184
barnacles 199, 281
Bartmann jugs 107
batteries 273
Battersea Shield 47–8
Bazalgette, Joseph 258
Bear Gardens 106
Bedford, Duchess of 252
Beechener, Robert 103
belaying pins 193
belemnites 53
Bella Court 237

Bellarmines 107, 136–7, 157, 294
Bennett, Robert 201
Billingsgate Dock 119
Billingsgate Market 186, 213
Blackfriars Bridge 31, 79, 93, 97, 145, 157, 180, 182
boar tusks 240
Board of Ordnance 178, 191
bodies, human 287
bodkin, seventeenth-century 74
Boleyn, Anne 164, 236–7, 242, 251
bombs, unexploded 178–80
Bonus Eventus figure 147
Bottle Beach 264, 271–3
bottles
    Victorian 47, 136, 280, 282, 289
    wine 16, 136–7, 187, 214, 277, 289
    see also Codd bottles
Boudicca 285
Bovril jars 271
Bow Church bells 207
bricks 47, 249–50
British Museum 49, 52, 82
Broad Arrow mark 191–2
brothels 95
'Brown Bettys' 270
'bulb of percussion' 57
Burns, John 43
Butler, John 104
buttons, naval 252–3
Byrne, Private John 183–4

cannon balls 176–7
Cannon Street Bridge 67, 72–3,
    146–7
Canterbury Cathedral 155
Cardinal Cap Alley 95
Careles, Robert 86
castration clamps 148–9
Catherine of Aragon 236
caulking irons 193
chafing dishes 239
chamber pot, eighteenth-century 137
Charles I, King 104, 168, 171
Charles II, King 249
chevron beads 76
Chick Lane 92
Childs, Maurice 37
Chinese mitten crabs 197–8
City of London 80
clay pipes 15, 50, 110–16, 122,
    128, 136–7, 141, 187, 195,
    201, 225, 231, 294
    fairy pipes 111, 246
Clayton, Rev. Philip Thomas
    Bayard 165
cloth seals 137
coal 92
Cobden-Sanderson, T. J. 21, 30–5,
    37–41, 291
cockerels, lead 248
cock-fighting 95, 247–8
coconuts 158
Codd bottles 15–16, 18, 137, 272
Cohn, John 104
coin weights 225
coins 89, 104–6, 128, 135, 137,
    151–3, 159, 168–72, 188, 200
    and 'buying the wind' 203–4
    clipping of 225–6
    counterfeit 224–5
    crooked sixpences 171
    engraved 'leaden hearts' 216

hammered 168–9, 213, 246
    maravedis 219
    in sewers 256
    thrown to mudlarks 231–2
    tin money 202–3
Colquhoun, Patrick 220, 222–3
comb, Viking 106
Cook, James 214
coral 199–200
cormorants 211
Cornwallis, Mrs 243
cosmetic set, eighteenth-century
    72, 74
cowrie shells 199
Cromwell, Oliver 171
Crow Stone 278
Crusades 190
Cuckold's Point 185–6, 218, 293
cufflinks 188
Cummins, Captain Kenneth 181
cupels 168, 174
Custom House 163
Cybele 148

Dartford Crossing 62
deadeyes 193
Defoe, Daniel 187
'devil's toenails' 53
dice 189
diyas (oil lamps) 158–9
dolls 210, 269
dominoes 189
Doomsday Ship 180
Doves Press type 30–41, 294
Drake, Francis 200
drinking vessels 106–8
Duchess ferry 264–5

East India Company 85
Eaton, Charles 49
echinoids 53–4

Edward I, King 164
Edward VI, King 200
Eel Pie Island 14
eels 198–9
electrolysis 152–3, 175
elephants 145
Elizabeth I, Queen 86, 111, 164,
    168, 186, 236, 243, 251, 267
English Civil War 213, 248
Erith 58–61, 94
erosion 121–2, 248, 268–9
etriers 71
Evely, John 196
Execution Dock 206, 217–19
executions 217–18
eye, prosthetic 260
eyots 12

fatbergs 260–1
feasting, Tudor 245
Ferryman's seat 96, 106
fids 209
First Anglo-Dutch War 249
fish traps, Iron Age 45
Fleet River 31
Fletcher, Lieutenant Commander
    Walter 289
flints 55–7, 166, 200
    Brandon gunflights 178
floods 291
floor tiles 77, 128, 249
fogs 62–3
fool's gold 84
Franklin, Colin 32
French, Francis Arthur 181–2
French Resistance 182
fruit and nuts 242–3
Frying Pan Stairs 206

Gabriel's Wharf 93
game counters, Roman 150–1

Ganesh statue 158
Ganymede 148
garnets 85–6
George II, King 252
George III, King 105, 170, 213
George V, King 135, 165
gin 92, 251–2
glass, Tudor 150–1
Globe Theatre 93, 95, 105, 109
Glover's Island 12
Goethe, Johann Wolfgang von 32
gold 83–4
Goodgame, William 103
Grant, Frederick 103
Great Fire of London (1666) 77,
    143–4
Great Stink 258
Great Storm of 1987 60
Green, Robert 35–41
Green, Robin 50
Greenland Dock 187, 195
Greenwich Palace 234–8, 243,
    247–51
Greenwich pensioners 251
Greenwood, James 139, 275
Guildhall Museum 50

hairpins, Roman 149–50
Ham Lands 13
Hammersmith Bridge, IRA bombs
    37–8
Hampstead Heath 23
Hampton Court 243, 248
hand grenades 178–9
handcuffs 223
Hanseatic League 67
Harriott, John 220, 223
hazelnuts, prehistoric 58
Heathrow Airport 11
Henry I, King 119
Henry III, King 166

Henry VIII, King 11, 126, 164, 176, 191, 236–7, 242, 245–8, 250, 267
Hindu objects 158–9
Hitler, Adolf 17
HMS *Haslemere* 288
HMHS *Llandovery Castle* disaster 181–2
HMS *Morea* 181
HMS *President* 182
HMS *Temeraire* 194
Honorius, Emperor 151, 153
Hoo Peninsula 276, 278
Horn Stairs 185–6
Howard, Catherine 164
Hughes, Private T. 281
human remains 157, 282–6
hypocaust, Roman 73

impressment 213
Inkerman, Battle of 183
Isis 148
Islamic prayer 157
Isle of Dogs 61, 197, 204, 208, 230, 233, 284, 287, 293

James I, King 111, 201
James II, King 203
jars, pressed-glass 272
Jeffreys, Judge 218
Jew's harps 189–90
Johnson, Amy 288–9
Johnson, Henry 58
Jones, Peggy 92–3
Jupiter 148
Justitia 215, 217

key, seventeenth-century 174
Kidd, Captain 218–19
Kidney Stairs 206
Kingsland, Robert 99–101

knife, folding 189
knife handles 245–6
Krauwinckel, Hans 159

ladders 69–71
Lalique, René 272
Lambeth Wells 74
land levels, rising 68
Layton, Thomas 48
lead shot 176–8
lead soldiers 128
Lepidodrendron bark, fossilised 55
Limehouse Cut 208
Limehouse Hole 206
lobsters 259
London Bridge 3, 7, 13, 48, 67, 69, 72, 89, 93–5, 142, 144–6, 148–50, 155, 159, 164, 196, 199, 217, 227, 233, 257, 279, 290, 294
    Old London Bridge 7–8, 48, 66, 94–5, 97, 119, 154
London clay 53
London Dungeons 283
London Gateway 276
London Stone 278
Lower Hope Point 275–6, 278, 293
Lower Thames Street 102–3
Ludgate Hill 147
lumpers 220–2

Maiklem, Robert 214–17, 224, 229
Maiklem family 207–9, 214–17
mail 174–5
Manby Smith, Charles 117, 163
maps 65–7
    see also Agas Map; Rocque's map
marijuana plants 226
Marine Policing Unit 286
Marryat, Frederic 205
Marshalsea Prison 217

Mary I, Queen 74, 164, 236
Mary, Queen 164
Mary, Queen of Scots 251
Mary Rose 126
Mason Stairs 96
Matilda, Queen 119
Maunsell Forts 278
May, William 102–3
Mayflower 200–1
Mayhew, Henry 185, 222, 255
medical waste 260
Mediolanum (Milan) 151
mercury syringe 129
Merxon, Cornelius 103
metal detectors 26–7, 97,
    182, 200
Metropolitan Board of Works 44
Millennium Bridge 67, 89, 91,
    96–7, 118
Millennium Dome 230
miller's thumb fish 259
Milton, John 32
Minié balls 177
Mithras 148
money boxes 108–10, 136
Mucking Marshes landfill 263–4
mudlarking permits 27–8
mudlarks
    categories of 26
    children 222–3, 231–2
    and criminality 222
    definition of 222
    and 'getting your eye in' 140–1
Museum of London 27–8, 49–50,
    68, 82–3, 113, 124, 126, 160,
    174, 182–3, 247, 284
musket balls 176–7
mustard pot, Georgian 137

Napoleonic Wars 178, 189, 194,
    251

Natural History Museum 55, 196,
    200, 259
needles 74, 88, 261
negative tides 5
Nelson, Admiral Lord 253
New Crane Stairs 211
New South Wales 214
Newton, Isaac 226
nicolo (onyx) 147
Noël Hume, Ivor 50–1, 65, 91
Nuremberg 89, 130

oakum 193–4
Old Surrey Canal 148
olive jar, Spanish 201
ordnance 176–80
Our Lady of Willesden 155
oysters 241–2, 259

Palace of Placentia 237
passports 226
peat, prehistoric 57–8
Pelican Stairs 206
Pepys, Samuel 58, 60, 143
pilgrim badges 155–6
Pinder, William 103
pins 86–7, 129, 159, 174
pipkins 238–9
Pitt, William, the Elder 113
Planters Marine Police Institution
    223
playhouses 109–10
Pool of London 186–7, 205–6, 220,
    242, 293
    Lower Pool 186, 203, 205–6, 222
Poor Law 100
Pope, Thomas 103
porcelain, Chinese 201
porpoises 197, 240
Port of London Authority (PLA)
    20, 27, 37, 80, 120

driftwood collectors 262–3
Portable Antiquities Scheme 28, 82, 121
posts, Bronze Age 45
posy rings 80–3
pottery
  blue-and-white 131, 135, 201, 270
  medieval 122, 131–4
  Roman 148–9, 158, 280
  Willow pattern 270–1
precious and semi-precious stones 84–6
Princess Alice 258
prison hulks 215–16, 224, 229, 285
Prospect of Whitby 206, 218
publicans 100–3
Punch & Judy shows 165

Queen Rat 257
Queen's Stairs 164–5, 176
Queenhithe 75, 78, 95, 117–20, 133, 197, 294

Raeren 133
rat-catchers 221
Regent's Park 23
Retribution 214
Rhine, river 53, 133
Richmond Weir and Lock 8, 21
Ricketts, Charles 41
river-glass 273
river pirates 221
Roach Smith, Charles 48–9
Rocque's map 97, 186–7, 205–6, 217
roof tiles, Roman 47, 69, 77, 144, 249
Rowe, Richard 229
Royal Armoury 175, 177
Royal Dockyards 237

Royal Hospital for Seamen 251, 253
Royal Mint 168, 203, 226
Royal Naval College 230–1, 251
Royal Observatory 229–30

sailor figurine 253
St Austell Brewery 17
St James's Gazette 7
St Mary's, Rotherhithe 194
St Paul's Cathedral 44, 66, 91, 182, 253
St Thomas Becket 154–5
Sargasso Sea 198–9
scabbard chape, Roman 160–1
seahorse, short-nosed 197
seals 196–7, 240
Seine, river 5
Sewell, Richard 101
sewers, and sewage 255–61
Shakespeare, William 32, 108
shark's teeth 55
Sheerness Docks 197
shies 248
ship dividers 193–4
ships, and ship parts 190–4, 208, 221
ships' ballast 54, 84, 148, 176, 197–200
shipwrecks 288
shoes 124–8, 136, 188, 212
Silchester 161
Skinners' Hall 203
Smith, Ambrose 101
Smith, Thomas 103
Smith, William 49
Society of Antiquaries 49
Society of Mudlarks 27, 75
Southwark Bridge 76, 93, 97
Southwark Cathedral 2, 283
Spanish Armada 267

spectacle lenses 269
spoons 174, 189, 245–6
spring tides 4–5
SS *Richard Montgomery* 180
SS *Empire Windrush* 265
stairs and causeways 96–7, 211–12
Stew Lane 95
stockings 270
stoneware, German 107–8, 134, 201
stoppers 15–18
stove tiles 245–6
Strand-on-the-Green 13
Strathfieldsay 214
sugar 243–5
sundial, ivory 129–31
swastikas 17
Sweetly, Jerry 257
swords, Bronze Age 49, 154
syphilis 129

tam 45
tarsal bone, pig's 210
Tate Modern 93
tea bowls, eighteenth-century 159
Teddington Weir 8, 290, 294
teeth, false 232, 260
teeth, human 243–4
tennis balls 261
tesserae, Roman 150
Thames Barrier 263, 291–2
Thames Discovery Programme 234
Thames Draw Off 8–9
Thames frost fairs 145–6, 248
Thames River Police 219–20, 223–4, 227
'Thames tummy' 259–60
Thames Waterman licences 20, 278
thimbles 88–9
Thirty Years War 252
Three Cranes Wharf 67, 75, 144

tide tables 3–4
Tilbury Fort 267
Tile Hill 76–7
tobacco, introduction of 111, 202, 244
tobacco and snuff tins 189
tokens 99–101, 104, 128, 156–7, 159–60, 170
  evasion tokens 224
  love tokens 171–2
  plantation tokens 203
toothpaste 289–90
tortoises 140
toshers 256–7
Tower Beach 165–6, 168, 172–5, 179
Tower Bridge 30, 72, 163–4, 261, 294
Tower of London 163–8, 174, 177, 186–7, 206, 236
Town of Ramsgate pub 206, 212–13
toys 209–11, 247, 269
Trafalgar, Battle of 194, 253
Trafalgar pub 231–2
Traitor's Gate 164, 176, 236
transportation 213–16
treasure trove 79, 83
Treasure Valuation Committee 80
Trevillick, Richard 103
Trig Lane 67–9, 79, 87–9, 91, 190, 294
Trinity Laban Conservatoire 230
Turk's Head Inn 217
Turner, J. M. W. 194

Vale type 41
van den Wyngaerde, Anthony 237
Van Diemen's Land (Tasmania) 214–16
Vaux, James Hardy 215–16

Vauxhall Bridge 43–4
Victoria, Queen 168, 290
Victoria Crosses 182–4
Victoria Deep Dock 230
Victory Medals 180–1
Virgin Mary 155–6
Virginia Settlers 201–2
Visscher, Claes Janz. 66

Walbrook, river 147–9
Walker, Emery 31–3, 35
Wapping Old Stairs 212
Warden Point 53
watch fobs 188–9
water, speed of 290–1
Waterman's Stone 278
Watts, John 184
wedding and engagement rings 29,
    83
Weller, Benjamin 103

West India Merchants 223
Westminster Bridge 95
wet wipes 260–2
whales and whalebone 195–6
whistle, pottery 247
White, James Sparrow 104
White Tower 166–7
Wiccan spell jars 157
Wild Man of the Woods 107
William III, King 89
Winchester Palace 95
witch bottles 157–8
Woolwich Marshes 215
Wordsworth, William 32
World's End pub 266
Wren, Christopher 230, 251

Yantlet Line 279

zebra mussels 197

NOTE ON THE TYPE

Most of the text of this book is set in Linotype Sabon, a typeface named after the type founder, Jacques Sabon. It was designed by Jan Tschichold and jointly developed by Linotype, Monotype and Stempel in response to a need for a typeface to be available in identical form for mechanical hot metal composition and hand composition using foundry type.

Tschichold based his design for Sabon roman on a font engraved by Garamond, and Sabon italic on a font by Granjon. It was first used in 1966 and has proved an enduring modern classic.

In homage to one of the river's best-held secrets, and thanks to the hard work of type designer Robert Green, the epigraphs are set in Doves, which currently has no italics or bold. Its story can be read in chapter 2, 'Hammersmith'.